BATTLEFIELDS IN THE AIR

Canadians in the Allied Bomber Command

Dan McCaffery

James Lorimer & Company, Publishers
Toronto, 1995

James Lorimer & Company Ltd. acknowledges with thanks the support of the Canada Council, the Ontario Arts Council and the Ontario Publishing Centre in the development of writing and publishing in Canada.

Cover photo courtesy of Jack Western.

Canadian Cataloguing in Publication Data

McCaffery, Dan
  Battlefields in the air : Canadians in the Allied Bomber Command

Includes bibliographical references and index.
ISBN 1-55028-491-6 (bound)

1. Great Britain. Royal Air Force, Bomber Command. 2. World War, 1939–1945 — Aerial operations, British. 3. World War, 1939–1945 — Aerial operations, Canadian. 4. World War, 1939–1945 — Destruction and pillage — Germany. I. Title.

| D786.M23 1995 | 940.54'4941 | C95-932257-4 |

James Lorimer & Company Ltd., Publishers
35 Britain Street
Toronto, Ontario M5A 1R7

Printed and bound in Canada

CONTENTS

This book is dedicated to my wife,
Val (Roberts) McCaffery who, for 21 years,
has put up with my obsession with airplanes
and the history of flight.

ACKNOWLEDGEMENTS

This book would not have been possible without the help of a great many people who, in one way or another, took part in the Second World War bomber offensive against Germany. My letters, telephone calls and interviews took many of them back to a time in their lives that they'd just as soon forget. Although it was extremely painful for some of them, they unhesitatingly shared their memories, photographs and letters with me. For that, I am extremely grateful.

First and foremost, my thanks go out to the courageous and often unfairly maligned Bomber Command veterans who were willing to discuss openly such sensitive subjects as the fears they felt while on operations and the morality of bombing civilians. They include the late Hugh Caraher, John Cunningham, J.D. Calvin, Bill DuBois, Lyle James, Charles LaForce, James Letros, Jim McCaffery, Daniel McCaffery, Ron Pickler, Geoffrey Pendrill and Jack Western. Thanks also to Dick Fisher, whose brother, Louis, was killed in action while flying with Bomber Command.

The brave people who were on the receiving end of the bombs were every bit as patient and frank with me, recalling in minute detail what it was like to endure the horrors of round-the-clock air raids. They include: Arthur Willi, Hans Richter, Elke (Gehrke) Taivassaalo, Ria Kurr, Ann (Hosseld) Dybczak, Ingrid Scheyk, Elisabeth Frey, Werner Kluger, Werner Bachmann, Edith Brackelmann, Trudy Ambridge, Inge Neame, A.F. Krings, Gerhard Nichau, Ulli Waschkowski, Agathe Ideler, Heidi Schaefer, Helga Schmidt, Ulrich Dankworth and George Busch. Special thanks to Luftwaffe fighter ace Franz Stigler for his riveting recollections of life-and-death encounters with Allied bomber crews.

Others who helped in various ways include Winifred Malley, who survived the London blitz; Norman Anderson, who was on the receiving end of Allied bombs while serving with the Canadian army in France; Bruce Langer, whose mother operated anti-aircraft searchlights at Hamburg; Second World War fighter pilots Charles Stover and Russ Bannock; writer Norma West Linder and Joe Egan, a veteran of World War II naval combat.

Thanks also to the Bomber Command Association of Canada, the Canadian Warplane Heritage Museum and to the staffs of the Imperial War

Museum in London, England, the Toronto Public Library and the University of Western Ontario Library.

I would also like to thank Diane Young at James Lorimer & Company for helping me to fine-tune the manuscript.

Last, but not least, heartfelt thanks to my wife, Val, and to special friend Mary-Jane Egan. Their support and encouragement was greatly appreciated.

INTRODUCTION

"It drives one mad to think some Canadian boor, who probably can't even find Europe on the globe, flies here from a country glutted with natural resources to bombard a continent with a crowded population."[1] German propaganda minister Josef Goebbels penned that bitter entry in his diary over half a century ago as thousands of Allied bombers, many of them operated by Canadians, ranged over the Third Reich, blasting it to flaming rubble from one end to the other. Goebbels was one of the earliest critics of Bomber Command's devastating Second World War aerial offensive against his homeland. He referred to the aircrews in his radio broadcasts as "terror fliers" who were ignoring military and industrial targets in favour of the deliberate and callous slaughter of hundreds of thousands of innocent civilians. After one particularly horrifying raid, in which a firestorm devoured much of the port city of Hamburg, killing 40 000 people in a single night, he described the event as "a catastrophe, the extent of which simply staggers the imagination."[2]

Royal Canadian Air Force aircrews were not surprised by Goebbel's charges. To be criticized by the enemy was something you expected. Something, indeed, that you could take pride in. If a leading German government official was actually singling out Canadians for special condemnation, it could only mean that the RCAF was causing the Nazis a lot of pain. Besides, it was about the only international recognition the Canadians ever got for their part in the bomber offensive. Certainly the British Broadcasting Corporation never mentioned Canada's role, always referring to the previous night's raids in morning newscasts as having been carried out by "RAF Bomber Command." This despite the fact that 50 000 of the 125 000 men who flew with Bomber Command during the war were from the Dominion of Canada. There were no less than fifteen RCAF heavy bomber squadrons flying out of air bases across southeastern England, and there were Canadians in all the British Royal Air Force squadrons as well. In fact, by 1944 there was hardly a single aircraft in all of the Bomber Command that didn't count at least one Canadian in its seven-man crew. In any case, there was something almost comical about being branded a murderer by one of Adolf Hitler's leading henchmen.

Canadian veterans, however, didn't find it very amusing fifty years later, when the Canadian Broadcasting Corporation and the National Film Board of Canada teamed up to produce a controversial documentary that many of them thought repeated Goebbels' charges and threw in a few new ones for good measure. The video, part of a three-part series called *The Valour and the Horror*, was entitled "Bomber Command: Death by Moonlight," and it caused an immediate sensation across the country. Angry veterans denounced it as a deliberate distortion of history and threatened to sue both the federal government and the film's producers unless it was withdrawn from circulation. A Senate committee held full-blown hearings in what turned out to be a vain attempt to determine whether the production's charges were valid. The proceedings were fraught with emotion — so much so, in fact, that the two sides appeared at times more interested in exchanging insults than they were in making their cases. There were groundless suggestions that the producers were pro-Nazi, with one Senator going so far as to ask a CBC official if he believed the Holocaust had taken place. More than one commentator suggested the film's producers, Brian and Terence McKenna, were trying to make Bomber Command look bad because it had been a British-run organization and they are of Irish descent. No evidence was produced to substantiate this rather childish accusation.

The McKennas stuck to their guns, insisting that they had hard evidence to back up their charges. Other defenders of the film expressed fears that its withdrawal would amount to censorship. Letters to the editor filled opinion pages of newspapers and magazines from Halifax to Vancouver, and, before long, few people could be sure where the truth lay.

Eventually, a judge ruled the veterans had no grounds for a lawsuit, at least partly because *The Valour and the Horror* had had nothing but praise for the courage of the young airmen who had carried out the raids. The documentary had criticized the policy of bombing cities and the senior air force commanders who formulated that policy, not the fliers who carried it out.

Exactly what had *The Valour and the Horror* said to whip veterans and others into such a frenzy? Among other things, it charged that Bomber Command had done such a poor job of hitting military and industrial targets during the first half of the war that the British had decided to revert to a policy of "area bombing." In plain English, it accused the Allies of conducting carpet-bombing raids on civilian centres. The film's narrator said bluntly that there was a change in policy in 1942 in which it was decided "Germany would be crushed through the deliberate annihilation of its civilians."

Sir Arthur Harris, the gruff commander-in-chief of Bomber Command, was painted in the video as a bloodthirsty killer with what the narrator called an "obsession" for killing civilians. "Killing civilians didn't bother Arthur Harris," viewers were told. "He wanted to win the war single-handedly by destroying every city in Germany and the people in them... His obsession with destroying German cities and civilians would continue until the end of the war." What's more, Harris was portrayed as a butcher who needlessly sacrificed the lives of many of his own men by removing armour plating and other safety features from their airplanes so they could be loaded with additional bombs. He also sent them out, viewers were told, on virtual suicide missions. In one raid in particular, the infamous Nuremberg mission of March 30–31, 1944, Harris is accused of squandering ninety-six bombers by forcing his men to fly despite impossible weather conditions.

The film was hardly any kinder to Canadian Wing Commander Marvin Fleming, who was depicted in re-enactment scenes as a sneering, greasy-haired bully who had no qualms about killing civilians or humiliating any airmen who could no longer stomach the enormous pressures that came with their jobs.

The Valour and the Horror also accused the British of deciding on a change of bombing policy without consulting the RCAF or the Canadian government. Canadian airmen, furthermore, were said to be in the dark about the change and were left with the impression that they were still attacking military and industrial targets. Finally, it accused Bomber Command of deliberately covering up the fearful casualties that the aircrews were suffering, so as to maintain morale on the bomber squadrons.

Many veterans were outraged by the sympathetic manner in which the video portrayed German fighter pilots. They felt the Luftwaffe airmen were depicted as particularly heroic figures who held the moral high ground. Indeed, the documentary quotes one high-ranking British official as saying that enemy pilots engaged in attacks on the bombers "ended the war morally undefeated. We had given them at the end of the war the one thing they lacked in the beginning — a clear cause to fight for."

The Valour and the Horror touched a raw nerve because the Second World War has always been a part of their history that Canadians have felt good about. It is seen as a glorious crusade in which the democracies defeated the dictatorships. Generations of Canadians have been told that Canada, which had a population of only twelve million at the time, played a crucial role in the defeat of Nazi Germany, Fascist Italy, and Imperialist Japan. The bomber offensive was arguably our most important contribution. Besides providing about 40 per cent of the aircrews and hundreds of the actual bombers (which were built in Toronto), Canada had been home to the enormously successful British Commonwealth Air Training Plan. This was the scheme that saw 137 000 Allied airmen from around the world trained in Canada. There were more pilots, navigators, bomb aimers, flight engineers, air gunners, and wireless operators who received their bomber training in Canada than in England and all the other British Commonwealth nations put together. If Germany was forced to surrender largely because of the bomber offensive, as has so often been claimed, then it's clear a great deal of the credit for the Allied victory belongs to Canada. But if the offensive did little more than kill civilians, while contributing virtually nothing to eventual victory, it follows that the 10 000 young Canadians who lost their lives in the skies over Germany did so in what was basically a dishonourable campaign.

Could the charges be true? Many would prefer not to think about the subject. Some have even argued that the whole question is irrelevant — that the razing of places like Hamburg and Dresden can be justified simply because the Germans bombed London and Coventry. But two wrongs don't make a right. The bomber offensive, in which 55 000 Allied airmen and more than 600 000 Germans died, can only be justified if it helped win the war. Otherwise, the critics of the campaign are correct.

As we glance back, two generations removed from the end of the Second World War, many things appear different than they did in 1945. Many of the cherished myths that were accepted at the time have been debunked or have taken on a far more complex appearance. The infamous raid on the French seaport of Dieppe, carried out in the summer of 1942 by Canadian soldiers, is a good example. At the time it was hailed in the Allied newspapers as a great victory. Only years later did the public learn it had actually been a bloody defeat. Truth, as the saying goes, is the first casualty in war. And although that may be understandable from a military viewpoint while the fighting is still raging, there can be no excuse for clinging to falsehoods after the war is long over. If we are to learn from the mistakes of our parents and grandparents we must know the whole truth, however painful it might be.

With that in mind, I set out to discover what the bombers had done to Germany between 1939 and 1945. Moreover, I wanted to find out the reasons for the bombing campaign, how it was carried out, what it was like to fly night after night through dark and hostile skies, and what it was like to be on the receiving end of the bombs.

I would be less than candid if I did not let the reader know that my father and two of my uncles served overseas with the RCAF during the war. Indeed my father, Jim McCaffery, participated in the horrific firebombing of Dresden, and my uncle, Daniel McCaffery, took part in the deadly Nuremberg raid. Another uncle, Ernest McCaffery, was seriously injured while attached to a Canadian night fighter squadron. I do not, however, think I am ancestrally sensitive to the issues raised by *The Valour and the Horror*. In fact my father, who flew twenty-two missions over Germany as a teenage tail gunner aboard a lumbering Lancaster bomber, has a profound anti-war streak running through him. I have heard him express grave reservations about the bombing of the ancient and beautiful city of Dresden, in which an estimated 135 000 people died in one night.

This book is not a blow-by-blow account of the entire bomber offensive. The official history of the Royal Canadian Air Force provides a good overview of that. The 1990 book *Reap the Whirlwind* gives an excellent day-by-day description of the activities of the fifteen Canadian bomber squadrons that made up Canada's famous Six Group. Instead, I have attempted to look at the campaign from the point of view of the Allied policy makers, the aircrews, the German night fighter pilots and anti-aircraft gunners, and the ordinary German civilians who lived through nearly six years of bombings.

I have interviewed dozens of veterans who participated in the offensive and have consulted letters, diaries, logbooks, combat reports, memoirs (some unpublished), and official documents related to this extraordinary campaign. I have, I believe, produced a work that gets to the bottom of the issues raised by *The Valour and the Horror* while, at the same time, allowing Canadians to fully understand what their bomber crews did so long ago.

Dan McCaffery
Sarnia, Ontario
April, 1995

CHAPTER 1

THE NEW BATTLEFIELD

The whole grisly business began on a warm summer day in 1863 at the height of the American Civil War, when a young German cavalry officer was sent to the United States to serve as a military observer with the Union Army. The indirect cause of the mighty aerial bombardments of the Second World War, Hamburg, London, Berlin, Rotterdam, Dresden, and Hiroshima, was the posting of twenty-five-year-old Count Ferdinand von Zeppelin as an attaché with the fabled Army of the Potomac. While in the United States the Prussian nobleman looked on in wonder as balloons were sent aloft to spy on Confederate lines and direct artillery fire. Although officially an alien neutral, Count von Zeppelin made at least one ascent in a captive balloon, peering four miles behind Rebel lines through powerful field glasses, while Southern riflemen fired vainly at him from far below. Before heading back to Germany, he took part in several mapping flights over the Mississippi River, thereby becoming one of the world's first aerial scouts. Gazing down on the rolling green hills and the muddy brown river, he became convinced the balloon could become a highly useful weapon of war — provided it could be motorized so that the crew could fly far behind enemy lines and then return safely to their own territory. The experience, he said later, brought him to the conclusion that he should dedicate his life to the construction of giant airships capable of travelling across whole continents.

Back in Europe in time for the 1870 Franco–Prussian War, Count von Zeppelin saw his French adversaries use balloons to successfully airlift bankers, industrialists, and important military figures out of the besieged city of Paris. More than sixty flights were made, with the intrepid balloonists bringing in valuable supplies and information before flying out with their human cargo. The Germans could only watch in frustration as the balloons sailed silently over their heads, taking the evacuees to the provisional French capital of Tours. Writing in his diary, the count laid plans for a steerable aerial battleship that would be powered by four engines. He went into great detail, expressing the opinion that such sky-borne dreadnoughts could be used for commercial transportation in peacetime and — most ominously — for reconnaissance and bombing in time of war.

Count von Zeppelin was a dreamer, but he was also a man of action. In 1892 he presented the Prussian army with blueprints for a huge airship and pleaded with the war ministry to sanction funds to help pay for full-scale production. The German generals, however, like their contemporaries across the globe, were slow to embrace change. These were men who had graduated from cadet schools in the 1840s, after studying from textbooks that had been written in the late eighteenth century. They were hide-bound traditionalists who dismissed the visionary von Zeppelin as some sort of eccentric. Two years later, at the age of fifty-six, he quit the military in a huff. At that stage it looked as if Count von Zeppelin's revolutionary ideas would die with his army career. But the indomitable old soldier wasn't about to go away. He kept refining his plans and raising money from sympathetic industrialists in his home town of Württemberg. Four years after leaving the army, he was ready to make his move. Moreover, he was prepared to put his money where his mouth was, putting up half the cash needed to build the world's first dirigible.

Scientists, generals, newspaper editors, and ordinary citizens ridiculed him mercilessly, dubbing his project "Zeppelin's folly." Kaiser Wilhelm derided him as a donkey. Undaunted, von Zeppelin unveiled his new airship on July 2, 1900. It was a behemoth, 420 feet in length and filled with half a million cubic feet of hydrogen. Slung beneath its cigar-shaped frame were three engines and a gondola capable of holding twenty people. The world had never seen anything like it. Thousands of spectators lined the shores of Lake Constance, on the Swiss border, to watch the maiden flight. There was a hush from the crowd as the airship lifted more than 1000 feet into the heavens. Sunlight reflected off its huge silver body. A journalist who witnessed the incredible sight wrote: "From where I stood on the shore, it resembled a shimmering arrow caught in motion."[1] The crowd, which minutes before had been highly sceptical that anything that large could get off the ground, broke into thunderous applause. A second flight came that autumn, with the elderly count piloting his creation for seventy-five minutes before landing. By the time a third trip followed a little later, he had proven conclusively that the dirigible was a viable form of transportation. Count von Zeppelin, however, was almost broke. He'd poured his life savings into the project and had no money left to continue his experiments.

Refusing to give up, the old fellow spent the next several years travelling the countryside, securing corporate sponsors. By 1907 he was back in business, flying a new airship a full 208 miles. An impressed German government helped pay for further construction. Just when it looked as if success was going to be his at last, disaster struck. His newest airship was caught in high winds and sent crashing into a forest, where it exploded in a gigantic orange fireball.

Lesser men would have thrown in the towel and gone quietly into retirement. But the seventy-year-old count persevered, and his spunk captured the hearts of a nation. Germans from all walks of life sent him money. Newspapers hailed him as a national hero. In all, more than $1.5 million came in, giving him enough capital to build his own airship factory. By 1910 there were giant dirigibles criss-crossing Germany, carrying passengers and goods from city to city. In a development that would have a profound impact on world history, he sold nineteen of his sky vessels — which were now popularly known as "Zeppelins" — to the German armed forces.

All of this was enough to convince a few farsighted people that airships might one day be used to bomb cities. Author H.G. Wells saw the potential danger, writing in his 1908 novel *The War in the Air* of a fictional air raid. "There is no place where a woman and her daughter can hide and be at peace," he wrote. "The war comes through the air, bombs drop in the night. Quiet people go out in the morning and see airfleets passing overhead — dripping death — dripping death."[2]

While all of this was going on a pair of Ohio bicycle makers named Orville and Wilbur Wright had invented the powered airplane, making their first flight in 1903. A few years later a French pilot demonstrated one of the new flying machines to Italian army officials in Rome. The flight was a failure; the plane, buffeted by strong winds, got less than a yard off the ground. Most of the onlookers were unimpressed, but a young major named Giulio Douhet predicted airplanes would prove useful in future wars. "Since the airplane is already capable of rising a few feet," he said, "soon it will be able to rise thousands of feet and cover a distance of thousands of miles." In a newspaper article he added prophetically, "To us who have until now been inexorably bound to the surface of the earth, it must seem strange that the sky, too, is to become another battlefield, no less important than the battlefields on land and sea. For if there are nations that exist untouched by the sea, there are none that exist without the breath of air."[3]

Before long many people in high places began to fear that in future wars the world's great cities would be destroyed from the air by Zeppelins and airplanes. There was enough concern, in fact, to persuade forty-four countries to sign a treaty that outlawed the aerial bombardment of open towns.

When the First World War broke out, in August 1, 1914, the German High Command waited precisely twenty-five days before breaking the anti-bombing agreement. It happened when a single Zeppelin sailed over the besieged city of Antwerp, Belgium, dropping 1800 pounds of bombs on its unsuspecting inhabitants. Two days later, a pair of airships attacked the city again. In fairness to the Germans, both raids were aimed at military fortifications on Antwerp's outskirts. But with no bomb sights, the airmen simply tossed their deadly cargo overboard by hand, aiming with nothing more sophisticated than the naked eye. The results were predictable. In the initial assault, a dozen people, all civilians, were killed. One bomb caused much of the carnage when it blew apart a wing of a hospital.

The attacks created worldwide headlines. In the neutral United States, editorial writers universally condemned the raids. There was outrage, too, in France and England. "Antwerp protests against this barbarous attack," a British newspaper declared. "Great excitement reigns throughout the town. The bombs exploded with terrific force."[4]

The anger felt in London and Paris was tinged with genuine fear. Rumours spread like wild fire that the Zeppelins were here, there, and everywhere. People anxiously scanned the night skies, reporting numerous false sightings. Before long, the absurd rumour spread that the Zeppelins were conducting nightly flights all over England and then landing just before dawn to spend the daylight hours hidden away in the Scottish Highlands. More often than not, reports of "bloody Zepps" turned out to be nothing more than clouds floating past in the moonlight. The situation was much the same in France, where a rural town was thrown into chaos one evening when a group of impish schoolboys set a homemade balloon aloft with a fire burning in its basket and then ran through the streets crying "Zeppelins!" In Russia, meanwhile, a battalion of infantrymen mistook the planet Venus for an airship and fired several volleys at it. Newspapers and magazines in all the Allied nations helped fan the hysteria with articles carrying such sinister headlines as "The Airship Menace" and "Foreign Airships as Nocturnal Visitors."

Most people were convinced the Zeppelins were all but invincible. Even England's War Office erroneously believed the monstrous dirigibles were protected from machine-gun fire by a layer of fire-proof gas. Authorities were certain the only way to destroy one was to get above it in an airplane and drop bombs on it. Unfortunately, there wasn't a plane in the entire Royal Flying Corps that could fly as high as a dirigible.

One young British night-fighter pilot named Arthur Harris was even ordered to attempt to harpoon a Zeppelin, should he ever manage to find one flying low enough to be attacked. A War Office inventor had come up with a crack-brained scheme that called on pilots to haul 500 feet of steel cable behind their frail BE2 biplanes, which were made of wood and canvas and held together with piano wires. At the end of the cable was a huge harpoon. "You get above the Zeppelin and pull the handle; the harpoon goes down through the envelope of the Zeppelin, opens its barbs and catches in the structure, and there you are," the inventor enthusiastically explained.

Harris retorted: "Well, where am I? The Zeppelin has three thousand horsepower and I have seventy-five, and what I should like to know before attempting this — who goes home with whom?"

To that, the inventor replied, "My subsequent intention is to provide an explosive grenade on a ring. When you have harpooned the Zeppelin, you slide the grenade down the wire and it bursts on reaching the harpoon."[5]

By mid-September, 1914, anxiety was so high that police ordered London blacked out. The resulting darkness only added to the gloom felt by the population. As the weeks and months passed with still no sign of the dreaded Zeppelins, however, England began to breathe a little easier. Some even confidently predicted the raiders would never come. What people didn't know was that the airships were being held in check by Kaiser Wilhelm himself. The German emperor, often portrayed by historians as a modern Attila the Hun, was in fact a man deeply troubled by the thought of making war on civilians, especially English civilians. The son of an English princess and the grandson of Queen Victoria, he hoped that a negotiated settlement could be reached with Great Britain. His misgivings were shared by German Chancellor Theobald von Bethmann-Hollweg. The chancellor, who had lived for a time in London prior to the war, was a devout Christian who abhorred the thought of bombing women and children.

All of this restraint was driving the German generals to distraction. As 1914 came to a close the war had already lasted a month longer than they had predicted at the outset. Both sides had lost close to a quarter of a million men, and the opposing armies were bogged down in trenches that stretched from the North Sea to Switzerland. With the machine-gun making frontal assaults totally ineffective, it looked as if there was nothing better to look forward to than years of bloody stalemate. The German admirals were even more irate about the ban on bombing. They were outgunned by England's powerful Royal Navy and realized full well that they could do little to contribute to final victory. About the only offensive weapon available to them was a small fleet of navy Zeppelins.

Rear Admiral Paul Behncke was one of the chief proponents of bombing, which he saw as a way to break the growing deadlock. As early as August 14, 1914, he had written a memo urging his superiors to attack London with both Zeppelins and airplanes. Ordinary citizens would become so panic stricken by such raids that the British government would have to consider suing for peace, he wrote. The German public, stung by England's naval blockade, was also calling for air raids. People in some of the Fatherland's cities were going to bed hungry, and they were in no mood to let British civilians off the hook.

Finally, in early 1915, the kaiser relented. But he issued strict orders that bombs were not to be dropped on historic monuments, Buckingham Palace, or over London's residential districts. Zeppelin captains were to aim for shipyards, docks, and war-related industries. If weather conditions made it impossible to bomb with a reasonable degree of accuracy, the airmen were to bring their bombs home. On paper, the edict seemed entirely reasonable, but Chancellor Bethmann-Hollweg thought the policy was insane, predicting it would tarnish Germany's reputation with neutral countries, including the United States. Nevertheless, the kaiser's word was law, and on May 31, 1915, the German High Command was finally given permission to bomb London. At the last minute, Kaiser Wilhelm even expanded the area of attack to include any military or industrial target east of the famous Tower of London. With the stroke of a pen he placed a full one-third of the British capital in danger.

Captain Erich Linnarz was given the dubious honour of carrying out the first aerial assault on one of the planet's great capitals. Taking off from his base near Brussels, he gained altitude over his field and then rode a brisk breeze towards England. The 536-foot Zeppelin LZ-38, powered by four Maybach engines, reached the mouth of the Thames River just after midnight. The city was blacked out but it stood out like a sore thumb in the lunar glow. Making navigation even easier was the fact that London's famous Crystal Palace shone in the moonlight like a beacon.

"We are at seven thousand feet," Captain Linnarz wrote later. "At full speed we steer for their capital city, the jewel of their civilization. I am stand-

6

ing at my command station, every fiber of my body taut. 'Let go!' I cry. The first bomb has been hurled at London! We wait with bated breath, listening. We lean over the side, watching. What a damned long interval between release and impact, the bomb falling those thousands of feet. 'It's a dud,' someone mutters, voicing the anxiety of us all — and then the quick flash, the faintly audible thud of the explosion, a chorus of hurrahs in the cabin. Already we have frightened them below. Away goes the second, an incendiary bomb, thrown out by hand, a pin being removed to activate its precussion cap. Suddenly, the searchlights come alive, right, left and all about us, stabbing the night, reaching after us like the legs of gigantic spiders."[6]

Seconds later anti-aircraft guns opened up far below, but the cannons couldn't be elevated high enough to hit their prey, and the LZ-38 slinked out of harm's way, heading for home. Linnarz, a thirty-five-year-old former schoolteacher, arrogantly dropped a weighted note that was found the next day. It read: "You English! We have come and we will come again soon. Kill or cure! Linnarz."[7]

In all, the Zeppelin had dropped fifty-five bombs. In his combat report, Linnarz claimed to have bombed London's docks but, in reality, he'd missed his target by more than a mile, killing seven civilians and wounding nearly forty more. Property damage was pegged at $100,000, which was a small fortune in 1915.

As the LZ-38 crossed the English Channel at a leisurely pace, a lone Canadian fighter pilot named Red Mulock climbed into his Avro 504 biplane and took off in hot pursuit. The German airship was gliding peacefully over the French town of Armentieres when the twenty-nine-year-old Winnipeg native closed in. Armed with only a pistol, two grenades, and a pair of bombs, Mulock was attempting the first night interception in the history of aerial warfare. Linnarz spotted him, however, and ordered his crew to dump water ballast. The airship skyrocketed out of sight, climbing at a rate of 1000 feet per minute. Four machine-gunners in the two gondolas opened fire at the same time, forcing the Canadian to dive out of a hail of red tracer bullets. Circling back around Mulock coaxed his rickety machine up at a rate of 350 feet per minute. He fired a few ineffective pistol shots before the Zeppelin vanished ghost-like into a cloud several thousand feet above him.

His adversary had escaped, but Mulock's evening was far from finished. Somehow, he had to get back to base in the dark, without radar or a navigational aid any more elaborate than a compass. "It was very dark, I could not see the sea or land and no stars or moon as I was in the clouds," he wrote in a letter home. "Talk about being alone in the world, very few people know what it means."[8] Heading east, he made for England, reaching the coast without incident. Then he hesitated, unsure of his ability to land at night. Mulock circled for several hours, finally touching down just as the first hint of daylight appeared on the horizon. There was hardly a drop of fuel left in his tank.

The Canadian was astonished to find himself something of a celebrity the moment he wearily climbed out of his cockpit. He was viewed as a David who had bravely challenged the aerial Goliath. Although he hadn't slain the sky monster, he had at least frightened it off. His pursuit of the Zeppelin was depicted on the cover of a British news magazine a week later, and Mulock proudly wrote home, pointing out to his parents that he had been the only pilot in the United Kingdom to go after the raider. In private discussions with his commanding officer he was less enthusiastic about the incident, feeling it had been a dangerous waste of time. "There's no use trying to swat one wasp with a wisp of straw," he said. "A wise man would pour a kettle of hot water down the hole and scuttle the lot. That's what we've got to do. Blast them out of their bloody sheds!"[9]

Mulock tried to do just that a few months later, carrying out a daring solo raid on the airship base near Brussels. He released four bombs and, amazingly, scored a direct hit on a giant canvas hangar, burning it to the ground. Unknown to him, the shed was empty. Clearly, if the Zeppelin menace was to be defeated, it would have to be done so in the air, by fighter pilots armed with more than just pistols, grenades, and bombs.

If Mulock was a hero in England, Linnarz was transformed into an almost godlike figure in Germany. He was instantly awarded the Iron Cross and hailed in the press as the man who had uncovered England's Achilles' heel. One newspaper wrote, "England no longer is an island! London, the heart which pumps lifeblood into the arteries of the degenerate huckster nation, has been mauled and mutilated with bombs by brave German fighting men in German airships."[10] The British press was indignant, branding the Zeppelin crews as "baby killers," "craven vandals," and "Huns."[11]

As the months rolled by, more and more Zeppelin raids were made on London, with new heroes emerging in Germany. The most celebrated was soon Lieutenant Heinrich Mathy, a bold young man with an uncanny ability to slip through the searchlights, fighters, and flak undetected to deliver his bombs right in the heart of London. Dubbed "the master" by his superiors, he was worshipped by his crew. Before long, he'd made a dozen successful nocturnal visits to London.

British fighter planes were now equipped with machine-guns, but no one seemed capable of getting close enough to a Zeppelin to bring one down. Scores of fighter pilots were killed in the attempt, crashing at night during take-offs and landings, or simply disappearing over the North Sea without a trace. All of that changed, however, on the night of October 1, 1916, when Mathy boarded the L-31, a new airship capable of carrying five 660-pound bombs. There was trouble for the Germans from the start. The British had installed new anti-aircraft guns that could be elevated high enough to draw a bead on the raiders, and Mathy encountered intense ground fire. Veering away from London, he dropped a few of his bombs over the town of Cheshunt, blowing up a greenhouse and injuring a woman inside. Then he circled back around and headed towards the capital again. At nearby Sutton's Farm airfield, meanwhile, the alarm had been sounded, and a Canadian from Perdue, Saskatchewan, named Wulstan Tempest jumped into his waiting BE2 fighter and took off. Just after 10:00 p.m. he spotted Mathy in the distance. His combat report, which is one of the most exciting official documents to come out of the First World War, tells what happened next. It reads in part: "There was a heavy ground fog on and it was bitterly cold, otherwise the night was beautiful and starlight at the altitude at which I was flying. I was gazing over towards the northeast of London, where the fog was not quite so heavy, when I noticed all the searchlights in that quarter concentrated on an enormous 'pyramid.' Following them up to the apex, I saw a small cigar-shaped object, which I at once recognized as a Zeppelin, about fifteen miles away and heading straight towards London. Previous to this I had chased many imaginary Zepps, only to find they were clouds on nearing them."

The two aircraft were on a collision course, and the distance between them closed quickly. "To get to the Zepp I had to pass through an inferno of bursting shells from the anti-aircraft guns below," Tempest wrote. "All at once, it appeared to me that the Zeppelin must have sighted me for she dropped all her bombs in one volley, swung around, tilted up her nose and proceeded to race away northwards, climbing rapidly as she went. I made after her at all speed at about fifteen thousand feet, gradually overhauling her."

Mathy was "climbing like a rocket" when Tempest made his move. "I gave a tremendous pump at my petrol tank, and dived straight at her, firing a burst straight into her as I came. I let her have another burst as I passed under her." Banking hard, he came at the dirigible from below, looking for all the world like a mosquito trying to bring down an elephant. "Flying along underneath her, I pumped lead into her for all I was worth. I could see tracer bullets flying from her in all directions, but I was too close under her for her to concentrate on me. As I was firing I noticed she began to go red inside like an enormous Chinese lantern and then a flame shot out from the front part of her and I realized she was on fire. She then shot up two thousand feet, paused, and came roaring down straight on to me before I had time to get out of the way. I nose-dived for all I was worth, with the Zepp tearing after me, and expecting every minute to be engulfed in the flames. I put my machine into a spin and just managed to corkscrew out of the way as she shot past me, roaring like a furnace. I righted my machine and watched her hit the ground with a shower of sparks."[12]

The Germans were not equipped with parachutes, but Mathy leapt from the burning airship anyway, choosing to slam into the ground from two miles up rather than burn to death. His body was found half buried in a farmer's field. Incredibly, he was still alive, although he died within moments of being discovered. His death sent a chill throughout Germany, where there was genuine sorrow over the loss of a man who had become a national icon. The German High Command, too, was shaken, now that it had been demonstrated that even the ablest Zeppelin commander could be shot down. It was obvious that as fighter planes continued to improve, the cumbersome Zeppelin would become increasingly vulnerable to air attack. Soon airship raids dropped off noticeably. When the raiders did come, they took increasing losses. Before the war was over, a dozen of them had been shot down by fighter pilots, including six by Canadians.

If there was any doubt that the Zeppelin was no longer a viable military weapon, it was erased for good when Stuart Culley, a nineteen-year-old British Columbia cowboy, caught the LZ-53 over the North Sea and shot it down in flames. His victory was of enormous importance because he scored it after taking off from a barge floating near the English coast. It was, in a way, the world's first strike from an aircraft carrier, and what it meant was the Allies were now capable of intercepting Zeppelins before they even reached land. Culley's graphic description of the kill, however, took some of the glamour out of "Zepp hunting." Indeed, it exposes readers to the full horror of war.

"It was the unbelievable size of the thing that most impressed me as I drew toward it," he wrote forty years later. "It was painted metallic silver, so that it resembled a giant mirror of reflected sunlight which some divine miracle-worker had suspended in the sky." Closing in unobserved, Culley opened fire with two machine-guns. In the next instant the gasbag erupted with a blinding flash that could be seen on land fifty miles away. To those looking on from afar it was an astonishing, almost beautiful sight. But for Culley, the experience was utterly sickening. "Maybe, had I not glimpsed their faces when I flew by the gondola, I would have been less affected by their ghastly fate. Without so vivid a reminder it was easy for a pilot to forget that enemy machines contained flesh-and-blood men such as himself, men whose fatal sin it was to be born German. I was horrified and sickened by what I had wrought. The memory of those frightened faces haunted me for weeks afterward and even nowadays, sometimes still does."[13]

So confident where the British that they had whipped the Zeppelins that they began directing new anti-aircraft guns to the navy to protect shipping from U-boats. Some existing cannons were even packed up and moved to the Western Front, along with several Home Defence fighter squadrons. The few gunners left in England were ordered not to fire on hostile aircraft during daylight hours. This bizarre directive was issued in the interest of reducing the number of men needed to man the guns — and to save ammunition. By early summer, 1917, London was even allowed to lift the blackout.

This serene sense of security was shattered at high noon on a warm and sunny May 25, when a formation of twenty-three twin-engine Gotha bombers appeared with unexpected suddenness over the sleepy resort town of Folkestone.

The Gotha! Here was the new secret weapon the Germans were counting on to win the war. It was history's first heavy bomber and one of the best airplanes produced by either side throughout the four years of fighting. Faster, more manoeuvrable, and better armed than the Zeppelin, it could also take a great deal more punishment. Powered by a pair of 220-horsepower Benz motors, it could climb to 20 000 feet, easily taking it out of the range of the few old BE2s still left on Home Defence duties. Even if more-modern fighters were recalled from the Western Front, the Gotha would be a tough nut to crack. It was literally bristling with machine-guns, including two covering the tail, a pair in the nose, and a fifth that poked out of a hole in the belly to guard the bomber's blind spot. With a wing-span of seventy-eight feet and a length of forty feet, it was a huge airplane for its time.

Folkestone was taken completely by surprise that Friday afternoon. The streets were crowded with shoppers preparing for the weekend, and long line-ups had formed in front of outdoor vegetable stands. When the drone of aircraft motors was heard directly overhead few thought anything of it. Some looked skyward, thinking they were gazing at British planes practising their formation flying. The last thing anyone expected was that the German Air Force would have the audacity to attack England in broad daylight. Seconds later, the terrifying whistle of falling bombs pierced the air. People began pushing and shoving in a mad scramble for cover. Too late. Shattering blasts toppled buildings, crushing scores of people to death in the streets below. Red-hot shrapnel ripped through the crowds, slicing men, women, and children to shreds. A soldier on the scene said later, "There were dead young mothers and dead children and babies all over the place. Buildings were on fire, people were screaming, or just stumbling around in stunned silence."[14]

The Gothas had actually been aiming for a nearby Canadian army camp at Shorncliffe, but there was no convincing anyone of that. Not with ninety-five civilians dead and nearly two hundred more seriously injured. In a single stroke the bombers had killed more people than all the Zeppelins in Germany had managed to slay during the entire previous year. Seventy-four fighter planes, mostly hopelessly obsolete BE2s, got airborne, but the raiders were long gone before any contact could be made.

To say England was shocked would be to put it mildly. Whole cities were gripped with fear for days afterwards. Attendance at several war industries fell off dramatically, as workers stayed home, fearful their factories would be the next target. Mobs stormed into foreign districts of London, ransacking shops owned by people with German-sounding names. Some even desecrated the graves of German Zeppelin crews buried in England the year before. In the House of Commons there were angry recriminations, with opposition MPs calling on the government to step aside and allow them to protect the nation. Member of Parliament Noel Pemberton-Billing created such a scene that he had to be bodily ejected by the Sergeant-at-Arms. Pemberton-Billing, a former actor and used car salesman, was a colourful character who constantly chided the government for its failure to protect the public from air raids. Once, with jowls flapping, he invited another MP, whom he accused of using "the most offensive, insulting and caddish language" to step outside where the matter could be settled with fists. According to the London *Times*, an "undignified scuffle ensued that had to be broken up by police."[15]

The public pressure to do something was so great that the War Cabinet agreed to withdraw Number 56 Squadron, the Royal Flying Corps' top-scoring fighter squadron, from the Western Front for Home Defence duties. The move, coming at a time when the British were about to launch their Ypres offensive, robbed the Allies of eighteen high-performance SE5 fighter planes and the services of several celebrated air aces. The Germans, alerted to the new danger over England, simply kept their Gothas grounded for a few weeks, striking again the very day Number 56 Squadron returned to France.

This time the raid was even more devastating than the Folkestone massacre. One stick of bombs fell on a London nursery school, killing sixteen children and wounding thirty others. Fourteen of the dead were under the age of five. A soldier who raced into the ruins to offer assistance never forgot the scene: "Many of the little ones were lying across their desks, apparently dead and with terrible wounds on heads and limbs, and scores of others were writhing in pain and moaning pitifully. Many of the bodies were mutilated, but our first thought was to get the injured. We packed the little souls on the lorries as gently as we could."[16] A group of rough-looking sailors helping to pull dead and maimed toddlers out of the rubble broke down and cried. Other rescue workers found casualties all over the city. In all, 162 were dead and 432 others were wounded.

For Prime Minister Lloyd George this was the last straw. British newspapers had been calling for reprisal raids for weeks, printing maps of Germany on their front pages that pinpointed cities within range of Allied bombers. A report from General Christiaan Smuts was already on the prime minister's desk that said "the day may not be far off when aerial operations with their devastation of enemy lands and destruction of industrial and population centres on a vast scale may become the principal operations of war."[17] Just as had happened in Germany two years earlier, the government was about to cave in to pressure from the military and the general public and sanction a bomber offensive against enemy cities. As happened in Germany, not everyone was in agreement with the policy. France formally objected, urging the British to use their bombers to attack the German army at the front. British General Douglas Haig, commander-in-chief of all Empire forces in France, was totally opposed to making war on civilians. The Church of England waded into the debate as well, with the Bishop of London denouncing a policy of vengeance.

In Germany, meanwhile, the doubts about the morality of bombing open cities were beginning to fade. Chancellor Bethmann-Hollweg opposed the Gotha raids as vigorously as he had the Zeppelin attacks, imploring the kaiser to put a halt to the bombings. With the Allied naval blockade now putting Germany on the brink of starvation, however, the kaiser was in no mood to call off his bombers. Indeed, his wrath was such that Berlin issued a mean-spirited communique warning civilians to get out of London or face the consequences. "The German people, under pressure of English starvation and the war, have become a hard race with an iron fist," it said. "The hammer is in our hands, and it will fall mercilessly and shatter the places where England is forging weapons against us."[18]

So the Gothas continued to come, but, as the defences improved, they also began taking losses. Wendall Rogers, a nineteen-year-old Canadian pilot from Charlottetown, Prince Edward Island, exposed the big bomber's weakness when he slipped under the tail of a Gotha and moved in to point-blank range before opening fire. Because Rogers' tiny Nieuport fighter wasn't much bigger than the Gotha's huge tail section, the German rear gunner found it virtually impossible to return the fire. Rogers emptied an entire drum of ninety-nine bullets into his target, sending it down in flames. All three crewmen perished, including Captain Rudolf Kleine, who was generally considered to be Germany's leading bomber pilot. Indeed, he had won the award for gallantry, *Pour le Mérite*, his nation's highest for leading a series of raids against London and Paris.

In all, defending fighters shot down twenty-four Gothas before the war ended, with Canadians bagging seven. In one particularly dramatic episode, Calgarian Harry Kerby shot down two raiders. His second victim was forced to land on the North Sea, where it promptly flipped over and broke up. Flying low, Kerby tossed his lifejacket to a German airman whom he could see clinging to a piece of wreckage. Then he flew off and fired signal flares to alert a Royal Navy ship to the downed man's predicament. The sailors, possibly fearful that there were U-boats in the vicinity, left the poor fellow to freeze to death or drown.

The new British bomber force went into action for the first time on June 5, 1918. Between that date and the end of the war, five months later, 543 tons of bombs were dropped on Rhineland cities. Berlin was never attacked, because it wasn't within range of the small aircraft of that era. A few of the raids helped the war effort directly. Once, for example, bombers blew up an ammunition train bound for the front, killing or wounding eighty-three German soldiers. And in one memorable thrust, Canadian pilot Walt Lawson knocked a chemical plant out of action at Mannheim. Flying at treetop level, he forced the German searchlights to dip so low that they illuminated the whole area, making it easy for him to pick out his target. Lawson quickly swooped down on the plant and dropped his bombs, putting every one on target. In that case the plant was out of action for several weeks. More often than not, however, the casualties were non-combatants. When the town of Düren was attacked, German civilians crowded into the streets to watch the circling aircraft, assuming, just as the people of Folkestone had done, that the planes must be friendly. Seconds later, bombs were exploding in their midst, killing or wounding scores of men, women, and children. At Bonn nearly ninety were killed or injured in just two minutes. Even Wiesbaden, a noted hospital town, was subjected to savage attack. The Allied fliers, just like the Zeppelin and Gotha crews, were trying to hit military and industrial targets. Like the Germans, they seldom had much luck in that department.

In any case, it hardly mattered to the British generals whether the bombs hit civilians or soldiers, so long as they killed Germans. That was made clear in a chilling exchange of letters between Air Marshall Hugh Trenchard and Sir William Weir of the Ministry of Munitions.

"If I were you," Weir wrote, "I would not be too exacting as regards accuracy in bombing railroad stations. The German is susceptible to bloodiness, and I would not mind a few accidents due to inaccuracy."

"I do not think you need be anxious," Trenchard replied. "The accuracy is not great at present, and all the pilots drop their eggs well in the middle of town generally."[19]

The Allies, like the Germans, also found the bombing of enemy cities could occasionally be a costly proposition. General Trenchard once lost ten of twelve planes he sent to bomb Mainz. Three of them came down inside Germany with engine trouble, and seven were shot out of the sky after being set upon by a swarm of forty German fighters. To make matters worse, the two survivors never did reach Mainz, dropping their bombs on Saarbrüken and then fleeing. When peace finally came, on November 11, 1918, the Allied bombers had killed 746 people and wounded 1800 more. The Germans, who had been bombing much longer, slew 1414 people and wounded almost 3500. Compared with the more than twenty million battlefield deaths, the losses were but a drop in the bucket.

The Germans felt the Zeppelin and Gotha raids had been a failure. They reasoned the amount of damage inflicted on British industry wasn't worth the effort that went into the offensive. That was true, if you only counted the damage done to industry. But the Germans failed to take into account the enormous strain they had placed on the Allied defences. At war's end, for example, there were nearly 500 anti-aircraft guns, more than 700 searchlights, and sixteen fighter squadrons tied down on the Home Front. All of that to guard against a Gotha bomber force that never consisted of more than forty-three planes at a time.

In Germany, too, valuable resources were used up defending the cities of the Ruhr Valley. In both countries there was a good deal of absenteeism in key factories the day after every raid.

Still, there's no denying the fact that the bomber offensives of 1914–18 were not decisive in any way, shape, or form. Airplanes of that period were too small, carried too few bombs, and were too few in number to make a real difference.

All of this, however, isn't to say their arrival on the scene was insignificant. Far from it. They were a vivid foretaste of what was to come. From the moment the first Zeppelin showed up over Antwerp in 1914 the nature of warfare had been changed forever. Fighting was no longer the province of professional soldiers. Modern war had become total war. Innocent civilians had been killed in their own beds, hundreds of miles from the front. The human race had stepped into a very black night.

CHAPTER 2

EARLY VICTORIES FOR THE LUFTWAFFE

As peace settled over a war-weary world at the end of 1918 the leaders of the victorious nations made a determined bid to put the lid back on Pandora's box. They wanted to make sure air power would never again threaten the great cities of Europe. British Prime Minister Lloyd George even discussed eliminating the Royal Air Force altogether. Opposed by several prominent Cabinet ministers, including Winston Churchill, he settled on a plan to gut it instead. The air force, which had consisted of ninety-nine front-line squadrons at the armistice, was reduced to just eleven squadrons four years later. Of the more than 27 000 officers on the payroll, half of them pilots, only 7,032 remained in uniform at the end of 1919.

Convinced that there would be no danger of war for at least a decade, the prime minister felt the RAF could forget about any sort of growth until 1929. And when that date finally arrived, the world had been plunged into the Great Depression, which put expansion of the air force off for another five years.

In Canada, meanwhile, the nation ended the First World War without a national air force. Although Canadians had made up fully one-third of the RAF during the war, there had been no all-Canadian squadrons. A separate Dominion air force was in the works late in late 1918, but it died on the drawing board with the peace treaty. Ottawa decided at that stage not to proceed with the establishment of an air arm. The country, after all, had only eight million people, and very few nations that size had military aircraft of any kind. What's more, most people believed the Great War, as it was called then, had been "the war to end all wars." When the League of Nations was formed in 1919 there was widespread hope that the planet had finally seen the end of war.

The situation changed less than a year later, when England unexpectedly shipped sixteen warplanes and $170,000 worth of spare parts to Canada. As the RAF scaled back, the British continued to send surplus planes to the dominions, shipping another one hundred aircraft, a dozen dirigibles, and six observation balloons to Canada before 1920 was over. Unsure what to do with all this expensive equipment, the federal government formed an air board, which promptly put it in storage to rot. There it sat, until 1924, when Ottawa decided it was time to form the Royal Canadian Air Force. At first, the new RCAF was something of a toothless tiger. Indeed, there was virtually nothing military about it at all. Its main duties were fighting forest fires and providing air transportation to remote northern communities. Most of the first planes to be taken out of storage were flying boats capable of landing on Canada's thousands of inland lakes. Virtually no thought whatever was given to building up a bomber force.

By the end of the first decade of peace the RCAF had 936 men in uniform. That figure was chopped back by about 300 as the Depression set in. Only when war clouds loomed on the horizon in the late 1930s did rapid expansion take place. Still, by the time Hitler's armies marched into Poland in September, 1939, the RCAF had only 4000 men and a scant 270 airplanes. Nearly half of those were trainers, and most of the rest were transport planes, reconnaissance machines, or fighters. There was only one bomber squadron, flying obsolete open-cockpit biplanes.

If the victors came out of the First World War with tiny air forces, at least organizations like the RAF and the RCAF actually existed. The German Air Force was dead, having been disbanded by the terms of the 1919 Treaty of Versailles. Still stinging from the Zeppelin and Gotha raids on their cities, the Allies outlawed the German Air Force, seized 14 000 airplanes and 25 000 aircraft engines and made it illegal for Germany to build any new military aircraft. To rub salt in the wound, they decreed that British and French warplanes had free rein to fly over German air space whenever they felt like it.

The destruction of Germany's air force actually began the day the war ended. A twenty-five-year-old wing commander named Hermann Göring got word on November 11, 1918, that he was to lead his pilots to the nearest French airfield, where they were to surrender their Fokker D-7 fighters. Göring, a highly decorated ace who had shot down twenty-two Allied planes over the previous three years, had no intention of carrying out such a humiliating edict. Instead, he assembled his men and ordered them to fly back to Germany. Confronted by his superiors, who bluntly told him he was putting the peace treaty in jeopardy, Göring instructed his fliers to crash land their planes on the French field, thus denying their former enemies the use of undamaged German aircraft. Göring himself refused to surrender, flying back to Germany, where he deliberately destroyed his own Fokker so it could not be turned over to the Allies.

At first, the victors had no trouble enforcing the Treaty of Versailles. International inspectors roamed Germany at will, making certain there was no attempt to build any new warplanes or to carry on any secret pilot training. They found nothing, mainly because Germany was too destitute to even think about rebuilding its air force. The Versailles agreement ruined the nation's economy, forcing Germany to pay a staggering $130 billion in war reparations. That was fully half the country's net worth. In an almost unbelievable move, the victors stripped Germany of much of its industrial might, handing over the Rhineland to France. In other words, the Germans were saddled with an impossibly large debt while at the same time being robbed of any realistic means of paying it off. The results were predictable. The nation's economy collapsed, and revolution was soon in the air. The conservative Kapp staged a brief coup, but gave up four days later when workmen across Germany went on strike.

Bitterly disillusioned by all of this, Hermann Göring went to Sweden to pursue a flying career. Returning home in 1922 with a Swedish bride in tow, he enrolled in the University of Munich to study history. There, he met a former army corporal named Adolf Hitler who led a radical new political organization called the Nazi Party. Fascinated by Hitler's pledge to restore Germany to its former glory, Göring quickly joined the movement. He was with Hitler a year later, when the Nazis attempted to seize the Bavarian government by force, sparking the bloody riot that is remembered in history as the Beer Hall Putsch. Shot in the thigh by police, Göring collapsed in the street. He lay unattended for several minutes, managing to get dirt in the wound. Eventually, he was taken to hospital and administered morphine. The treatment deadened the pain, but it also made Göring a drug addict.

Hitler was sent to prison but was soon released. The economic and political situation in Germany continued to deteriorate until it was so desperate that the population was ready to take a chance on a bold energetic radical promising to put an end to all the suffering, and in 1933 Hitler became chancellor. The Führer, as he insisted on being called, sought out Göring the day he took office, asking him to head up a secret German air force. He made no bones about what he intended to accomplish, declaring "in the air we shall of course be supreme." The airplane, he continued, was "a manly weapon, a Germanic art of battle: I shall build the largest air fleet in the world."[1] The Treaty of Versailles was still in effect, and Hitler knew he would have to move slowly before he could openly defy the Allies.

In many ways Göring didn't belong in the Nazi Party at all. His grandfather was half Jewish, and he had several Jewish friends. Privately, he believed Jews were similar to other people, although perhaps a little more intelligent. Whenever Hitler launched into one of his loathsome anti-Semitic speeches, Göring was deeply depressed for hours on end. He even wanted to appoint Helmut Wilburg, a Jew, as state secretary for aviation. That proved impossible, but Göring made him a general as soon as the Luftwaffe, as the new German air force was to be called, was unveiled to the world. And he concocted an elaborate scheme to appoint Erhard Milch, whose father was rumoured to be Jewish, as deputy commander of the Luftwaffe. Göring ordered an investigation that produced new "evidence" that Milch's real father had been a Christian who had had an affair with Milch's mother. Frau Milch signed a statement to this effect, and Göring issued strict orders that the matter was never to be discussed again. "I am the one to determine who in the Luftwaffe is a Jew and who is not!" he declared.[2]

Göring had to operate covertly on other fronts as well. International inspectors were still making periodic searches to make sure Germany had no air force. They found nothing, mainly because the Germans had worked out a secret deal with the Soviet Union in 1922 that allowed German pilots to train in Russia. A rather large sports flying club was set up. Officially, it was a civilian organization but, in truth, it was a sort of reserve air force partly funded by the Third Reich. Milch, meanwhile, was using government funds to convert locomotive and shipbuilding firms into aircraft factories for the production of bombers and fighters.

The growth of this secret industry was incredibly rapid. When Hitler became chancellor at the beginning of 1933 there were a scant 4000 workers in Germany's civilian aircraft industry. A year later, there were 20 000 men making warplanes. Two million others were busy constructing air bases, flying schools, barracks, and other facilities that would be needed to accommodate the greatest air armada the world had ever seen. When famed airplane builder Hugo Junkers protested, insisting he wanted to continue to construct airliners and planes to transport mail and other goods, he was placed under arrest. Tortured by the Gestapo, the elderly father of twelve, who had designed his first plane in 1910, agreed to sell both his airline and his factories to the government. Within weeks the Junkers complex was churning out bombers. The Dornier aircraft company was also ordered to build warplanes at a factory to be established in Switzerland.

Hitler had set an initial target of 4000 military aircraft, including 1000 bombers. The key man behind the bomber program was General Walter Wever, a fanatical Nazi who, unlike Göring, had taken the time to read Hitler's book, *Mein Kampf*. Because of that, he knew full well that the Führer had no intention of making war on England and France. At least not yet. He dreamed instead of creating "living space" to the east, and to do that he planned to conquer Russia. Therefore, Wever set out to build a bomber force capable of dealing with the Soviet Union.

Wever was a man ahead of his time when it came to military thinking. He reasoned it made far more sense to destroy an enemy's ability to wage war by blowing up his factories *before* they could build the guns, tanks, and planes needed at the front than it did to attempt to knock out that same equipment *after* it had reached the battlefield. So he decided what Germany needed was a heavy bomber capable of flying as far as Russia's Ural Mountains — some 1000 miles from the Reich's eastern frontier. By 1936 the prototypes for two such super-bombers were ready to be tested. Germany was on the verge of producing a four-engine airplane known by the code name "Ural Bomber."

Had production gone forward, the Second World War might have taken a very different turn. Fate stepped in, however, and Wever was killed in a flying accident before the first Ural Bomber came off the assembly lines. His replacement, General Albert Kesselring, thought the program was too expensive and would put too much of a strain on Germany's rather limited oil resources. Each Ural Bomber would need six tons of fuel per mission, and Kesselring thought that was asking too much. So he cancelled the program, replacing it with a plan to build smaller, twin-engine bombers designed to support the German army in the field. They would be great when it came to attacking enemy troops, but would be far less effective than a four-engine bomber when it came to going after industries — or entire cities. Although no one knew it yet, the Germans had just committed the first major blunder of the Second World War.

A superbly confident Adolf Hitler announced his new Luftwaffe to the world in 1935. In the Allied nations there was open despair. A confidential British government report concluded the Germans would be capable of killing 150 000 English civilians by bombing in the first week, should war come. Not surprisingly, Prime Minister Stanley Baldwin was heard to utter, "I wish for many reasons flying had never been invented."[3] It was a sentiment shared by many. Famed Irish author George Bernard Shaw warned the world was entering an era where "a boy in a bomber" could destroy a great city in thirty minutes.[4] British Army Colonel J.C.F. Fuller predicted in future wars swarms of bombers would target civilian areas in order to force governments to surrender. Historian Basil Liddell-Hart expressed the opinion that bombers would cause people living in slums to riot, thus putting pressure on the government to sue for peace. Railways would be severed and factories knocked out of commission. And because modern industries depended on each other, if one was destroyed, the whole economy would collapse, he believed.

In a debate in the House of Commons, Prime Minister Baldwin warned there was no way to stop bombers from reaching their targets. The only defence, he said flatly, was to destroy an enemy nation's cities before he could destroy yours.

The fears mounted appreciably in 1937, when Hitler sent the Luftwaffe to Spain to help General Francisco Franco overthrow the Spanish government. Although less than pleased with the results of their Zeppelin and Gotha raids a generation earlier, the Germans decided to give terror bombing another try over Madrid. So Luftwaffe planes pounded the Spanish capital for three days and nights without let-up, using both incendiaries and high explosives. The incendiaries, nicknamed "flambos" by the Germans, were twenty-two-pound cans filled with airplane fuel and motor oil that were ignited by a tiny fragmentation grenade. As pilot Adolf Galland noted many years later, the world had just been introduced to the "early prototype of the modern napalm bomb."[5] These hideous new weapons were dropped in the daylight, creating fires that guided night bombers to their targets. Attacking around the clock, the Germans knocked out the telephone exchange, damaged several municipal buildings, and killed 150 civilians. At least twice that many were wounded, and thousands more were left homeless, but morale remained remarkably strong. Some even thought the raids stiffened the resolve of the survivors. Indeed, the city held out for many more months, beating back several thrusts by Franco's ground forces.

The next target was the historic Basque town of Guernica, which was literally blown off the map on April 26, 1937. As the supper hour approached on that warm spring night, the inhabitants heard the faint drone of approaching aircraft. Minutes later, the thunderous roar of forty bombers could be heard directly overheard. Church bells rang out in warning, and the townspeople ran for their cellars and a few sandbag air raid shelters. Wave after wave of Heinkel 111 and Junkers 52 bombers dropped their bombs right in the centre of the town. The Germans said later they were aiming for the stone bridge that crossed the Oca River at Guernica, but while the bridge escaped unscathed, row after row of wooden townhouses and apartment buildings went up in flames. Incendiaries slammed through rooftops, pouring out red hot liquid that caused everything it came into contact with to burst into flames. Hundreds died in their cellars when buildings caved in. The front of the Julian Hotel, one of the town's largest buildings, was blown off, exposing all four floors to the elements. The train station was blasted into separating junk, the church of San Juan was gutted by fire, and the hospital crumpled after taking a direct hit from a string of bombs. Dazed survivors stumbled into the streets, only to be cut down by machine-gun fire from low-flying aircraft. Three hours after it began, it was all over. More than 1600 were dead and close to one thousand more were wounded. In one afternoon the Luftwaffe had killed more people than the Zeppelins and Gothas had slain during the entire First World War.

The Germans had dropped an incredible 100 000 pounds of bombs, totally destroying three out of every four buildings in the town. Almost all the rest were damaged, some seriously. A London *Times* reporter who was on the scene witnessed an eerie sight as the sun set on the dead town. "The total furnace that was Guernica began to play tricks of crimson colour with the night clouds," he told his shocked readers.

Luftwaffe General Wolfram von Richthofen, in his report to headquarters, described the raid as a complete success, but his men were not nearly as enthusiastic. Pilot Galland said later the airmen were ashamed of having destroyed an utterly defenceless village and never talked about it afterwards, not even among themselves.

Around the globe the reaction was one of horror and revulsion. Franco, taken aback by the bad publicity, denied Guernica had been bombed at all, claiming government forces had torched the town themselves to win international sympathy. But the *Times* exposed the lie, quoting a Fascist officer who openly declared, "Of course it was bombed. We bombed it and bombed it and bombed it, and why not?"[6]

Franco tried to call his German and Italian allies off after that, but they would have none of it. Hitler and Mussolini were more interested in testing equipment and theories than they were in helping either side win the civil war. So, a few months later the Italian Air Force went to work over Barcelona, bombing around the clock for two days. When the smoke cleared, 1300 civilians were dead. Other targets swiftly followed. Bulbao, Valencia, Durango, and Granollers were all hit. Some of the raids appeared to have no purpose other than spreading terror. In Granollers, where there was nothing of any military or industrial importance, more than one hundred people, many of them children, perished. Another 248 died in one afternoon in sleepy Durango. Before the war ended, an estimated 10 000 civilians had been killed by bombers. That represented only 2 per cent of the war's casualties, but it was enough to send shock waves throughout Europe. If Madrid could be bombed, could the continent's other great metropolises be spared in the event of a major war?

While the rest of the world cringed in fear, the Germans were privately disappointed with the bombing results in Spain. They felt Spanish civilians had held up rather well, and, as a result, the Luftwaffe was more determined than ever to build light bombers for use on the battle front, instead of heavy bombers with which to destroy cities.

There was, however, an unexpected side benefit to the terror raids that Hitler skilfully exploited. Stories about air attacks on such places as Guernica and Madrid made the French and British governments more determined than ever to avoid war. They were willing to bend over backwards to appease Germany. When Hitler sent his armies marching into the Rhineland in open defiance of the Treaty of Versailles, they didn't lift a finger to stop him. He had given his troops strict orders to retreat at the first hint of resistance, but his three battalions occupied the region without firing a shot. Some one hundred French divisions stood idly by and watched the operation unfold in front of them. A year later the German army marched into Austria, and again the West did nothing, fearful that war would mean the end of civilization. Next Czechoslovakia was gobbled up, and still the British and French sat on the sidelines. As one American reporter so succinctly noted, "It is blackmail which rules Europe today, blackmail made possible only by the existence of air power."[7] But by September 1, 1939, when the Nazis moved into Poland, Britain and France had finally had enough. Both declared war on Germany. A few days later, Canada followed suit. The Second World War was under way.

Hitler, who was a veteran of the First World War's long years of frustrating trench warfare, had no intention of getting bogged down in another hopeless quagmire. This time the Germans would use so-called *Blitzkrieg*, or lightning war tactics to win swift victories. The plan was simple. Armoured divisions would smash through enemy lines, while dive-bombers destroyed the Polish Air Force on the ground and wreaked havoc with enemy communications systems. As all of this was going on, Luftwaffe bombers would give terror raids another try, in the hope that they could add to the general panic and confusion.

On the first day of the war, in fact, German bombers were over the Polish capital of Warsaw. A Polish government communique admitted that forty-one enemy planes appeared over the heart of the city in broad daylight. "Several houses caught fire, and the hospital for Jewish defective children was bombed and wrecked,"[8] it said. In all, 130 people, only twelve of them soldiers, were killed. The bombers were over Kolo the next day, killing 111 refugees who had fled from border towns to escape the fighting. The death toll was even higher on September 3, when the undefended city of Sulejow was hit. Its peacetime population had swelled from 6500 to nearly 10 000, thanks to an influx of frightened refugees. The centre of the community was torched by incendiaries, and low-flying planes strafed anything that moved. No one knows how many died, but survivor Ben Helfgott recalled later, "People were falling, people were on fire. The night sky was red from the town burning."[9]

By mid-month the German army was at the gates of Warsaw, demanding unconditional surrender. When the Poles stubbornly refused to give up, Hitler ordered the Luftwaffe to destroy the city. An incredibly brave colonel named Seybold flatly refused to carry the order out, declaring he hadn't come to war to kill civilians. He was quickly sacked and Wolfram von Richthofen, the destroyer of Guernica, moved in to take his place.

Richthofen wasted no time, sending his planes into action on September 14 — the Jewish New Year. Hundreds of people were caught packed in Warsaw's synagogues. Scores were killed as bombs slammed into crowded churches. There was so many dead that graveyards quickly filled, and victims had to be buried in parks. But Warsaw's ordeal was far from over. Richthofen threw everything he had at the city on September 25, dispatching some 1150 planes in an all-out assault. With no enemy fighters and very few anti-aircraft guns to protect it, Warsaw was a sitting duck. The Germans even sent in low-flying transport planes loaded down with "flambos." Airmen actually used shovels to hurl incendiaries out of cargo doors. Fires broke out all over the city, making it difficult for other airmen to see their targets. As a result, some bombs landed on German troops on the city's outskirts, inflicting dozens of casualties. A fierce debate broke out at headquarters, with the army demanding that the Luftwaffe call off the bombers. Richthofen was engaged in an especially heated confrontation with furious army commanders when Hitler himself strode in unexpectedly. The Führer listened intently to the arguments, then turned to the Luftwaffe general and said simply, "Carry on!"[10]

Hitler was determined to reduce the Polish capital to rubble. "At the time, he announced he was not going to allow the city to be rebuilt," German Armaments Minister Albert Speer wrote later. "I remember his reaction to the final scene of the newsreel on the bombing of Warsaw in the autumn of 1939. We were sitting with him and Goebbels in his Berlin salon watching the film. Clouds of smoke darkened the sky; divebombers tilted and hurtled toward their goal; we could watch the flight of the released bombs, the pull-out of the planes and the cloud from the explosions expanding gigantically. Hitler seemed fascinated."[11]

In the city itself the agony was almost indescribable. On the night of the worst raid, when seventy-two tons of firebombs fell, a Polish woman named Jadwiga Sosnkowska was helping out in one of Warsaw's hospitals. "On the table at which I was assisting," she recalled later, "tragedy followed tragedy. At one time the victim was a girl of sixteen. She had a glorious mop of golden hair, her face was as delicate as a flower, and her lovely sapphire-blue eyes were full of tears. Both her legs, up to the knees, were a mass of bleeding pulp, in which it was impossible to distinguish bone from flesh; both had to be amputate above the knee. Before the surgeon began I bent over this innocent child to kiss her pallid brow, to lay my helpless hand on her golden head. She died quietly in the course of the morning, like a flower plucked by merciless hand."

Before the night was over Sosnkowska was to see still more horror. "On the same table, there died under the knife of the surgeon a young expectant mother, nineteen years of age, whose intestines were torn by the blast of a bomb. She was only a few days before childbirth. We never knew who her husband and her family were, and she was buried, a woman unknown, in the common grave with the fallen soldiers."[12]

When the Polish army finally surrendered, more to save the city from any further torture than anything else, German soldiers who marched into Warsaw were numbed by what they saw. One of them, the famous Field Marshal Erwin Rommel, wrote to his wife, "There is hardly a building not in some way damaged. The people must have suffered terribly. For seven days there has been no water, no power, no gas, no food. The mayor estimated there are forty thousand dead and injured. The people are probably relieved that we have come and that their ordeal is over. The field kitchens are besieged by starving, exhausted people."[13]

The Germans turned their attention on the Polish city of Modlin next, bombing it into submission on September 27. The air raids alone did not cause the Poles to throw in the towel. Warsaw and Modlin were both surrounded, and it would only have been a matter of days before they would have been overrun by German troops. But the bombardments certainly speeded up their surrender. Polish commanders in those cities were not willing to incur any more civilian casualties in a lost cause, so they gave up without further fighting. That undoubtedly saved the Germans heavy losses that would have resulted from house-to-house fighting. In other words, terror bombing of a civilian population had finally achieved real military advantage for the attackers.

While flames consumed Warsaw there was an almost surreal calm on the Western Front. American President Franklin Roosevelt issued a public plea, calling on both sides to refrain from the bombing of open cities. Both instantly agreed, but for different reasons. The British and French acquiesced because they didn't have bomber forces as large as the Germans, and they feared they'd come out on the short end of the tit-for-tat raids. Britain's Royal Air Force, for example, had only 300 front-line bombers, compared with 1500 for the Luftwaffe. Hitler, for his part, was still hoping to reach a negotiated settlement in the West. He knew air raids on London and Paris would make that next to impossible. In addition, the Nazi dictator didn't want to provoke a fight with the British and French until after he had finished off Poland. He knew full well that the German army had only thirty divisions in the West facing one hundred French divisions. What's more, all of his Panzer tank units were in the East. So he issued orders forbidding the Luftwaffe to bomb any target — military or civilian — anywhere in England or France.

For a few weeks, at least, it was a delightful little war for the men of RAF Bomber Command. Canadian pilot Billy Macrae, a fun-loving Calgarian who had joined the RAF in 1939, spent much of his time buzzing the town of Norfolk, which was situated near his air base. Diving to treetop level, he would fly hell-bent-for-leather right at the church steeple, only lifting his wing at the last possible moment to avoid a collision. Another Canadian, John Griffiths of Niagara Falls, Ontario, actually looped his bomber under

Tail gunner John McDougall. Courtesy of Jim Letros.

London's Tower Bridge. It was all great fun, and, before long, the newspapers were referring to the inactivity in the West as the "Phony War."

Although the RAF couldn't attack Germany, it was given the green light to go after Nazi ships, provided they weren't tied up in dock. Every effort had to be made to ensure not a single bomb fell on German soil. So, hobbled by the politicians — and faulty equipment — Bomber Command went to war very slowly indeed. The first mission came on September 3 when a lone Blenheim twin-engine bomber set out in foul weather to look for the enemy fleet. The four-man crew managed to spot several ships, but because their radio equipment was frozen solid, it was several hours before they could pass the information on to the Royal Navy. By that time the Germans had slipped away. The next day, led by Canadian navigator Selby Henderson, twenty-nine bombers went after the German fleet, scoring four direct hits on the battleship *Admiral Scheer*. Not a single explosion was observed because all four bombs were duds! German anti-aircraft gunners were shooting back with real ammunition, sending five of the attackers down in flames. Two other bombers were lost the same day in an unsuccessful strike against other German warships. About the only positive development from an Allied point of view was that Henderson, a Winnipeg native who had just become the first Canadian of the Second World War to see action, was awarded the Distinguished Flying Cross for his brilliant navigational skills.

It wasn't a very impressive start for Bomber Command, but the worst was yet to come. These raids were being made in broad daylight, without any fighter escort, because the RAF was convinced its planes could get to their targets simply by flying in tight formation, where the combined firepower of many gunners would provide the protection needed. Each Wellington bomber, after all, came equipped with six machine-guns, and the RAF was the only air force in the world that had hydraulically operated gun turrets.

The early losses had been bad, to be sure, but they were far from crippling, mainly because the bombers had been attacking ships at sea, far from Germany's fighter bases. Pilots with RAF Fighter Command had tried to warn the bomber boys that they wouldn't stand a chance against the Luftwaffe in daylight raids. During one mock exercise over England, a flight of British Spitfire fighter pilots returned to base reporting they could have wiped out a whole squadron of bombers in just a few minutes, but Air Chief Marshall Sir Edgar Ludlow-Hewitt, the head of Bomber Command, dismissed their claims with haughty contempt. He thought most fighter pilots were undisciplined show-offs whose opinions weren't worthy of consideration. And his theory seemed sound enough on December 3, 1939, when twenty-four Wellingtons raided German shipping near Heligoland Island. The planes failed to score any hits on the ships, but they did manage to beat off a flight of German fighters without loss. What Ludlow-Hewitt didn't know, however, was that his men had run into a particularly indifferent Luftwaffe fighter squadron, led by a pilot who was not very aggressive. The Germans had simply failed to press home their attacks with any sort of vigour.

A more realistic example of what daylight bombers could expect to face over enemy territory came on December 14, when twenty-five German fighters descended on a formation of forty-two Wellingtons led by John Griffiths. Five of the bombers were shot down, and the gunners managed to bag just one German Messerschmitt in return. But the British High Command remained undaunted, concluding that their missing planes had actually fallen to anti-aircraft fire, despite reports to the contrary from their own bomber crews.

There was, however, no denying the fact that fighters were responsible for the bloody massacre inflicted on Bomber Command just a week later when two dozen Wellingtons set out alone on a sunny and clear day to bomb shipping near the German port of Wilhelmshaven. There was no cloud cover, and it was fiercely cold. So cold, in fact, that the gun turrets moved slowly as hydraulic oil thickened in the frigid air. Fifty miles from the target the formation was detected by German radar operators on Heligoland Island, but when this news was telephoned to the Luftwaffe, the German fighter pilots didn't take it seriously. They couldn't believe that many unescorted bombers would be approaching their territory in broad daylight. The radar operators must have detected a flock of seagulls, they decided. As a result, the first Messerschmitt 109s only took off after German naval officers reported visual sightings of the bombers.

More by luck than anything else, Bomber Command had taken the Germans by complete surprise. But as the Wellingtons moved in, the commanding officer gave the order not to drop any bombs. The enemy ships were too close to shore and he had orders to make absolutely sure none of the bombs fell on land. So the Wellingtons circled slowly around and headed back to England. The German fighter pilots weren't about to let them get away. Wave after wave of single-engine ME 109s and twin-engine ME 110s waded into the bombers like a pack of hungry wolves. These fighter pilots were highly aggressive. One of them, Helmut Lent, had scrambled into his plane while a mechanic was still sitting on the wingtip, loading the guns. So anxious was Lent to get airborne that he gunned his engine and began taxing into take-off position before the mechanic could climb down. The poor fellow had to leap from the wing and only just managed to roll out of the way of the fighter's tail section. Quickly gaining altitude, Lent had no difficulty overtaking the Allied formation. His fighter was, after all, a full one hundred miles per hour faster than the Wellingtons. It was also better armed and considerably more agile. Moving in close, he killed the tail gunner of the nearest bomber with one burst, then knocked out one of its engines with a second salvo. The British pilot somehow managed to set his crippled machine down on land, where he and his surviving crewmen were taken prisoner. Lent, meanwhile, was closing in on another victim. "Both of the enemy's engines began burning brightly," he wrote in his combat report. "As the plane hit the water the impact broke it apart, and it sank."[14] A few minutes later, his blood-lust still not satisfied, he sent a third bomber down in flames.

Lent's deadly marksmanship broke up the RAF formation, and the sky was now a virtual shooting gallery for the German pilots. Several discovered their cannons had longer range than the Wellington machine-guns, so they just sat back and blazed away, completely safe from return fire. In many ways they were like a boxer who has longer arms than his opponent. Others took advantage of the fact that the Wellingtons couldn't defend themselves from below, diving under the bombers before riddling their fat underbellies. One after another the big planes were hit and went tumbling into the North Sea.

Calgary pilot Billy Macrae was one of the few to escape. He gamely tossed his bomber all over the sky like a cowboy riding a bucking bronco. At least three German fighters were after him, and his tail gunner's fingers were so frozen that he couldn't return their fire. Cannon shells tore into the plane, wounding the gunner, puncturing both fuel tanks, and chewing gaping holes in the wings. Macrae put the tricks he'd learned by buzzing that Norfolk church spire to good use, diving so low that his propellers were actually skimming the tops of the waves. One German recklessly pursued him and ended up crashing headlong into the sea. The other two fighters wisely withdrew. Macrae just managed to coax his battered bomber back to England, where he was promptly awarded the DFC, but few of the others were so fortunate. Ten of the Wellingtons had been shot down, and several came back with dead crewmen on board.

At first Bomber Command wasn't willing to accept that nearly half the raiders had been lost to enemy fighters. It blamed the airmen instead, saying they'd exhibited sloppy formation flying. When one of the survivors protested, claiming it was impossible for bombers to operate over enemy lines in broad daylight without a fighter escort, his patriotism was called into question.

The Phony War ended with unexpected suddenness on May 10, 1940, when Hitler sent his armies crashing into Belgium, Holland and France. Bomber Command was thrown into the breach and was quickly cut to pieces. If there was any doubt that bombers couldn't survive in daylight without fighter protection, it was removed now. On May 12 eleven of forty-two Blenheims were shot down while attempting to bomb bridges just behind the battle front. Two days later, a shocking forty out of seventy-one Fairey Battle bombers were blown out of the sky while attempting to destroy the German bridgehead at Sedan. Three days after that, eleven of twelve RAF planes were lost trying to bomb German troop concentrations. Between May 10 and June 26, 1940, no fewer than 147 British bombers were shot down while inflicting almost no damage on the German army. New bomber crews, some only partially trained, were rushed into action, but with as little as 200 hours of training under their belts (compared with the pre-war average of 600) they had even less chance than the seasoned airmen who had been slaughtered prior to their arrival.

The carnage was so great that one Canadian Blenheim pilot, Alan Brown, was shot down three times in three weeks. Amazingly, he lived to tell the tale, somehow managing to crash inside friendly territory each time.

The Allied armies weren't faring any better than Bomber Command. German Panzer units rolled over them like a tidal wave. France, which had held out so gallantly for four years in the First World War, collapsed after just six weeks of fighting. The British army was badly battered, but 380 000 weary soldiers managed to escape to England via the port of Dunkirk.

In Holland the Nazis scored an even quicker victory, thanks partly to a devastating air attack on the city of Rotterdam. Some one hundred Heinkels took off around 2:00 p.m. on May 14, 1940, and headed for the city. "Just before take-off," pilot Hans Lackner said later, "we received information from operations headquarters on the telephone that General Kurt Student had radioed that the Dutch had been called on to surrender Rotterdam. On our approach we were to watch for red Very lights [signal flares]. Should they appear we had orders to attack not Rotterdam, but the alternative target of two English divisions at Antwerp."[15] The Dutch agreed to surrender the city at the last moment, but fifty-seven of the German pilots failed to see the red flares and dropped their bombs anyway. That wasn't very many planes, com-pared with the massive air fleets that would routinely darken Europe's skies before the war was over, but they did an almost unbelievable amount of dam-age. Some of the first bombs to fall burst Rotterdam's watermains, and as a result fire hydrants went dry. Others hit a margarine warehouse, causing a spectacular fire that soon spread for blocks in every direction. Within hours a full square mile of the city had been burned to ashes. Nearly 1000 civilians were dead and another 80 000 were homeless. Fearing that Amsterdam would be next, Holland surrendered that very evening.

If the world was shocked by what had happened to Madrid and Warsaw, it was utterly stunned by the destruction of Rotterdam. Newspapers reported the death toll had been 40 000, and although that was a lie, the truth was bad enough.

Hitler now turned his bombers on England, hoping to win control of the skies in order to pave the way for an invasion of the United Kingdom. The Battle of Britain, as the ensuing aerial campaign became known as in the pop-ular press, raged throughout the summer of 1940. At first, the Luftwaffe kept to military targets, blasting British airfields and radar stations. During one night raid, however, a flight of Junkers 88s strayed off course and accidentally bombed London. The damage was light, but British Prime Minister Winston Churchill ordered Bomber Command to carry out a retaliatory raid on Berlin. The attack was a failure. The German capital was covered in clouds, and strong winds slowed the return of the bombers, giving the defenders time to shoot six of them down. Only a handful of bombs fell on Berlin, destroying a summer cottage and slightly injuring two civilians. Most of the rest landed in the countryside, where they caused some crop damage and started the joke that the Allies were trying to starve Germany into surrender.

Adolf Hitler wasn't laughing, however. Incensed, he ordered the Luftwaffe to destroy London. The first day of the blitz, as the German bombing campaign came to be called, was horrifying in its intensity. More than 300 bombers, escorted by 600 fighters, pounded London for eight solid hours. British teenager Len Jones never forgot the experience of being bombed for the first time. "Bombs began to fall, and shrapnel was going along King Street, dancing off the cobbles. The suction and compression from the high explosive blasts just pulled and pushed you... you could actually feel your eyeballs being sucked out. The suction was so vast, it ripped my shirt... I couldn't get my breath, the smoke was like acid."[16] More than 300 tons of high explosives and incendiaries fell, causing fires to break out all over the city's east end. "Send all the pumps you've got," one exhausted firefighter radioed back to his station. "The whole bloody world's on fire."[17]

In all, more than 2000 Londoners were killed or wounded that night, and it was just the beginning. Before the month was over, nearly 7000 British civilians had perished under one savage air attack after another. In addition to London, the Luftwaffe hit Liverpool, Coventry, Southampton, Bristol, Plymouth, Manchester, Belfast, and Glasgow. Some of the worst devastation took place in Coventry, where the city's thirteenth-century cathedral was destroyed. More than 1000 "flambos" were dropped, and fires roared out of control all over the city, devouring hundreds of buildings. Some 1800 people were killed or wounded. Across the United Kingdom, four million of the nation's thirteen million homes were destroyed or damaged in the blitz and more than 60 000 civilians were killed.

Surprisingly, public morale stood up fairly well. Winnifred Malley, a nineteen-year-old letter carrier at the time, told the author fifty years later that the bombings actually "brought people closer together." The raids were "scary," but Londoners dug shelters in their backyard gardens, shared their food rations, and generally learned to live with the danger.

So far, while the Luftwaffe had been mercilessly blasting Madrid, Warsaw, Rotterdam, London, and countless other places in Spain, Poland, Holland, France, and England, Bomber Command had done little more than carry out a few nuisance raids over Berlin. But at least one senior RAF officer was already plotting revenge. Arthur Harris, the commander of Bomber Command's Five Group, drew up his plans as he witnessed the worst night of the blitz from the rooftop of London's air ministry building. "I watched the old city in flames, with St Paul's standing out in the midst of an ocean of fire — an incredible sight," he wrote later. "One could hear the German bombers arriving in a stream and the swish of the incendiaries falling into the fire below." Turning to a fellow officer, Harris said calmly, "They have sowed the wind and now they are going to reap the whirlwind."[18]

CHAPTER 3

THE BOMBER COMMAND FALTERS

"When I look round to see how we can win the war I see that there is only one sure path. There is only one thing that will bring Hitler down and that is absolutely devastating, exterminating attack by very heavy bombers from this country upon the Nazi homeland. We must be able to overwhelm them by this means, without which I do not see a way through."[1] So wrote a desperate Prime Minister Winston Churchill in 1940, as German troops took control of virtually all of mainland Europe. The threat of an enemy invasion of England had diminished, thanks at least partly to the fact that Bomber Command has destroyed 12 per cent of the German army's landing barges in the French ports. If the Wehrmacht couldn't set foot on English soil, the British army couldn't get at the Wehrmacht either. The Royal Navy still ruled the waves, but with the German surface fleet refusing to come out and fight, there was little opportunity to engage the Nazis on water. If the Allies were to conduct any sort of offensive operations, therefore, they'd have to do so in the air, and that meant bombing. The only other options were to continue to sit on the defensive while enemy submarines, known as U-boats, tried to starve Britain into submission, or to attempt to negotiate a peace treaty that would leave Adolf Hitler permanently in charge of Europe.

In reality there really was no choice at all. Even if Hitler could be persuaded to sign a deal, only the most deceived of fools thought he could be trusted to respect it for very long. Britain's War Cabinet decided to launch a "strategic bombing offensive." Aircraft factories were ordered to begin work on four-engine bombers that would be capable of carrying three times the bomb load of the old Wellingtons, Blenheims, Hampdens, and Whitleys. Next, the High Command began casting about for suitable targets. At first there was no thought of making war on civilians. Bomber squadrons even received specific instructions to take every precaution to avoid hitting the residential districts of German cities. Instead, the airmen were to go after industrial and military targets, especially oil refineries, aircraft factories, airfields, and government buildings.

The man put in charge of the offensive was Sir Richard Peirse, whom Churchill hoped would be more aggressive than the departing Ludlow-Hewitt. Ludlow-Hewitt, a deeply religious individual, wasn't believed to be tough enough — or perhaps mean enough — for the task at hand. He had fallen out of favour with his superiors at least partly because he showed so much open anguish over the loss of air crews. Indeed, Ludlow-Hewitt would often personally telephone squadron commanders after particularly rough missions to discuss losses and offer condolences. Although an admirable trait in many ways, the practice tended to make him look weak and afraid. His critics feared he didn't have the stomach to press home the offensive with the vigour that would surely be needed if Germany was going to be bombed into giving up its dreams of world conquest.

One of Peirse's first steps was to ban daylight bombing inside German territory, where fighter escort was not possible because of the short range of the British Spitfires and Hurricanes. Losses on daylight raids had been ten times higher than what was considered the acceptable level, if Bomber Command was going to remain a viable force over the long haul. It hadn't escaped his attention that the Blenheim and Fairey Battle bombers had been slaughtered during day attacks over France, while the Wellingtons, Whitleys, and Hampdens had escaped with relatively few losses during night operations over Germany in the same period.

What Peirse didn't know was that the night strikes had been utterly ineffective. Bomber crews at this stage of the war lacked the navigationa aids necessary to find their targets with anything approaching accuracy. They relied on a system of dead reckoning, which was nothing more than guessing where the target lay based on air speed and how long the planes had been airborne. If there was cloud cover or heavy industrial haze over the target, the crews often couldn't see the ground, even in bright moonlight. Enterprising airmen began flying low, dropping flares in a bid to pinpoint specific targets. But searchlights and withering anti-aircraft fire soon forced them to such high altitudes that there was little hope of hitting their objectives. In the lunar glow they soon discovered they were easy prey for the small, but rapidly growing force of German night fighters.

Bomber pilot Ron Pickler in the cockpit of his Lancaster bomber. Courtesy of Ron Pickler.

Had the Allies known just how badly the bombers were faring during the first months of the offensive, the whole campaign would almost certainly have been called off. It got off to a terrible start on May 15, 1940, when 111 bombers carried out the first raid of the strategic offensive, going after factories in Cologne, Dortmund, and a few other locations in the Ruhr Valley. At Cologne, the bombers missed the city almost completely, scattering the great majority of their high explosives in the adjacent countryside. The only fatal German casualty was farmer Franz Romeike, who was killed in his outhouse. The luckless fellow had turned on a porch light before going out to relieve himself around midnight, and the glow had attracted the attention of the bombers. In Cologne itself, five people were injured by the few bombs that landed inside the city limits. There was some damage in Münster, where two people were hurt, but neither of them required hospitalization. One bomber was shot down that night, so in return for some minor property damage, the killing of a lone farmer, and the wounding of two civilians, Bomber Command had suffered six fatal casualties and the loss of an expensive airplane.

The attacks were even less successful a fortnight later, when two dozen bombers went after the oil refineries at Hamburg and Bremen. Seven bombs landed in Hamburg, totally missing the plant and causing no injuries. At Bremen there was no damage of any kind. Presumably the bombs had landed somewhere in open country outside the darkened city. Another attempt to destroy the Hamburg plant followed before the end of May. It injured one civilian but left the refinery untouched. Over the next several months Bomber Command would go after this important industrial city no less than thirty-six times, killing a grand total of nineteen people. At Münster over the same period, two civilians perished in fourteen raids. Only once did more than ten bombs fall inside the town.

Frequently, the raiders suffered more losses than the Germans. At Cologne on June 17, 1940, for instance, six German civilians died in exchange for the lives of twelve Allied airmen. Even attempts to hit coastal towns, which were much easier to find in the dark than inland communities, met with frustrating failure. That was amply demonstrated at Wilhelmshaven, where twenty-one attacks on the city's dockyards over a four-month period caused what the Germans described in official records as only "trifling" damage.[2] As summer came, the Allied effort became even more inept. On July 3, a Blenheim bomber force missed Hamburg's docks by three miles, killing nineteen people, including eleven children. And a month later Brunswick was bombed, although no planes had been ordered to attack the city.

The most humiliating failure of all came when a bomber crew that set out to attack a German airfield in Holland somehow got turned around during a severe lightning storm over the North Sea. Not realizing they were headed straight for England, the men pressed on with their plan of attack. In some ways the error was entirely understandable. Their magnetic compass was no longer functioning and when they spotted the Thames River below they mistook it for the Rhine. Certain they were on the right course, they kept flying towards what they were sure was the Dutch-German border. Trigger-happy British anti-aircraft gunners helped convince them they were on the right track by sending up a hail of red-hot steel. Undaunted, the airmen kept coming, somehow finding a Royal Air Force fighter station in the dark. For once their bombing was accurate, and they tore up several hundred feet of runway. Fortunately, there were no casualties. The fiasco did nothing to improve Bomber Command's slumping morale — especially not after a flight of Spitfires flew over the offending bomber crew's airfield the next day and sarcastically dropped a box of home-made German Iron Cross medals.

A whole series of disasters now followed in quick succession. At Kiel, more than one hundred planes failed to find the city, dropping their entire bomb load into open country through thick cloud cover. One house was damaged when an unexploded anti-aircraft shell fell into Kiel, but there were no German casualties. Four bombers were, however, shot down in flames. During another even more galling raid, ten planes were lost in exchange for the killing of a few goats in a barnyard near Berlin.

Even attempts to hit a target as large as the Black Forest proved difficult. Aircraft dropped numerous loads of phosphorus-coated strips into that vast woodland, hoping to set fires that would hurt Germany's pulp and paper industries. Despite dozens of attempts, and the loss of several more planes, no major fires were set — at least not in the Black Forest. Several conflagrations did, however, break out aboard bombers carrying these controversial weapons.

About the only major Bomber Command success of this period was achieved quite by accident. It happened over Cologne, when a Canadian Wellington bomber crashed into the streets, attracting a large crowd once the raid was over. As people milled about hoping to gather souvenirs from the wreckage, the plane's bomb load suddenly went off, killing sixteen Germans.

The War Cabinet persisted with the offensive mainly because it had no idea how poorly the bombers were doing. Businessmen from neutral countries often returned from trips to Germany reporting widespread damage in places such as Cologne, Hamburg, and Berlin. This was the result of being too close to the scene. A person standing in the middle of a bomb-ravaged street was often left with the impression that the raid had been devastating, but those looking on from the air in daylight could see that the rest of the city was completely intact.

Adding to the problem was the fact that the airmen were continuously returning to base with glowing reports about the accuracy of their raids. They were expected to get the job done, and they weren't about to come back from every mission reporting failure. Besides that, many genuinely believed they were causing massive damage to German industry. That's clear by reading the reports filed by Royal Canadian Air Force bomber squadrons during the early days of the bomber offensive. The first RCAF bombers went into action on June 12, 1941, over Hamm, Soest, and Schwerte. Many Canadians had flown with RAF outfits prior to those attacks, but this marked the initial appearance of all-Canadian squadrons. More than 200 planes attacked the three cities and five were shot down. At Soest, visibility was so poor that less than half the raiders got anywhere

near the target. Few of those that did managed to hit anything of consequence. At Schwerte the results were no better. And at Hamm a grand
total of seven bombs landed inside the city, killing no one. At least one of
the bombs even failed to explode.

All of this calamity was not an indication that the airmen weren't trying.
Canadian pilot A.C. Clayton, for example, circled over Hamburg twenty minutes one night in September, 1941, trying desperately to pinpoint the big
Blohm and Voss shipyards. It would have been easy for him to simply drop his
bomb load and flee, but he braved heavy flak and the very real risk of fighter
interception in a determined bid to find his target. Eventually, it was spotted,
and RCAF records claim "most satisfactory" fires were started. The flames, however, were actually confined to residential districts far from the intended target.

Nor were the airmen lacking in enterprise. Canadian D.H. Campbell
once flew his twin-engine Hampden so low over a German airfield that his
plane was nearly blown out of the sky by the blast from his own bombs. Still,
he missed the airfield completely, as did all the other forty-four bombers
involved in the operation. The German anti-aircraft gunners had better
luck, shooting down one of the raiders.

In most cases the failures could be blamed on poor weather conditions,
inadequate navigation tools, or inexperience. When Canadian pilot H.V.
Dadson smelled gunpowder from his own gunners' weapons, for instance, he
mistook it for evidence that his plane was on fire and ordered the crew to bail
out. Quickly realizing his mistake, he cancelled the order, but not before one
man had gone out an escape hatch, heading for four years of captivity in a
prisoner-of-war camp.

Adding to the headaches of the bomber crews was German ingenuity.
The defenders often set large decoy fires in open fields, successfully tricking
the bombers into flying away from their cities. A pilot would see the flames,
assume they were caused by bombers that had arrived over the target ahead
of him, and proceed to drop his bombs in the middle of nowhere. On literally dozens of occasions entire bomber forces were fooled in this manner. On
other nights anti-aircraft gunners would purposely withhold their fire, hoping to trick the airmen into thinking they were nowhere near their targets.
Nazi party officials vehemently protested, declaring the population should
see the flak gunners blazing away at the intruders. Flak commanders, however, were more interested in fooling the Allies than they were in scoring
political points, and they often withheld their fire, successfully diverting the
planes away from their intended victims.

Nasty weather was often the biggest headache of all for Bomber Command during the winter of 1940–41, forcing hundreds of aircraft to turn back long before reaching Germany. At first, crews were ordered to bring their bomb loads home if they couldn't find their targets, but after several men died in shattering explosions as bomb-laden planes crashed on landing, the airmen were ordered to ditch their lethal cargos in the North Sea before returning to base.

Crews that pressed gallantly onward that winter despite all the obstacles found they had even more difficulty than usual in finding their targets. Heavy clouds meant bombs often had to be dropped strictly by guesswork. On November 7, 1940, for instance, a large force claimed to have wrecked the giant Krupp Works at Essen, only to be told the next day that daylight reconnaissance photos showed their bombs had landed in a forest several miles away. Wings often iced up in winter as well, forcing pilots to fly dangerously low whether they liked it or not.

While all of this was going on the Luftwaffe was carrying out indiscriminate bombings of London and other British cities, hoping to pressure Churchill into accepting a negotiated peace. The cigar-chomping prime minister responded by ordering Bomber Command to carry out its first so-called area attack on a German city. And so it was on December 17, 1940, that the Allies deliberately went after German civilians for the first time. Some 134 planes carpet bombed Mannheim, an industrial town in southwest Germany, killing thirty-four people and leaving 1200 homeless. Seven bombers were lost, however, costing the attackers forty-two casualties. Once again, from a human point of view, the bomber boys were taking more fatalities than they were dishing out.

Ann Hosseld, who was a teenager in Mannheim at the time, says her town escaped heavy losses because it was well prepared for air raids. "Mannheim was better off than many cities because it had a lot of big underground bunkers where everybody went. Some shelters had ten thousand people in them. And it had highrises that were five or six storeys high with three or four feet of concrete on top. Some smart mayor had the foresight to build these things up." People felt so secure that there wasn't the same hysteria that would be reported in other cities later in the war. "On the whole it was quite orderly in the shelters," she said. "You just sat there and waited. What else could you do? People reacted differently. You tried not to get hysterical. You could feel the vibrations from the bombs even inside the shelters. But I remember my mother was always very calm."

The raid was a failure in other respects too. Although it was led by eight of the best crews in Bomber Command, the bombs were scattered over a wide area, with many missing the city altogether.

After the Mannheim mission Bomber Command reverted back to a campaign of attacking industries and military targets. It was viewed by the Allies as a one-time event, designed to warn Hitler that if he kept bombing British cities the Royal Air Force would strike back at his towns. There were some people in high places, however, who wanted to make area bombings a regular feature of the aerial offensive. Sir Charles Portal, the British Chief of Air Staff, suggested that radio warnings be broadcast alerting the Germans that Bomber Command intended to raze twenty major cities to the ground. He argued strategic bombing just wasn't working, and that area attacks would be far more fruitful. If a bomb missed a factory, Portal reasoned, it would still hit something of value inside the city, provided that the aiming point was the centre of town. However, the idea was rejected, mainly because Bomber Command still believed it was hitting German industry hard.

In March 1941 the Allies took an unintentional step towards area bombing. It happened when Churchill ordered the airmen to go after enemy submarine pens and U-boat factories. He was deeply concerned that England would lose the Battle of the Atlantic if more wasn't done to curb the Nazi submarines. "We must take the offensive against the U-boats whenever we can," he wrote. "The U-boat at sea must be hunted, the U-boat in the building yard or dock must be bombed."[3] The campaign lasted four months, but it was hobbled from the beginning by the clever tactics of the defenders. The Germans laid down thick smoke screens during daylight raids on their French-based U-boat pens, causing thousands of tons of high explosives to fall harmlessly short of their targets. Even direct hits on the concrete pens did little damage.

As one failure followed another Bomber Command became more desperate — and reckless. Before long it was frequently hitting residential districts adjacent to the U-boat factories. The factories were located in Hamburg, Germany's second-largest city, and the raids produced far more bloodshed than had earlier attacks. In all, Hamburg suffered 331 dead in eighteen bombings during this period. That was three times as many as had been killed in seventy-two previous strikes. At Kiel, another important U-boat base, 254 civilians died in seventeen assaults, or ten times as many as had perished in sixteen prior raids. Clearly, Bomber Command was being less careful about where its bombs landed.

None of this was a concern to Air Marshal Arthur Harris, who wrote a memo saying one of the benefits of attacking submarine engine factories at Stuttgart and Mannheim was that the raids were having a negative impact on civilian morale in those communities.

In any case, the truth is that as the late summer of 1941 approached, the bomber offensive was a shambles. The Germans, it was later established, didn't even know Bomber Command had been trying for over a year to attack their oil industry. Making all of this even harder to swallow was the mounting cost. Dozens of aircraft were being lost every month, along with some of the most experienced airmen in Bomber Command. An examination of RCAF records shows the Canadian bomber squadrons had already lost three commanders, including R.C. Biset and P.A. Gilchrist, both of whom had been in on the first Allied propaganda leaflet-dropping operations in 1939. W.B. Keddy, who had been in the air force for four years, was also dead. Even the redoubtable Moose Fulton, considered to be Canada's leading bomber pilot at this stage of the war, had gone missing over Hamburg.

The story of Montreal pilot Bruce Campbell, who was shot down in July, 1941, shows just how unprepared the airmen were for the task at hand. "This was very early in the war," he said later, "and we didn't have radar, as such. As a matter of fact, we were being fed Brussels sprouts and special pills and eating carrots to improve our night visions."[4]

The special diet didn't allow his crew to spot an attacking German fighter one night over Düsseldorf, and his plane was riddled with cannon fire. Smelling smoke, he went to an escape hatch and prepared to bail out. "There was a handle you twisted and a door would open up. You had a chest 'chute, and you'd just fall out. I remember trying to get this door open and just a portion of it would open. I could see, down on the ground below, fires and everything else. But I couldn't get this door open. I lived my whole life over again. And all was peaceful.

"The next thing I remember, I was falling through the air. It was a moonless night, no sign of aircraft. And as I went to pull my 'chute I said to myself, 'I've got to hang onto this, because you'll be fined if you don't return it.' You could be fined two shillings if you didn't return the 'chute. The things you think of in that situation." Hitting the ground with terrific force, he lost a shoe, said a quick prayer and headed for Holland on foot. He was sheltered for a time by a Dutch woman, who hid him in her barn. But the Germans soon caught up with him, shot the woman, who was a mother of three, and shipped Campbell off to a prisoner-of-war camp.

While Bomber Command continued to falter, the Nazis were rolling from one stunning victory to another. In May 1941 they invaded Yugoslavia, occupying most of that country within weeks. The Luftwaffe helped pave the way to victory with a crushing raid that killed 17 000 civilians in Belgrade in a single afternoon. Unopposed by either flak or fighters, the bombers came in low, in broad daylight, raining their bombs onto the city with astonishing accuracy. Days later Hitler sent his armies crashing into Russia, hurling the Red Army back hundreds of miles in just a few days with a series of punishing blows. Within weeks Nazi bombers would be pounding Moscow.

By August, with the Germans appearing virtually unbeatable on all fronts, Churchill received a chilling report from War Cabinet Secretary D.M. Butt, who had been carefully studying the effects of the bomber offensive against Germany. Butt had analyzed thousands of aerial photographs, taken both during and after raids and had read the combat reports of hundreds of crews. His findings were startling. Among other things, he concluded one third of the airmen didn't even claim to find their target on the average raid. Of those who did, only one in three came within five miles of hitting it. Over the Ruhr Valley, where industrial pollution made navigation even more dicey, only one in ten got that close. Bomber Command's top brass protested that the study was flawed, but the British government's faith in the strategic bomber offensive had been shaken to the core.

Butt's report couldn't have come at a worse time, as far as its impact on Allied morale was concerned. That's because the Axis powers were on the verge of total victory. Hitler's legions controlled virtually all of mainland Europe and, in the east, they were almost to the gates of Moscow. One more thunderous blow would send the Nazis straight to the Caucasus. In the Atlantic Ocean, German U-boats were sinking Allied ships faster than they could be built, thus threatening England's vital North American lifeline. Indeed, more than 1000 transport vessels had already gone to watery graves, and the German submarine fleet was only just hitting its stride. To the south, Italian and German troops had captured Greece, Yugoslavia, and much of North Africa. Celebrated Field Marshal Erwin Rommel's vaunted Afrika Korps, fresh from a string of spectacular victories, was poised to run the British Eighth Army right off the continent. After that, the Desert Fox, as Rommel was called, planned to seize Egypt, the Suez Canal, and the entire oil-rich Middle East. If that happened, Britain would lose up to a quarter of its supply of oil. In the Far East, meanwhile, the Japanese Imperial Navy had destroyed the American Pacific fleet at Pearl Harbor on

December 7, 1941. Since that time, Japan's forces had trounced British, Canadian, Dutch, and American troops at Hong Kong, Singapore, Manila, Baatan, and Wake Island. With those rapid-fire conquests Japan now ruled much of China, which it had overrun prior to Pearl Harbor, most of Southeast Asia, and much of the Pacific. In fact, Japanese soldiers controlled fully one third of the globe, including the vital oil fields of Borneo and Indonesia, along with 85 per cent of the earth's natural rubber production. What's more, the Rising Sun threatened Australia, where the northern city of Darwin had already felt the sting of enemy bombs, as well as India and Hawaii. Even North America wasn't safe. Nazi U-boats were prowling openly in the St Lawrence River, sinking ships just north of Quebec City. Japanese submarines were operating off the coast of California. A few Japanese planes had even been spotted over Alaska's Aleutian Islands.

With their armed forces triumphant virtually everywhere, the Axis dictators began rounding up so-called sub-humans in the conquered territories. In Europe, Hitler shipped millions of Jews, Gypsies, Slavs, Russians, and others deemed unfit to live off to concentration camps and the gas chambers. In the Far East, the less-methodical Japanese relied on bullets and bayonets to slaughter a million non-combatants in China. Hundreds of thousands of others, including thousands of prisoners of war, were herded into slave labour camps where they would work until they dropped dead from exhaustion or hunger.

As 1941 came to a close, it is no exaggeration to say that the barbarians were at the gates. It looked very much as if the dictatorships were going to overwhelm the democracies and enslave the entire world.

CHAPTER 4

THE EARLY RAIDS ON GERMANY

As 1942 dawned the Allies faced a crisis. They had to decide whether to continue the strategic bomber offensive or resign themselves to fighting a strictly defensive war, waiting fearfully for the Nazis to make their next move.

There was open debate about what to do next. In Britain's House of Commons, opposition MP Stafford Cripps argued that with the entry of the Americans and Russians into the war the British Commonwealth was no longer standing alone and, therefore, no longer had to rely on bombing. MP A.V. Hill was even more blunt, openly declaring the bomber campaign had been a colossal failure. "We know that most of the bombs we drop hit nothing of importance," he said. "The disaster of this policy is not only that it is futile, but that it is extremely wasteful."[1] Lord Beaverbrook, the New Brunswick businessman who was now Britain's Minister of Aircraft Production, sounded a similar theme. He urged Prime Minister Churchill to call off the offensive and send the bombers to other theatres of war, such as North Africa and the Far East. In the Canadian House of Commons, meanwhile, there wasn't a whisper of debate about the campaign, despite the fact that thousands of RCAF personnel were helping to carry it out.

Churchill decided he had no option but to continue the bombing. The only question that remained was whether the airmen should carry on with largely ineffective raids against military and industrial targets or adopt a policy of carpet bombing German cities. Air Marshal Charles Portal favoured carpet bombing, which the high command preferred to call "area bombing." He called for the creation of a massive air armada of 4000 planes, which he said would be capable of forcing the enemy to surrender within six months. Such a huge fleet of bombers could destroy all of Germany's major cities and the industries in them, he said. The chaos that would result from such a relentless aerial assault would surely cause domestic collapse. In a blood-curdling paper delivered to the Chiefs of Staff, Portal frankly predicted 4000 aircraft could obliterate six million homes, kill 900 000 civilians, and leave twenty-five million more homeless by 1944. Forty-three major German cities could be utterly destroyed. The campaign could also be counted on to wreck at least a third of Germany's industries.

Lord Cherwell, the prime minister's scientific advisor, was in full agreement. He predicted that area bombing would make one in every three Germans homeless. Studies carried out in England following Luftwaffe attacks had found civilian morale sagged noticeably when homes were destroyed. In fact, individuals seemed more distraught when their homes were lost than they were when loved ones were killed, he said. A bomber force such as Portal envisioned, he added, could smash fifty-eight German cities and break the spirit of the population. British scientist Frederick Lindemann, a favourite of Churchill's, also confidently predicted destroying the homes of workers would break morale and produce victory.

Churchill, whose faith in bombers had been shaken by the Butt report, vetoed the idea of building 4000 of them. For one thing, England couldn't afford it. Each plane would cost tens of thousands of pounds and that would put an intolerable strain on the economy. Even if Britain had the money, it didn't possess enough workers for the task. Such a program would consume millions of hours of work. In fact, it took 76 000 hours to build just one four-engine bomber. Besides all that, Churchill no longer believed Bomber Command could win the war by itself. "It is very disputable whether bombing by itself will be a decisive factor in the present war," he wrote Portal. "On the contrary, all that we have learnt since the war began shows that its effects, both physical and moral, are greatly exaggerated."[2] What's more, he added, Germany could probably continue to fight even if all its cities were blown off the map. The Nazis, after all, controlled all of mainland Europe and could build factories in occupied countries. If that happened, the Allies would be helpless to do anything, unless they were willing to destroy such places as Paris, Amsterdam, and Brussels.

Why did Churchill decide to continue with the offensive? Because he was by nature a man of action. To sit idly by and do nothing wasn't in his make-up. Bomber Command was the only offensive tool available to him, and he was going to use it, come hell or high water. Besides that, he knew if the bombers couldn't win the war they could at least *help* bring victory. And that was better than nothing. There were also political considerations. If the Western Allies simply sat back while the Russians fought for dear life against the whole might of Nazi Germany, Soviet leader Joseph Stalin might try to negotiate a separate peace with Hitler. One way to keep the Russians in the war was to show them that the West was serious about coming to grips with the enemy. It wasn't yet possible to open up a second front by invading Europe, but there was no reason why the air offensive couldn't be stepped up.

The bomber raids were therefore allowed to continue. Churchill, however, wasn't going to put all his eggs in one basket by building 4000 bombers. Nor was he willing to permit the disastrous policies of 1940 and 1941 to continue. During that period Bomber Command had lost 4000 highly trained airmen — or about the same number of German civilians that it had slain. At that rate, the air force would be wiped out long before Germany. Churchill sanctioned the controversial "area bombing" policy on February 14, 1942. A directive from his War Cabinet went out to Bomber Command on that date spelling out exactly what was expected. It reads in part: "It has been decided the primary objective of your operations should now be focused on the morale of the enemy civil population and in particular of the industrial workers... the aiming points are to be the built-up areas, not, for instance dockyards or aircraft factories."[3] In other words, Bomber Command was under direct orders to attack German civilians. Portal was the man who had pushed hardest for area bombing, but it was Churchill who made the final decision.

At the same time, it was decided that the public should not be informed of the change in policy. Minutes from British Cabinet meetings show the government felt that "it was better that actions should speak louder than words in this manner."[4] It was obvious the Allies were keeping the new policy under wraps for fear that there would be widespread public disapproval. They needn't have worried, at least not in Canada, where a Gallup poll conducted that year found 57 per cent of Canadians approved the bombing of German civilians. Only 38 per cent disapproved. That same year, a Maclean's magazine article raised the issue of whether all Germans should be sterilized after the war. Clearly, after three years of bitter fighting, the public was in a ruthless and hateful mood.

The new policy was in place, and now Churchill had to find someone to carry it out. He had no faith in Bomber Command's chief, A.M. Peirse, who had overseen a whole series of disasters after taking over for the equally ineffective Ludlow-Hewitt. The final straw had come in November, 1941, when Peirse had sent a large force out in extremely bad weather, losing nearly forty bombers to the elements in a single night. The prime minister was so anxious to get rid of him that Peirse was dumped even before the new bombing directive was issued. In his place, Churchill appointed the commander of Five Group, Air Marshal Arthur Harris.

Harris! For the first time since war had broken out Bomber Command was headed by a fighter. Born in England on April 13, 1892, the forty-nine-year-old Harris was the son of a civil servant who had left home as a sixteen-year-old boy to seek his fame and fortune in Rhodesia's gold fields. He didn't find it, ending up instead as a driver of horse-drawn wagons. Later, he settled into a life of farming. It was hard work but he loved Africa and it's doubtful he would ever have left — or that the world would ever have heard of him — if not for the outbreak of the First World War. As soon as fighting broke out Harris joined the Rhodesian army as a bugle boy. Quickly tiring of the ceaseless marches, he volunteered for pilot training with Britain's Royal Flying Corps. Ironically, the man who would go down in history as "Bomber" Harris, started his air force career as a night fighter pilot. He spent hundreds of hours dodging British anti-aircraft fire over London as he carried out fruitless searches for German Zeppelins. Although he never caught up with one of the giant dirigibles personally, one of the men in his command, Lieutenant Leefe-Robinson, gained lasting fame by shooting a Zeppelin out of the sky right over the heart of the capital.

Posted to France for daylight combat over the Western Front, Harris proved himself a brave and resourceful pilot. There were few aviators on either side as aggressive. In one of his combat reports, he described how he attacked a giant yellow Albatros two-seater, getting in so close that all he could see in his telescopic gun sight was the fuselage of his opponent. Ignoring the presence of a pair of nearby enemy fighters, he fired thirty bullets from point-blank range, blowing both wings off the German machine, which crashed in flames. On another occasion, Harris shot down a bomber, killing the rear gunner before zooming over the German's top wing at the last possible moment, barely avoiding a collision. Another victory was scored at twenty yards range — an incredibly close distance in aerial combat.

Noted for his penetrating blue eyes, forthright manner and blunt speech, Harris was not an especially popular flight commander. Some were undoubtedly jealous of his success. Harris, after all, had only been a front-line officer for two months when he was made the leader of a flight of six fighter pilots. More than a few pilots were put off by his willingness to take losses in order

Bomb aimer Ron Evans with his hand on a 4,000 lb. bomb. Courtesy of the author.

to gain victories. The best example of that trait came when he led his flight against a much larger German formation, losing two men in exchange for six kills. In one three-day period he lost half his flight. By the time the war was over Harris was an ace, with five single-handed victories to his credit and the Air Force Cross pinned to his chest. He'd also gained attention by inventing a device that allowed pilots to count the number of bullets they had fired, so they would know in the midst of a dogfight if they were running low on ammunition.

After the war, Harris stayed in the RAF where, despite his obvious talents as a fighter pilot, he was given command of a bomber squadron. The posting was not as inexplicable as it seems today. The theory at that time was that the days of dashing young fighter aces were over. In future wars, it was thought, bombers would be the principal air weapons. In any case, when the Second World War broke out, Harris was given command of his own bomber group, where he quickly gained a reputation as a crack leader.

Regardless of how talented he was, Harris faced what looked like an impossible task. He had orders to knock out four major cities in the heavily industrialized Ruhr Valley, plus fourteen other lesser towns, all during the first three months of his command. Harris was expected to do it with a front-line force of just 378 serviceable bombers, including only seventy of the four-engine Halifax heavies. All the rest were twin-engine medium or single-engine light bombers, capable of providing the army with excellent front-line support, but totally inadequate for the task of destroying cities.

If Harris was perturbed he didn't show it. He was determined to inflict the maximum possible damage on Germany with the tools available to him while, at the same time, pressing the high command for new and bigger bombers at every opportunity. He instituted immediate changes designed to make the offensive more effective. He demanded and got larger bombs. No longer would the airmen drop piddly 250-pounders on their targets. Instead, they'd carry 500-pound and even 4000-pound blockbusters capable of knocking down whole rows of buildings. He also sharply increased the use of incendiaries, reasoning that it would be far easier to burn a city to the ground than to attempt to blow up every building. He'd use the big blast bombs to blow out windows and tear off rooftops, then shower the target with incendiaries, which could do more damage if they fell directly inside buildings. On a typical mission, high-explosive bombs would not only knock out buildings, they'd rip apart streets, making it difficult for fire trucks to get to the places where they were most needed. Harris also introduced bomb aimers who were specifically trained to hit targets accurately. Until that innovation, navigators had been expected to both locate the target and drop the bombs. His next move was to continuously throw his whole force at a single city in a single night. Gone were the days when three or four separate forces of forty or fifty planes each would try to hit three or four different targets a night. Now, 200, or even 300 bombers would plaster a single community. Harris would send his men back night after night until the area had been utterly destroyed.

Finally, to get concentration over the target, Harris was willing to send all his planes over a city in one or two hours. This greatly increased the risk of collisions, but it cut in half the time his men had to spend over the most dangerous parts of Germany, making it far more difficult for the defenders to respond to a raid.

Harris had no time for critics. He made that clear in a newsreel interview granted soon after assuming his post. Staring straight into the camera, he said ominously, "There are a lot of people who say that bombing alone cannot win the war. My reply is that it has never been tried. We shall see."[5]

He ruthlessly stripped his planes of armour plating and even took out a bed designed for the use of sick or wounded crewmen, so each aircraft would be able to carry more bombs. Partially because of such actions he quickly became known as "Butcher" or "Butch" to the airmen who served under him. Indeed, reaction to his methods was decidedly mixed on the bomber stations. Canadian Dave McIntosh is scathing in his memoirs. "Butch Harris didn't give a damn how many men he lost as long as he was pounding the

Stirling bomber about to take off. Courtesy of Jack Western.

shit out of German civilians," he wrote. "Butcher was the deserved nick-name of the RAF chief of Bomber Command. An air force twin for Haig of the Somme, Ypres and Passchendaele. One thing about Harris, though, he played no favourites. He was just as willing to sacrifice Brits as Canadians."[6]

Ontario pilot Lyle James took a much more charitable view. "I worshipped him. If you're going to war with a general, he was the one you wanted to go with. The Russians were screaming for a second front and for the first four and a half years we couldn't get at the Germans with our army. He made a second front in the air. He was a pilot's pilot."[7]

Besides that, it soon became evident that Harris was demanding — and getting — better equipment for his men. And when he couldn't secure new planes fast enough, he simply retired some of the more obsolete aircraft under his command. He immediately ordered several dozen Stirling and Hampden bombers put on the shelf because they were no longer up to the task at hand. It was a courageous decision because he needed every plane he could get.

There's no doubt Harris faced a daunting task, but making it a little easier were two new navigation and bombing aids that came on stream just as he took charge. Called GEE and OBOE, the devices would prove to be of enormous help in locating targets in the dead of night. They would be so beneficial that the bombers would eventually stop coming by moonlight. That, in turn, made it much harder for the German night fighter pilots to locate them. GEE was an instrument that allowed a navigator to calculate the bomber's location by receiving pulse signals from a trio of widely scattered stations in Britain. GEE calculated the differences between the signals, giving the navigator an immediate fix on his own position. Its range, however, was limited to about 400 miles, which meant it couldn't be used much beyond the Ruhr Valley and a few North Sea port towns. OBOE was a bomb-aiming device that was also controlled from the United Kingdom. A pair of stations transmitted pulses to the bombers, which received them and retransmitted them back to England. By calculating the time it took to get the pulses back, the people in the ground stations could get a fix on the plane's position and tell it exactly when it should release its bombs. If everyone did their jobs right the typical bomb-aiming error could be slashed from the average of five to ten miles to a scant 300 yards. Of course to achieve such accuracy the pilot had to fly in a straight line for several minutes, making him highly susceptible to enemy fighters and flak as he approached the target. Nevertheless, OBOE would prove to be a real breakthrough.

Another important development was the arrival of the fabled Lancaster heavy bomber. Affectionately known as the "Lanc" to all aircrew, it would turn out to be the finest bomber of the whole war. It was both sleek and powerful. Weighing 65 000 pounds when fully loaded, it could reach speeds of 277 miles per hour and climb beyond 20 000 feet. What's more, its four Merlin engines and large fuel tanks gave it an amazing range of 1700 miles, making it capable of striking any target in the Third Reich. And its payload, which could be as much as 18 000 pounds of bombs, made it the terror of every town in Germany. Airmen loved it because it could take an unbelievable amount of punishment and stay airborne. Pilots soon discovered the highly reliable Lanc could even land after three of its four engines had been knocked out.

If there was a drawback it was the plane's armament, which consisted of eight .303 machine-guns, including two in the nose, two in the mid-upper turret, and four in the tail. They had good range and a rapid rate of fire, but lacked the deadly punch of the cannon carried by enemy night fighters.

Most Lancasters were painted in green and brown camouflage patterns, although some were coated entirely in black to make them more difficult to spot at night. Red, white, and blue RAF roundels were painted on the wings and fuselage.

The Lancaster normally bombed from 20 000 feet, not out of the range of flak, but higher than the old Wellingtons and Stirlings, which were much easier to shoot down. Harris immediately fell in love with the powerful new

Bomber crew in front of Lancaster bomber. Courtesy of the author.

bomber and began demanding that all of his squadrons be equipped with it. It would take time, but with his relentless badgering, Harris would eventually be successful in securing this deadly new weapon for most of his men.

So, Bomber Command headed into the third month of 1942 with an aggressive new leader, improved navigation and bomb aiming devices, better aircraft, and a whole new strategy. The High Command held its breath, anxiously awaiting results. Harris wasn't long in delivering.

Harris's first major operation, against a truck factory in the French town of Billancourt, just outside Paris, was in many ways an example of what the new offensive would look like from now on. Bomber Command set several records that March 3 evening, sending 235 planes after the Renault factory, six more than had been deployed against Kiel a year earlier. And the concentration of bombers over the target was estimated at 121 per hour, well in excess of the previous mark of eighty. In addition, a record number of bombs fell — 470 tons. The mission was unique in other ways, too, featuring as it did the mass use of signal flares to light up the target. Also, for the first time, the raid was led by handpicked crews. It was, in many ways, similar to the famous Pathfinder raids that would be seen in years to come.

From a military point of view the operation was a complete success. Some 300 bombs fell smack in the midst of the plant, destroying nearly half its buildings. Production ceased for a full month, and it was early summer before the facility was running again at full capacity. In all, the disruption cost the German army an estimated 2300 trucks. The triumph came with an appalling price tag. Although no bombers were shot down, scores of apartment buildings near the target were flattened. Because no one had expected an Allied attack on a French town, few had taken shelter. When the smoke cleared, more than 700 French men, women, and children lay dead or injured. Nine thousand more were left homeless.

The Nazis tried to whip up anti-Allied feelings among the survivors, claiming that the RAF had callously slaughtered French civilians, but they had little success. In fact, George Gorse, who was a prominent Billancourt citizen living in England, wrote a newspaper article declaring the people of France would have to accept some casualties from Allied bombing if they were to be liberated. "Those who died have also bought their own contribution to the coming of dawn," he wrote. It would be easy to dismiss his words as flowery rhetoric not shared by the people who were under the bombs that night. There is, however, evidence that Gorse's views were widely held because, after the war, he was elected mayor of Billancourt.

Next came the controversial raid on the Baltic port city of Lubeck. There were a few U-boat building yards in the town but, essentially, it was a rather unimportant place that was not well defended. Harris was perfectly blunt about why he picked it, writing in his memoirs that he wanted to test out his city-burning theories. Lubeck, a Medieval community constructed of half-timbered wooden buildings with narrow streets, was ideal for such an experiment. "From the nature of its buildings it was easier than most cities to set on fire," Harris wrote. "The main object of the attack was to learn to what extent a first wave of aircraft could guide a second wave to the aiming point by starting a conflagration. I ordered a half hour interval between the two waves in order to allow the fires to get a good hold before the second wave arrived."[9]

If Harris wanted to create a hell on earth he was successful. In all, 234 bombers dropped 160 tons of bombs. The results were devastating. Aided by a full moon, the airmen carried out the first truly punishing attack on a German city since war had begun. More than 60 per cent of this beautiful old town was destroyed, including many buildings of historic and/or architectural importance. More than 300 civilians died and 700 more were wounded. Canadian airmen taking part in the raid reported that the fires could still be seen for one hundred miles on the return trip.

In the Allied nations, where war-weary populations were starving for some good news, Harris was hailed as a genius. The British Air Ministry announced to the world that Lubeck's industries would be out of production for two months. In fact, they were back on line within seven days. Clearly, most of the bombs had landed in residential districts.

At first the Germans downplayed Lubeck, not wanting to admit publicly that they'd been badly mauled. The Luftwaffe, in particular, was not anxious to concede that it had failed, for the first time, to protect a German city from major devastation. The Nazis were howling from the rooftops a month later, when Bomber Command burned much of the North Sea port of Rostock to ashes.

Once again Harris had gone after a relatively unimportant — and lightly defended — city. And once more he was out to burn it to the ground. Like Lubeck, Rostock was also an ancient town, filled with wooden structures packed closely together. It was home to the Heinkel aircraft factory but, like Lubeck, it really was of only minor industrial importance.

It was considered such an insignificant target that many people didn't bother to seek shelter whenever they heard the air raid sirens go off. They assumed the planes were merely passing overhead on their way to some other destination. Hans Richter, who was a thirteen-year-old schoolboy in Rostock at the time, told the author his parents sometimes didn't even bother to get out of bed when the alarm sounded. "This gave my brother and me the opportunity to watch the spectacle of searchlights in the night sky and tracer bullets flying all around. It was a thrill for us." But that all changed soon enough. "Heavy bombing raids on Rostock started on April 22, 1942, at nighttime by Lancaster bombers. Sitting in the basement we heard the bombs exploding and the flak guns shooting. Sometimes consecutive bomb explosions became louder and louder, then we always wondered if the next one would hit our house. At one time an incendiary stick came through the roof tiles and got stuck in a roof beam. My father saw it on one of his frequent inspections of the attic. He hacked the burning stick out of the beam and threw it on the street."

The Richter family moved to a nearby village where, two nights later, young Hans looked on from a distance as his home town was destroyed. "We could see from the distance the sky lighting up as the city was again bombed. As we returned the old city centre was destroyed."

Indeed, flames had raced through the entire city, devouring 1200 buildings and killing more than 200 people. Nazi propaganda chief Josef

Hans Richter (centre), a German schoolboy at Rostock. Courtesy of Hans Richter.

Goebbels told his diary "community life in Rostock is practically at an end."[10]

For once Germany's state-controlled media didn't attempt to downplay an attack. Radio reporters used the term "terror raid" for the first time and the magazine *Signal* printed an emotional account of what had happened weeks earlier in Lubeck. Writer Benno Wundshammer's heart-wrenching account of the destruction of Lubeck's oldest church has survived. It reads in part:

"A truck rattles in the principal nave of the burnt out Mother Church of Lubeck. Sappers and men belonging to the emergency service have dug a round bronze vessel out of the charred rafters and using their combined strength they push it into the truck standing ready. 'This is the only thing remaining over from all the treasures, pictures, carvings and works of art in this church,' an elderly gentleman says to me. 'This half-melted bronze is a baptismal font dating from the fourteenth century and we are going to see if it can be restored.' The old gentleman precedes me making his way across grating splinters of glass, ruined walls and smouldering pews. 'This is where our famous organ stood. That, too, was devoured by the flames and is now buried under the ruins of the roof which caved in.' The worst loss of all is probably that of a famous danse macabre by an unknown Medieval master. But there are such a lot of things I could tell you. Not only this church is burnt out, but nearly all the churches, to which Lubeck owed its name, the city of the golden towers, were destroyed during the night when the British attacked our town.

"We leave the church and outside bright sunshine is streaming over the yellow ruins of the burnt down Old Town. The streets of Old Lubeck have been turned into quarries. The market place is surrounded by ruins. The town hall is completely burnt out. The rich carving on the doors and panels, the magnificent tarsia work, the wonderful alabaster friezes, and valuable treasures of the Renaissance were gutted in a single night. All the romantic alleys in the craftmen's quarter of the town no longer exist. In the air there is a penetrating odour of marzipan coming from what remains of the largest cafe in Lubeck which was famed for its marzipan.... An inestimable number of art treasures, gathered together in the old patrician houses by generation after generation, were destroyed. There was the 'Schifferhaus' with its magnificent wood carvings and iron work, models of Medieval ships, there was the famous old museum... the Lubeck Cathedral suffered severely. During the night a soldier penetrated into the burning interior of the church and out of the inferno of crashing rafters and caving vaults saved the famous Memling Altar, a masterpiece of Flemish wall painting. The Cathedral Museum and Cathedral School were damaged by bombs, the Church of St Peter was burnt down as well as the Agidia Church and the Katherineum, which housed the municipal library."

As Wundshammer continued to write he grew increasingly bitter. "Blind destructive fury and murderous vandalism raged over the town and no attempt to alter the facts, however ingenious, will be able to make it appear credible that these were military objectives. I flew over the town in the afternoon and convinced myself that the centre of the town, lying between broad stretches of water, cannot possibly be mistaken. There can be no question in this case of bombs missing their mark, or mistakes, particularly when it is taken into account that the moon was shining brightly over the town during the night of the attack. I am an airman myself and am able to judge."[11]

Readers of *Signal* could be forgiven if they felt indignant. Few likely remembered that the same publication had written a gloating article about the bombing of Rotterdam two years earlier. Under the heading "The Spectacle of Total War," the writer had noted, "after Warsaw it was Rotterdam that, issuing a challenge, learned how hopeless it was to resist the German Luftwaffe — and paid for the lesson by the destruction of the centre of the city."[12]

After Renault, Lubeck, and Rostock, morale on the bomber stations literally soared. There had been an enormous amount of positive publicity in the Allied newspapers about all three raids, and the airmen felt that, at long last, they were getting somewhere. They knew large numbers of planes were going out on every mission and, from the fires they could see burning below, they knew they were hitting the Germans hard.

Harris had proven he could hurt the enemy, now he wanted to demonstrate to the world that Bomber Command could win the war by itself. And to do that, he planned to send 1000 bombers out to destroy a major city in a single night.

On the surface, his idea seemed like sheer lunacy. Bomber Command only had 400 aircraft available at any one time. But Harris reached into the training schools, calling up instructors, student pilots, and the planes they flew. When he still didn't have enough men and machines, he borrowed crews and aircraft from Coastal Command to attain the magic 1000 figure.

What Harris was planning was the most spectacular gamble of the war. With so many planes airborne at once, the risk of collision over the target was greatly magnified. Indeed, some air force officials glumly predicted at least one hundred bombers would be lost. Undaunted, Harris ordered each pilot to fly at a specific height, hoping that would cut down on the casualties. Finally, on May 30, 1942, the greatest aerial armada ever assembled set out in bright moonlight with orders to blast the cathedral city of Cologne to bits.

In Cologne that warm spring night the first hint of trouble came when journalist Josef Fischer's dog suddenly wet the living room floor and rolled over on its back, yelping in terror. The family knew from past experience that the dog could hear planes groaning across the sky long before human ears could detect the sound of their engines, so they quickly headed for the cellar. Minutes later, bombs were raining out of the night. The family, Fischer wrote afterwards, spent the next few hours huddled together "like animals during a violent thunderstorm."[13]

Others were caught in the open. Bank employee Richard Frank was strolling home from a pleasant evening of bowling when the air-raid sirens began wailing. He dashed to the nearest shelter, only to find the door locked. Keeping cool, he ran to the Rhine River, taking refuge beneath one of its many bridges. Moments later several soldiers joined him. "We huddled together in this hail of bombs, watching with horror the reflection of the burning city in the waters of the river,"[14] he recounted later. Suddenly, a bomb exploded right beside them, tearing off a leg of one of Frank's young companions.

The bombed-out buildings in Cologne, Germany. Twenty thousand of the city's residents were killed in air raids. Courtesy of Ulli Waschkowski.

Within minutes much of the city was in flames. Canadian pilot Johnny Fauquier, who was in the second of three waves of bombers, reported seeing smoke billowing 10 000 feet above the burning city. He estimated seven-eighths of Cologne was on fire and told a reporter afterwards, "It didn't seem possible we could do any more damage than had already been done."[15]

In fact, 10 000 buildings were engulfed in flames, and smoke was choking people to death all over the city.

Firefighter Erich Behnke was haunted forever afterwards by the cries of terrified people trapped in smoke-filled basements. He saw cellars filled with corpses, many of whom were clinging pathetically to steel-barred windows.

One of those who survived the smoke was brewer Hans Sion. He couldn't make it to a bomb shelter in time but managed to scramble into the basement of Cologne's great cathedral. Within minutes the whole place was filled with smoke, and his eyes stung so badly that he was blinded for nearly a week. At least he was still alive.

In all, almost 500 people lay dead and 5000 were injured. Forty-five thousand more were homeless. For the loss of just forty-one airplanes Bomber Command had all but wrecked Germany's third-largest city. Amazingly, the Cologne newspaper was still able to get an edition on the street the next day. In it, reporter Franz Berger summed up the tragedy this way: "To all who surveyed the attacked city May 31 it was instantly clear they had bid their farewell to Cologne. Destruction is tremendous everywhere. Destroyed buildings, damaged schools, churches, hospitals, museums, monuments, many warehouses and shops are still burning. Whole quarters of the town are empty, the windows in ruins."

In Allied nations the newspapers were reporting Bomber Command could win the war by itself. Reporter Drew Middleton of the Associated Press was telling his readers, "Germany can be knocked out of the war by fall, crushed by huge fleets of British and American bombers, air experts predicted today as the German city of Cologne lay in flaming ruin under the most devastating air raid in history."

"When the RAF sent more than one thousand bombers with the greatest weight of steel and explosives ever borne on wings into the Rhineland Saturday night," these sources declared, "its fliers heralded not only an eventual invasion of Hitler's Europe, but also the systematic destruction of his war machine, city by city, factory by factory."

The Cologne raid had silenced Bomber Command's critics. There would be no further talk of abandoning the bomber offensive. Instead, a major effort would be made to bomb Germany right out of the war.

CHAPTER 5

THE COMMONWEALTH AIR TRAINING PLAN

The decision had been made to destroy Germany by bombing, and now it was necessary to build up a force powerful enough to carry out such a grim task. Although Prime Minister Churchill had rejected as too expensive Portal's call for a 4000-bomber air armada, he realized Bomber Command would have to be dramatically expanded if it was to have any hope of achieving its objectives. And that meant tens of thousands of airmen would have to be trained for combat. This was no minor task. Dozens of training schools, recruiting centres, and airfields would have to be established.

It was obvious from the start that the United Kingdom was not the place for such an undertaking. For one thing, Britain didn't have the vast, wide-open spaces required. For another, England was still under the constant threat of air attack. The last thing the Allied commanders wanted was to have scores of rookies flying around the countryside in unarmed trainers when experienced Luftwaffe fighter pilots might show up at any moment. Therefore, it was decided that the British Commonwealth Air Training Plan (BCATP), as it came to be known, would have to be established overseas. Three countries were considered, including Egypt, Cyprus, and Canada. The first two were a gamble, because the Germans and Italians still controlled the Mediterranean Sea and much of North Africa. Canada, on the other hand, was located an ocean away from the nearest Axis soldier, and there wasn't an enemy plane in existence capable of flying across the Atlantic and back. On top of that, Canadian Prime Minister Mackenzie King was lobbying hard to have the air training plan set up in the dominion. He had been opposed to the idea prior to the war, mainly because he feared it would cost too much money. However, the prime minister had a change of heart shortly after fighting broke out. In fact, he even went so far as to promise Canada would pay much of the cost and provide up to half the airmen. King had his reasons. First, he was anxious to avoid raising a large army. During the First World War the nation had lost more than sixty thousand of its sons in the trenches of France and Flanders, and he didn't want a repeat of that bloody debacle. Of course, the air force would lose men too, but not at anywhere near the same rate as the army. Second, by pouring Canada's resources into the air force King hoped to avoid a repeat of the 1917 conscription crisis that had nearly torn the country apart. He realized there would be no shortage of volunteers for the RCAF, so he was confident the draft would not be necessary. That would avoid the type of ugly scenes that had cropped up a generation earlier, when English Canada had supported conscription at the same time that Quebec had bitterly opposed it.

What's more, putting such a vast operation into action would take time, and King wanted to put Canada's participation in any European bloodbath off as long as possible. In a radio address to the nation the prime minister made it clear he was not going to rush the country into combat. "In making provision for this vast undertaking the government has done so knowing that nothing can be left to haste or chance," he declared. "The intricate machine must be perfect. In every phase of their work, the men must be trained by the highest skill, and under the best conditions it is possible for the country to provide."[1]

Before long, workmen were cutting down trees and clearing bush as airfields sprang up from British Columbia to Prince Edward Island. There were centres designed specifically to train air gunners and bomb aimers, flight schools to turn out pilots, and institutions to produce navigators. Just as King had predicted, thousands of young Canadians flocked to RCAF recruiting stations, anxious for some of the glory that the famous Spitfire and Hurricane pilots had won in the Battle of Britain. Many of them had been raised on thrilling tales of heroic aviators. Indeed, throughout the 1920s and 1930s no profession in Canada was more prestigious than that of pilot. No schoolboy could grow up without reading or hearing about such legendary Canadian First World War aces as Billy Bishop and Roy Brown or the equally glamorous 1920s bush pilots and barnstormers. When war came in 1939, young men had swamped RCAF recruiting stations. The tiny air force had been forced to turn most of them away. Now it would swing the doors wide open. Almost all of them wanted to be fighter pilots. As navigator Doug Alcorn recalled later, his dream "was to be another Billy Bishop, fearlessly shooting down Nazi fighters by the dozen. And just when that dream was starting to unfold smoothly, it had been shot down in flames as suddenly as one of Billy's victims."[2] What happened to Alcorn was what was in store for thousands of other RCAF recruits. They were accepted for aircrew training, but were soon informed they'd be flying with Bomber Command, not Fighter Command. More often than not, they'd be going into combat as gunners, navigators, wireless operators, or bomb aimers. The majority would never get into a pilot's seat.

Young men were soon signing up right, left, and centre, but Canada alone couldn't begin to provide all the volunteers Bomber Command was going to need. So, thousands more poured into the country from all over the Commonwealth. Australia alone sent 10 000, and there were thousands more from England, New Zealand, South Africa, and elsewhere. Indeed, when a plane crashed on landing at one BCATP flight school, the rescue party found a Russian, Czech, three Frenchmen, two Norwegians, and even a veteran of the Moroccan Camel Corps among the dazed survivors! Even this flood of volunteers, however, wasn't going to be enough to meet the demands of Arthur Harris. Some of the recruits would be sent to fighter squadrons, and others would end up flying transport planes for the army. Still others would have to hunt submarines for Coastal Command. Ottawa sent out letters to every commercial pilot in the country, inviting them all to sign up.

The response was overwhelming. Romeo Vachon, the famous Quebec bush pilot, was one of the first to accept. The federal government even went so far as to offer one hundred dollars to private clubs for every pilot they could train. One enterprising First World War flier took out newspaper advertisements in Moose Jaw, Saskatchewan, offering to split the reward with his students if they'd train with him. Even Wop May, the legendary bush pilot who had helped track down the infamous Mad Trapper, was rushed into uniform.

Still there was a shortage of airmen. Ottawa turned to Billy Bishop for help. The old ace, now an overweight, hard-drinking, retired businessman, was named RCAF director of recruiting. There was never a better salesman for any branch of the armed forces. Bishop was a showman who believed in bands, colourful parades, and all the newspaper ink he could generate. He stumped the country, giving speeches, pinning wings on new pilots, and even going so far as to set up a recruiting station in New York's posh Waldorf Astoria Hotel while the United States was still a neutral nation. Before long, more than 6000 Americans had joined the ranks of the RCAF.

Thanks to Bishop there were now enough volunteers, at least for the moment, but the BCATP was still plagued by a serious shortage of planes. Canada alone couldn't possibly build all the aircraft that would be needed so the British shipped over hundreds of trainers. Bishop came up with a brilliant scheme to get American-built planes into the country. Officially, the neutral Americans could not ship or fly warplanes to one of the belligerent nations. In Bishop's plan, American pilots would land their machines within a few yards of the Manitoba border, where Canadian personnel would lassoe them with ropes and then drag them north of the forty-ninth parallel. After Pearl Harbor, of course, this deception was no longer necessary.

Once the men and planes were in place, training began in earnest. Volunteers who had signed up expecting glamour and excitement were in for a shock. Instead, they received a steady diet of unremitting drudgery. It started out with a miserable "boot camp" period in which sadistic drill sergeants tried to whip the undisciplined newcomers into shape. Airman Robert Collins, who later became an accomplished author, remembered it as three weeks of day-long marches interspersed with the nightly ritual of polishing boots and brass buttons. That last task alone required thirty minutes of work, but no one dared face the drill sergeant with even a speck of dirt on his shoes or a smudge on his cap badge. Trainees were rousted out of bed before dawn, with lights suddenly bursting into life and an NCO barking out "wakey, wakey, wakey!" As soon as they were up, they showered, made their beds, and put the finishing touches of Brasso on their badges, all the while living in mortal fear of an unexpectedly early inspection. Moving at breakneck speed, they stored everything except their blankets in a kit bag at the foot of their beds.

"Our instructors were lean, mean sadists with hard muscles," Collins wrote later. "There were knee bends, arm stretches, running on the spot, jump bends, push-ups that I could barely do… pain in the feet, back, legs, the whole body screaming."[3]

The most humiliating experience of all came during the infamous "short-arm" inspection. This consisted of being lined up with a long row of other recruits and then dropping your pants to expose your private parts to a medical officer. The doctor, who usually behaved much like a veterinarian inspecting cattle, ordered each man to squeeze his penis while he watched for any signs of discharge or disease. After that came mandatory viewing of revolting colour pictures that illustrated in graphic detail what venereal disease could do to various parts of your body.

Adding to the inhumanity was the fact that there was no privacy to be found anywhere. Even the washroom stalls were without doors. But for farm boys accustomed to using outhouses with an Eaton's catalogue for toilet paper, just having indoor plumbing could be a real treat. There were hot showers, which were a joy for lads accustomed to baths in old porcelain tubs. The pay was good too — about forty dollars a month. In fact, the 500 dollars

Canadian tail gunner Jim McCaffery.
Courtesy of the author.

per year was more than most of them had made in their lives. The extra cash, however, didn't get them out of taking a whole battery of medical tests — or from being pricked with fierce-looking needles. There were shots for small-pox, typhoid, and lockjaw, as well as scarlet fever and diphtheria. The federal government, which had insisted throughout the 1930s that it couldn't afford a public health system, suddenly discovered it had plenty of money to vacci-nate the one million Canadians in uniform.

Food in the boot camps was bland, to say the least. Bored cooks in white aprons ladled out generous portions of unidentifiable slop that some of the men thought might be stew. It was nourishing but virtually tasteless.

With boot camp mercifully over, it was on to flight school. Now this was the adventure they'd signed up for! "On clear days the station crackled with action," Collins recalled. "Pilots with parachute packs flopping over their rear ends as they strolled to the planes. Armourers checking the machine guns. Student gunners taking their seats, as nervous in their new jobs as I was in mine. Motors revving and trumming. Fairey Battles taking off and landing. In the sky, planes trailing behind them the drogues that the gunners would use as targets. Air scented with gasoline and glycol. All of it very exhilarating."[4]

Looking back today, in the age of heat-seeking missiles and smart bombs, this training appears to have been almost comically primitive. Student-gunner

Jim McCaffery found himself riding in the back of old Fairey Battle and Bolingbroke bombers, firing machine-guns at targets being hauled over northern Manitoba. "Another aeroplane would let out a long sock, perhaps three hundred feet long and three feet in diameter," he said years later. "Our aeroplane, containing three gunners, would sweep up close to the tow plane and each gunner would fire perhaps two hundred rounds." They usually began blazing away from 200 or 300 yards out, with the maximum range being 600 yards. Scoring hits was no easy task. "You were moving at a different forward speed and your elevation relative to the target was changing," McCaffery noted. "We were supposed to lead the target on our gun sights to compensate the distance it would travel while our bullets were on route. You never aimed straight at it or you'd get a zero score. We fired colour-coded bullets so they knew how many hits each gunner achieved."[5]

McCaffery wasn't the only gunner who found the drogue difficult to hit. One veteran admitted later that he graduated without ever scoring a single hit. Another confided he once missed the drogue and damaged the tow plane by mistake.

Reactions to the training planes were mixed. Ontario pilot Lyle James was thrilled just to be allowed to fly. "Coming out of the Depression where I couldn't afford a bicycle, I had an airplane and two thousand gallons of gasoline. When I got my first one I wrote and told my mother it was like flying the house."[6] A former gunner, on the other hand, remembered the Fairey Battle as "noisy, rough, and oily. There were no seats or anything in it. You just sat on the floor. But we enjoyed it. We were all young and stupid."[7] The planes were cold, and in some of them the gunners actually stood up in the open air to fire their weapons. "A G-string held you in so you wouldn't go into the wild blue," one of them said later. "You felt like you were in World War I."[8]

The training wasn't without its hazards. Jim McCaffery recalled one gunner dying a particularly gruesome death in a freak accident. "You were not supposed to touch the control column when you exited the turret. He did and it came down and filled the hole where his body was and crushed him."[9] After that, the rookie gunners were extremely careful while getting in and out of their turrets.

Nor was it just the gunners who faced danger. Flying instructor Red Henderson, who later flew combat missions, thought the most harrowing experiences of his career came in Canada while trying to teach greenhorns how to fly. He never forgot the hazards of sitting in the back seat of a beat-

Lancaster bomber pilot Lyle James.
Courtesy of Lyle James.

up old trainer while a student pilot attempted to land on a snow-covered runway. Certainly flying instructor Max Ward wouldn't have disagreed with Henderson's assessment. He survived a close brush with death when his student pilot collided with another training plane. Ward lived to tell the tale, but his pupil died in the mishap. Another tragedy took place when a young recruit accidently fired a signal flare off inside his plane, which promptly crashed in flames, killing both him and his teacher.

Some of the danger came not from antiquated planes or even the inexperience of the young airmen. There were times when the exuberance of youth created its own special hazards. Lyle James found that out while flying over duck blinds near Windsor, Ontario. Together with his flight instructor, he decided to buzz hunters along the Detroit River. It was a near-fatal mistake. "We flew down through the reeds and ripped the top off a duck blind with the wheels of our airplane," he told the author. Coming back around for a second pass at an altitude of just ten feet, the two were greeted by the shotgun barrels of three very irate hunters. All three opened fire from point-blank range, raking the Tiger Moth biplane from nose to rudder. "There were two hundred shotgun pellets in the plane and sixteen in the pilot," James said. "I had pellets in my fingers, knee and hips. I don't blame those guys, though, we could have killed them."

Somehow, the two men managed to bring the crippled plane back to base for an emergency landing. Both were rushed to hospital, and the Royal

Canadian Mounted Police launched an immediate investigation. The two airmen didn't dare tell the truth because they would have faced a court martial for flying so low. James managed to convince the authorities they had been flying several hundred feet up when they were hit, probably by accident. Needless to say the duck hunters, who could have faced attempted murder charges, kept quiet too. Eventually, the police dropped the matter.

Student pilot George Flinders was less fortunate. He was court-martialed for flying too low over a residential area in order to show off to his wife. He spent time after that standing on the end of runways, using a flare gun to signal pilots. Eventually, he became a flight engineer aboard a bomber, but he was never allowed to fly again.

Sometimes, civilians living near the air bases found themselves in unexpected danger. Once, bombs were actually dropped on the west end of Toronto by a student bomb aimer. Fortunately, there were no casualties. A gunner in Macdonald, Manitoba, narrowly missed hitting a group of terrified fishermen in a lake below when he open fire at a flock of ducks.

The wildest pilots seemed to be the Australians. It wasn't unheard of for two of them to set their wingtips together, one on top of the other, and then to push them violently upward, breaking away in a so-called push up stunt. If all of this seems rather childish, it should be remembered that most of them were just teenage boys. The average age was nineteen, with the oldest member of the seven-man crew usually being a twenty-one-year old. Just how youthful they really were is captured by recounting the story of a recruit who was posted to guard a hangar full of aircraft. Awestruck by the machines, he set his gun down and was found later seated in the cockpit of one of the aircraft, playing the role of a pilot. Once, when another guard fired his rifle into the air one evening, the whole station spent the night searching for enemy spies. The culprit, fearing a court martial, didn't dare report what had really happened.

Despite the pranks and adventures in the air, it was by no means always exciting. One student pilot said later, "It was very hectic. It was a morning-to-night thing; it was a grind. There was not too much time for fun, because you had so many hours to put in and you had to accomplish so many things in that time. And then we also had the ground work: navigation, weather, this sort of thing. I can remember going to bed sunburned and tired, just beat!"[10]

Eventually, after more than six months of training in Canada, the airmen graduated from their various schools and were issued smart-looking blue RCAF uniforms. The garments looked dashing, but because they were made of wool, they itched from head to toe. Over time, as the fabric wore down, the airmen could relax. Until then, the best an excited new flyboy could say was that his new garb gave him instant prestige everywhere he went. Soldiers and sailors could turn the young ladies' heads too, but the airmen were considered a breed apart. Jealous members of other services referred to them as the "Brylcreem boys" but there was no denying the fact that, with the public at large, they were the most popular fighting men in the armed forces.

Events now accelerated. The airmen headed to Halifax upon graduation and boarded troop-ships for the crossing of the grim North Atlantic. There was always some apprehension when they pulled out, because German U-boats were sinking dozens of Allied vessels every month. Indeed, more than 2500 ships would be sent to the bottom by Nazi subs before the war ended. Assuming they made it to England in one piece, the recruits discovered they weren't going to be allowed anywhere near an airplane until they had completed, of all things, a commando course! Men who had trained to fight in the sky were now thrusting bayonets into dummies, tossing hand grenades, firing rifles from the shoulder and Sten guns from the hip. Scores of Canadians found themselves spending their days hanging upside down over water from ropes, climbing cliffs, and crawling in the mud while live machine-gun bullets whistled just above their ears. Precisely why they were put through these exercises is not clear. Perhaps the authorities needed to keep them occupied while they waited for positions to open up on operational bomber squadrons. Or maybe they felt the newcomers needed more discipline — or better physical conditioning.

In any case, once commando training was over with they were sent to operational training units (OTU) on the east coast of England. Here, they took more practical exercises, brushing up on the skills they'd learned in Canada. At last, it was on to the Lancaster Flying School at Lindolme for the final stage of their training. In many ways this was the most unpleasant experience of them all. Pilot Jack Currie, who reported to Lindolme expecting a brief stay in a cozy pre-war facility, was in for a shock. "The spacious brick-built quarters were not for us," he wrote later. "With the other crews from OTU we were segregated like a leper colony, in a muddy little hutted camp a couple of miles away from the airfield. For four depressing days, we ran in our white vests and baggy blue shorts, doing PT and other violent exercises. By the end of the second day I had had a bellyful of the prison-camp atmosphere."[11]

The most exciting thing to happen here was the simulated night combats that pitted Lancaster crews against Mosquito fighter pilots. The bomber gunners were armed with powerful flashlights that they were to turn on to indicate they were opening fire. The fighters, on the other hand, would signal they had launched their attack by blinking red and green navigation lights on and off. It was a crude arrangement, and more than one argument ensued about who had opened "fire" first, or who had flashed his light from too far out to be effective.

Jimmy Rawnsley, a Mosquito navigator engaged in these war games, recalled how the fighter crews played cat and mouse with the lumbering bombers. "Time and again we found that we could make our usual stalk and pull up and hold the bomber in the gunsight and sit there for several minutes before there was a response. Sometimes we would even finish the attack and pull alongside the bomber, flashing our lights. The rear turret in the bomber would then suddenly swing around and the gunner would happily report another fighter shot down!"

"The odds, of course, were all in our favour.... But I had a feeling that many of the less experienced bomber crews paid far too little heed to the unseen but very real danger from night fighters, compared to the very healthy respect they had for the all-too-visible flak."

Rawnsley had no doubt the flak was deadly. He'd seen Lancasters take direct hits from anti-aircraft shells and "that was a sight to appall the stoutest heart. Whenever a damaged Lancaster came limping in to West Malling — and it happened quite often — the minds of the crew of the bomber were nearly always occupied with the flak. 'Night fighters?' they would comment, 'we shoot them down.' And there was a ring of very real conviction in the way they said that. How could we explain that the ones they shot down were the bunglers and the inexperienced, and that they would never see the one that would probably get them in the end?"[12]

Clearly, despite all their training, many of the airmen were not ready for combat. Ready or not, however, the bomber boys found themselves reporting to operational squadrons after a preparation period in Canada and England that had lasted more than a year. While they were doing that, scores of new Lancasters had been coming off factory assembly lines in Toronto. With Canada churning out hundreds of aircraft and literally tens of thousands of new airmen, Bomber Command was ready during the second half of the war to make an all-out effort to blast Hitler's Third Reich to pieces.

CHAPTER 6

THE BATTLE OF THE RUHR

On a cold winter evening in 1943 several hundred Canadian and British bombers flew over Germany, visiting virtually every important town in the Reich. Anti-aircraft guns barked into life, fighter pilots scrambled into their planes, and civilians dashed for air-raid shelters. Strangely, no bombs rained down out of the night. The bombers roared overhead and then disappeared. When people emerged from their cellars they found the streets littered with millions of leaflets. Most were relieved. It was far better to be showered with paper than with high explosives or fire bombs. Many didn't even bother to read the material, which they assumed was more of "Churchill's propaganda." Some did scan the contents, however, and what they read must surely have sent a chill down their spines.

The message, signed by Arthur Harris himself, was a blunt warning that unless the German people overthrew their Nazi masters, Bomber Command would conduct wholesale slaughter. It read in part: "We in Britain know quite enough about air raids. For ten months your Luftwaffe bombed us. Forty-three thousand British men, women and children lost their lives. Many of our most cherished historical buildings were destroyed."

"You thought, and Goering promised you, that you would be safe from bombs. And now we are bombing Germany heavily. Why are we doing so? It is not revenge — though we do not forget Warsaw, Rotterdam, London, Plymouth and Coventry. We are bombing Germany, city by city, and even more terribly, in order to make it impossible for you to go on with the war. That is our objective. We shall pursue it remorselessly. City by city. Let the Nazis drag you down to disaster with them if you will. That is for you to decide."

"I will speak frankly about whether we bomb single military targets or whole cities. Obviously, we prefer to hit factories, shipyards and railways. It damages Hitler's war machine most. But those people who work in these plants live close to them. Therefore, we hit your houses and you... Soon we shall be coming every night and every day, rain, blow or snow. We are going to scourge the Third Reich from end to end if you make it necessary for us to do so."

"It is up to you to end the war and the bombing. You can overthrow the Nazis and make peace."[1]

Having delivered fair warning, Harris opened what would go down in history as the Battle of the Ruhr. His objective was to win the war in short order by destroying every city in the enemy's industrial heartland. With new navigational aids and much bigger bombers than had been available earlier in the war, Harris was confident he could wreck the Ruhr in a matter of months.

At first, the offensive got off to a spectacular start. More than 400 bombers attacked the giant Krupp Works at Essen on the night of March 5, 1943, scoring hundreds of direct hits. The plant, which produced thousands of tanks, guns, and planes, was the biggest of its kind in Europe. It was so vast that the airmen had little trouble finding it, even at night. By the time the smoke cleared, fully a third of this important target had been blown to pieces. A follow-up raid a week later did less damage to the factory, but it did wreck 500 nearby homes. There was success at the big inland port of Duisburg, too, where four important steel plants were blasted to rubble. Bombs that missed the plants hit 18 000 homes and sank dozens of ships and barges. Other raids, however, proved less fruitful. At Munich and Stuttgart, only about a quarter of the bombs fell within three miles of the targets, which were covered by industrial haze. On one particularly unfortunate night, Pathfinders accidently dropped flares onto an asylum for the insane in the Czechoslovakian town of Dobrang, and the poor souls below felt the full brunt of a major attack. Another disappointment took place over Düsseldorf, when a 700-plane raid was foiled by overcast weather.

Anxious to revive sagging morale after these disasters, Harris now agreed to attempt a mission that heretofore he had rejected as being little more than a foolish publicity stunt. British scientist Barnes Wallis approached him with the idea of flooding the entire Ruhr Valley by knocking out three massive hydro-electric dams in one night. If it worked, most of Germany's war industries would be put under water in a single stroke. At first, Harris had been sceptical, to say the least. He knew the dams were massive. Indeed, the concrete Mohne Dam was 130 feet thick, and it was the smallest of the three. The nearby Sorpe Dam was made of virtually impregnable earthworks. Despite the size of the dams, Harris had always considered them to be impractical targets. He knew at 20 000 feet they would appear rather small to his bomb aimers. Besides that, conventional bombs couldn't possibly breach them. Not even the big 4000-pound "cookies" would be effective. Torpedoes wouldn't work either, because the Germans had laid nets in the lakes in front of each dam. But Wallis had come up with a secret weapon that he was sure would do the trick. He proposed to knock the dams out with five-ton cylindrical-shaped bombs that were designed so they could skip over water, much like a flat stone. That would make it possible for them to evade the torpedo nets and slam directly into the dams. A few hits on each dam, Wallis believed, would create huge cracks. After that, water pressure would do the rest.

Of course, there was one hitch. The airmen would have no margin of error, which meant they'd have to fly extremely low to have any chance of success. Realizing this, Harris turned to Bomber Command's top pilot — Englishman Guy Gibson — and asked him to lead the raid. Gibson, a handsome twenty-four-year old who had already survived an unbelievable 170 missions, was given permission to hand pick his team. In all, nineteen bombers would carry out the raid, and Gibson selected 133 airmen, including many of the best crews in Bomber Command. Thirty of the men chosen were Canadians, including two who would fly in Gibson's own plane. After that, the men trained for two solid months before setting out on the evening of May 16, 1943.

As they took off, Calgary pilot Ken Brown was convinced they were all dead men. He knew they'd have to fly a scant sixty feet off the deck to avoid radar detection and to be sure of placing their bombs on target. At such a low altitude there was no room for mistakes. If a pilot let a wing dip even slightly at that height it would go straight into the ground. Then there was the very real danger of running headlong into hills, transmission lines, or trees. On top of that, planes flying at sixty feet would be sitting ducks for German flak gunners.

Nevertheless, Brown and the others pressed on, with Gibson's navigator, Canadian Terry Taerum, leading the way. Next to Gibson himself, Taerum was the most important man on the mission. As navigator of the lead plane it was up to him to bring them right to the target for a precision attack. This was one raid where it would do no good at all to come within three miles of the target. Fortunately, with thirty-five operations to his credit, Taerum was more than qualified for the task at hand.

With the Canadian providing expert direction, the raiders found the dams in the bright moonlight and went straight to work. Gibson led five

Lancasters against the Mohne Dam, diving so low that the tips of his propellers were almost touching the water. To the Englishman the target appeared "squat and heavy and unconquerable; it looked grey and solid in the moonlight as though it were part of the countryside itself and just as immoveable."[2] Seconds later, all hell broke loose. Anti-aircraft gunners opened up on the charging Lancasters and Gibson's nose gunner, Canadian Tony Deering, returned fire. Within seconds the planes and the dam seemed to be joined by glowing green, yellow, and red tracer shells. For men on both sides the suspense was almost unbearable. "The tracers began swirling towards us," Gibson recalled later. "Some were even bouncing off the smooth surface of the lake. This was a horrible moment: we were being dragged along at four miles a minute, almost against our will, towards the thing we were going to destroy."[3]

For German flak gunner Karl Schutte, who was located in a gun tower directly beside the dam, the awesome sight of five big bombers coming straight for him, their front guns blazing, the strange-looking bombs bouncing off the water, was every bit as unnerving. The lead Lancaster, he remembered half a century later, "roared towards us like a beast as if it would ram the tower and us. We fired... the shells whipped into the face of the attacker."[4] Somehow, neither Deering or Schutte scored a fatal hit, but the first bomb exploded against the Mohne with shattering force. "A gigantic water spout rose into the air and waves swept over the wall," Schutte recalled.[5]

Gibson's plane had weakened the dam but Schutte held his ground, firing at the next Lancaster to come thundering down on top of him. This time the German got the best of the exchange. The attacker exploded in flames and crashed, just missing the Mohne. Its bomb had already been released, but it somehow skipped right over the dam and destroyed an adjacent powerhouse. Schutte was blown off his feet by the force of the blast and a hail of debris whizzed past his head. Undaunted, the German scrambled to his feet, taking up his position behind what was now a red-hot anti-aircraft gun. More planes were diving on him. Schutte found himself in an impossible position. "Banking planes dropped more flares and also showed their directional lights to draw our fire. We restarted firing which was returned by the machines. While they were still trying to draw our fire another plane raced towards the wall. Target change, and again the shells whipped towards the attacker and several hits were scored. The plane was now also shooting at us. Just like a string of pearls, the luminous trail of the shells came towards the tower like large glow-worms."[6] One Lancaster came so low that

Schutte felt he could almost have reached out and touched it. So low, in fact, that he could clearly see the outline of the pilot's head in the moonlight. His flak gun jammed, but still the courageous German refused to give up, firing away at the raiders with a bolt-action rifle!

The attackers, however, were as determined to destroy the dam as Schutte was to save it. In the end they succeeded. There was another direct hit, the dam trembled, and then collapsed. As Schutte looked on in horror, millions of gallons of water cascaded into the valley below. Looking over his shoulder, Guy Gibson was just in time to see the Mohne give way. "The water, looking like porridge in the moonlight, was gushing out and rolling into the Ruhr Valley… It was the most amazing sight. The whole valley was beginning to fill with fog from the steam of the gushing water."[7]

Gibson now led his men to the Eder Dam. One Lancaster, flown by Ottawa pilot Lewis Burpee, was hit by flak and spun into the ground. Burpee, whose wife was nine months pregnant, died along with the rest of his crew, including two fellow Canadians. But the raiders pressed home their attack relentlessly, delivering several bombs right on target. The Eder shuddered and then toppled over like a deck of cards. Two hundred ten million gallons of water came crashing down with it. The planes were flying so low that Canadian tail gunner Harry O'Brien's Lancaster was almost engulfed by the tidal wave. The bomber barely outran the wall of water and climbed to safety. Looking on as they headed for home, O'Brien watched as an avalanche of water washed away a bridge and came crashing down on top of a fleeing automobile.

Now came the Sorpe Dam's turn. Again heavy flak rose up to greet the raiders. Another bomber crashed in flames. Its bomb aimer, Canadian John Fraser, somehow had made it to an escape hatch and prepared to jump, but when he looked out his heart was in his throat. In the moonlight he could clearly see the tops of individual trees below. There was no way his parachute would have time to open before he hit the ground. Thinking quickly, Fraser pulled his rip-cord inside the plane, sending the chute billowing out into the fuselage behind him. It was an unorthodox solution to be sure. The odds were that the chute would catch onto something and either tear to pieces when he jumped, or become so hopelessly entangled that he would be trapped inside the burning plane. There was no other alternative, though, so he took a deep breath and dove head first out the hatch. Miraculously, the parachute came out behind him totally intact, and he landed safely. The rest of his crew, including Ken Earnshaw, an Alberta schoolteacher who was slated to return to Canada right after the dams mission, perished.

Calgary pilot Ken Brown, meanwhile, was having a devil of a time just finding the target. On the way he'd narrowly missed slamming into a castle that had appeared out of nowhere at the top of a hill. A few minutes later, he'd been forced to raise a wingtip to avoid hitting a darkened church steeple. He was flying so low that his gunners had spotted three troop trains on the way to the dam. They peppered all three with lead, killing nine German soldiers and wounding four others.

By the time Brown got to the Sorpe Dam his gunners were low on ammunition and his plane had been damaged by flak. Nevertheless, he pressed home his attack, trying to find the target in a valley shrouded in thick fog. Brown, like Guy Gibson and Karl Schutte, was an exceptionally brave and determined man. He made eight runs down the valley, straining his eyes in a fruitless attempt to find the dam. Flying sideways to dodge hills at every turn, he slowed at times almost to stalling speed. Still unable to locate the target, he dropped incendiary bombs on his ninth pass, setting fires to trees adjacent to the dam. Finally he could see his prey and, on his tenth run, in a magnificent display of airmanship, brought his plane in perfectly, allowing his bomb aimer to score a direct hit. Three hundred feet of earthworks crumbled but the Sorpe held.

There was nothing more anyone could do. The surviving airmen banked away and headed for home. Only when they got back did they realize how costly the operation had been. In all, eight of the nineteen planes had been shot down. Fifty-six airmen were dead, including fourteen Canadians. When he heard the news, scientist Barnes Wallis wept openly and declared he would never have embarked on the project had he known it was going to be so costly.

In the documentary *The Valour and the Horror*, it is argued that the Dam Buster Raid, as it came to be known in the popular press, was a costly failure that did more harm to the Allies than to the Germans. That is not correct. Only those who weren't in the Ruhr Valley when the dams came tumbling down that unforgettable night could say the attack was anything but an overwhelming success for Bomber Command. There was widespread chaos throughout the Ruhr. Coal mines fifty miles away were flooded, factories had to be closed temporarily, and one of the biggest Luftwaffe airfields in Germany was swamped. Roads, bridges, and rail lines were washed away, disrupting communications for weeks. Foundries denied water were unable to make steel for days on end. A newspaper in neutral Sweden reported, "The flooding after the dams raid has created great havoc. Entire buildings have been swept away. In Dortmund many streets were submerged and traffic restricted to flat bottom boats." German veterans of the First World War told the newspaper that "not even the gunfire in Flanders had done more destruction than the British attack on the Ruhr."[8]

Eventually, with almost superhuman effort, the Germans were able to clean up the mess, but they were only able to do so because thousands of troops engaged in other tasks, including the building of the Atlantic Wall, were brought in to effect repairs.

Still, it would be a mistake to glamorize what happened that night. For as successful and as important as the mission had been, there was a terrible human cost. Besides the fifty-six Allied airmen who died, almost 1300 people were killed by flooding, including 493 Ukrainian women who were serving the Nazis as slave labourers.

Nor would it be appropriate to think all the heroism was confined to the Allied side. In addition to the German flak gunners, scores of ordinary civilians performed courageously that night, giving their all in bids to save others from the high waters. In one village a priest heard the approaching tidal wave and dashed to his church, where he rang a bell to warn the inhabitants of the impending disaster. He kept tugging on the bell's rope until both he — and the church — were washed away.

A farmer named Kersten sounded the alarm in the village of Niederense, where waves fifteen feet high roared over the buildings. A woman he was helping to safety was washed right out of his hands, along with a mother carrying a baby. All three drowned. Throughout the village dead farm animals and human corpses could be seen dangling in trees. One eighty-eight-year-old lady with an exceptionally strong will to live managed to survive by climbing onto the roof of her house and strapping herself to the chimney with a rope.

Regardless of what impact the raid had on Germany, it was a huge boost to the morale of Bomber Command and to people throughout the Allied nations. Seizing on the propaganda value, the British government presented medals to thirty-four airmen, including nine Canadians. Gibson was awarded the coveted Victoria Cross, the Empire's highest gallantry award. Two of his crewmen, Canadians Terry Taerum and Tony Deering, both received Distinguished Flying Crosses. Ken Brown, who surely deserved a VC as well, had to settle for the Conspicuous Gallantry Medal.

Bouyed by the success of the Dam Buster Raid, Arthur Harris closed out the Battle of the Ruhr with several punishing blows aimed at cities that

A Canadian Lancaster bomber crew. From left to right: Hank Tims, Fred Graham, Geof Haight, Don Squires, Bill DuBois, F. Valentine, Robert Geisel. Courtesy of Bill DuBois.

had hitherto escaped relatively unscathed. Almost half the town of Krefled was burned out in a single night, with 1000 people dying and 72 000 more being left homeless. Next it was Mulheim's turn. Five hundred residents were slain and 64 per cent of the city was smashed. Following that, Wuppertal felt the wrath of Bomber Command and 1800 died. Finally, Cologne was hammered again, with devastating results. More than 4000 people were killed and this time the city's great twin-spired cathedral was damaged.

Five months after it began the Battle of the Ruhr was over. More than 1000 bombers had been lost and 7000 young airmen had been killed, wounded, or captured. Harris, who was frequently given to over-optimism, reported to Churchill that Germany's heartland had been all but destroyed. The Ruhr had indeed been badly mauled, but it was far from finished. With literally tens of thousands of people toiling around the clock, the Germans would have much of the damage repaired before the year was out.

Having finished with the Ruhr, at least for the time being, Harris switched his attention to the giant port city of Hamburg, which he planned to bomb back into the Stone Age. In four nights in late July 1943 he proposed to raze a city of two million souls to the ground. He would send his whole force to Hamburg four times in just over a week, showering it with hundreds of thousands of tons of bombs.

In many ways Hamburg was a legitimate military target. Besides being Germany's second-largest city (after Berlin) it was the country's biggest seaport and home to the Nazi fleet. Indeed, Hamburg's shipyards had built the mighty battleship *Bismarck*, not to mention more than 200 U-boats since the start of the war. There were hundreds of other military and industrial facilities in the city as well. Harris, however, despite the success of the Dam Buster Raid, had no confidence that his men could hit specific targets with any degree of regularity. Besides that, nearly half the Dam Busters had been lost in one mission, and he could hardly afford to throw away his best crews for very long at that rate. Therefore, he reasoned, he'd have to return to area bombing.

Harris ordered his crews to make the aiming point the vast residential areas of Hamburg. More than one hundred aircraft factories, power stations, and oil refineries were located on the south side of the Elbe River, but no attempt would be made to hit any of them. According to the official history of the Royal Canadian Air Force, what Harris was planning was "a terror campaign, pure and simple."9

Unlike the 1000-bomber raid on Cologne the year before, Harris planned an utterly exterminating series of blows on Hamburg. Besides sending his entire force after it four times in a row, he had talked the United States Army Air Force into launching a pair of massive daylight assaults on the city during the same time frame. In other words, Hamburg was to be pulverized virtually around the clock.

There was something else that would make this assault different. For the first time Bomber Command would employ a secret weapon known by the code name of "Window." As the airmen approached the target they would toss hundreds of thousands of strips of aluminum foil out side doors to confuse German radar. Tests conducted in England showed Window would work, jamming both ground control radar and detection sets aboard night fighters. The Allies had known about Window for over a year, but had been afraid to use it for fear that the Luftwaffe would copy it and use the same trick over British cities. Unknown to Bomber Command, the Germans had discovered Window at about the same time and had been keeping it hushed up so the Allies wouldn't use it against towns in the Reich!

In any case, on the night of July 24, 1943, as just under 800 planes went into their bomb runs over Hamburg, millions of strips of aluminum foil came floating down out of the darkness, poking out the eyes of the German radar system. Fighter pilot Otto Kutzner was climbing swiftly to greet the bomber stream when his radar screen suddenly revealed more targets than he knew what to do with. Time and again he manoeuvred into position behind "bombers" that didn't exist. In the end, he returned to base without a single kill. Rolf Angeresbach, a radar operator aboard a JU 88, couldn't find a thing for his pilot to shoot at, despite the fact they were right in the midst of the bomber stream. They too returned without registering a successful interception. Radar operators on the ground were panic stricken. If their screens were to be believed, there were 8000 bombers overhead. Not sure what to do, the flak crews simply fired blindly, putting a curtain of steel over the whole city. In many instances they were firing at patches of sky completely devoid of aircraft.

Canadian pilot Harry Gowan, who was flying one of the Pathfinder planes, was the first Allied airman over the target. Flying straight and level so as to mark the city properly, he was soon caught in several searchlights. Now, at last, the defenders had something concrete to shoot at, and virtually every flak gun in Hamburg zeroed in on Gowan's plane. One shell exploded directly in front of the cockpit, sending a jagged piece of shrapnel through the windscreen. It missed the Canadian's head by less than an inch, but flying glass cut his face in several places. Another shell killed the mid-upper gunner, and still another knocked out the Lancaster's electrical system, forcing the bomb aimer to release his load manually. Still, Gowan held his course, not taking evasive action until the last flare was gone.

With the target now lit up like a Christmas tree, the main force went to work, dropping almost 2300 tons of bombs. In less than an hour some 1500 people died.

One of those caught in the inferno was A.F. Krings, a German lance corporal who had just been posted to Hamburg to work on U-boat diesel engines after two winters on the Russian Front. "Shortly after midnight on July 24 the air raid sirens started to wail," he wrote in a letter to the author. "My mother woke me and insisted we should go into a shelter. I really did not want to, but finally agreed. I put on a raincoat over my pyjamas, put on shoes [no socks], a hat and put the keys in my pocket." Along with his mother and a younger brother, Krings took shelter in the basement of an office building across the street from his apartment. Within minutes he realized they were in extraordinary danger. "Because the groundwater level is quite high there the basement was only a few steps down from street level."

But now it was too late to go anywhere else. "The lights were out and we could hear the detonations of the bombs and the fire of the flak batteries. I always felt that as an 'old' soldier one develops a sixth sense. As I heard a bomb coming in I grabbed my little brother and pushed him onto the floor, with me on top. The bomb hit close by, the windows and the sandbag barricades came flying into the basement. I did not want to remain in this building. The air raid warden refused to let me out, but when I opened the spy hole in the door, I could see the building was on fire. I grabbed my mother and brother and we took off."

Stepping into the street was akin to walking into a furnace. "The house I lived in was gone and so were all the others on that side of the street. Everything was burning. We ran along the street and came to a police station close by. Here I dipped my hat and raincoat in a barrel of water and covered my mother.... We kept on running in the general direction of Hamburg's well-known St Michael's Church. There were craters in the middle of the street in which the gas from broken gaslines was burning. I saw the curtains in holes, where windows used to be, burning. A strong windstorm started to develop and made breathing more difficult. Finally we reached St Michael's and went into the crypt deep underground. Here the walls are very thick. But the smoke came in. It was pitch dark."

When the trio emerged the next day at noon, all they could see was devastation in every direction. What they didn't know was that the damage, which seemed so terrible at the time, would appear absolutely trifling compared with what was coming three nights later.

July 27, 1943, was the night that Hamburg died. Seven hundred eighty-seven planes hit the city, and this time the bombing was much more concentrated. So concentrated, in fact, that the flames of dozens of fires converged together, creating something that had never been seen before — a firestorm. As the flames of different fires joined forces, temperatures shot up to an estimated 1800 degrees Fahrenheit. This searing heat caused a ferocious updraft that drew oxygen right into the fire. That, in turn, created a whirlwind of unbelievable force. It was so powerful that people were literally swept off their feet and sucked into the raging inferno.

An official Hamburg report gives some inkling as to what it was like for those on the ground. It says, "The scenes of terror are indescribable. Children were torn from their parents' hands and whirled into the fire. People who thought they had escaped fell down, overcome by the devouring heat, and died in an instant. Refugees had to make their way over the dead and dying. The sick and infirm had to be left behind by the rescuers who, themselves, were in danger of burning."[10] Another German document says the whirlwind was so powerful that "trees three feet thick were broken off or uprooted, human beings were thrown to the ground or flung alive into the flames by the winds, which exceeded one hundred and fifty miles per hour. The panic-stricken citizens did not know where to turn. Flames drove them from their shelters but high explosive bombs sent them scurrying back again. Once inside, they were suffocated by carbon monoxide poisoning and their bodies reduced to ashes as though they had been placed in a crematorium, which was indeed what each shelter proved to be."[11]

If the official reports make grim reading, they are tame compared with the tales told by survivors. Agathe Ideler, a mother of two, was one of those who had to face the terrible decision of whether to risk suffocation in her shelter or the flames and exploding bombs outside. She chose to flee. "It was terrible," she recalled half a century later. "I was crying with my kids, trying to get out. There were no wagons or cars. You had to go by foot. The street was bubbling, both sides were burning. Ashes were falling on our heads."[12] Seventeen people who stayed in the bunker beneath her apartment building died.

Arthur Willi, a young German sailor, left the relative safety of the docks in a desperate bid to rescue civilians in nearby residential areas. "It was awful, seeing people walk around in flames, stuck in asphalt up to their knees. I saw a lot of people, including Russian prisoners, with burned faces. Their skin came right off. I helped an old lady who was sinking in asphalt. It burned my feet a little but I got her out. A lady, maybe twenty-eight years old, with two babies, twins maybe one year old, maybe less, was in trouble. My friend picked up the babies, which were stuck in the asphalt. He got them out and placed them on a wagon."

"I saw people burning in the water. The air was burning. All the sailors from my boat went in and helped them out. People were burning and jumping into the water. We took ropes to the water and helped get them out. I saw a lot of crying. It was unforgettable. I was a lot of time in the Atlantic and it was much worse than that. In the Atlantic it was men against men."[13]

German schoolgirl Elke Gehrke. Courtesy of Elke Gehrke.

Heidi Schaefer, a young office worker, remembered the sheer terror in the shelters. "One woman was trying to stop a baby from crying," she recalled, choking back tears. "She was hysterical and she hit the baby. Of course it was a stupid thing to do… it only made him cry more. But she was out of her mind with fear. The decision was made to leave [the shelter] and we all ran into the street. Coming around a corner I heard a terrible howling noise and saw the baby being swept out of the woman's arms by a gust of wind so strong it knocked her down. He was sucked into the fire before our eyes. She could never forgive herself for hitting her baby. Please don't ask me to tell you any more."[14]

Elke Gehrke was only four years old but she still remembers the terror of that night. "We lost everything. I lost a lot of my family — brothers, sister, mother, grandparent, cousin, uncle, and aunts. I have a lot of memories coming back, like riding through the city in a truck with housing burning and people jumping out. People were killed just left and right. I remember people jumping into the water and when they came out they were still burning because of the phosphorus. We had a lot of water in Hamburg, I remember that."[15]

The firestorm raged out of control for three solid hours, only subsiding when it had burned out a residential section three miles wide and two miles long. The next day at high noon the sun still couldn't be seen through the thick clouds of smoke that blanketed the whole city. At least 40 000 people were dead, and countless more were homeless. Indeed, more than one million people, fearing that there was more to come, fled Hamburg that very day. Many had nowhere to go and were simply getting out of town as fast as their legs could carry them.

Hiltgunt Zassenhaus, a schoolgirl who survived the night in a shelter, witnessed incredible scenes as people streamed out of the city. "Children were being pulled along, tripping and stumbling over their own short legs, trying to keep pace with the grown-ups… some sat on the curb to pull shoes off swollen, aching feet. Others simply lay down in the middle of the road, staring vacantly up into the smoke-filled sky. No one cried or complained. The faces were dark and empty, as if life had gone out." Many soon abandoned their belongings and got out as quickly as possible.

Some were too dazed to flee. They sat dejectedly beside scorched pieces of furniture in the middle of the street, looking for all the world as if they were waiting for a moving van.

Hiltgunt Zassenhaus headed home with a deep sense of foreboding, breaking into a cold sweat every time she thought about her night in the shelter. Miraculously, her home was still standing. But she found little comfort there because of a sickening smell that came wafting through broken windows. It was, she quickly realized, the stench of burnt flesh.

Agathe Ideler and her two children were among those who got out of the city. Her apartment had been badly damaged, and there was no electricity or running water. "We slept in straw" that first night out of Hamburg. "Nobody had anything. There was just a terrible feeling that they would come back."

Those who stayed behind soon lived to regret their decision. For on July 29 Bomber Command was back. This time, 777 planes dropped bombs. Once again mostly residential areas were hit. Four nights later there was yet another raid, with 740 bombers involved. Between these blows came a pair of daylight strikes by the Americans. The United States Army Air Force (USAAF) didn't believe in area bombing, and its planes aimed strictly for the shipyards and industrial areas. But with so much smoke covering the city, many American bombs landed in residential districts as well, adding still further to the suffering below. By the time the last plane had departed for England, the six raids combined had killed close to 50 000 civilians, most of them old men, women, and children.

Gerhard Nichau, a schoolboy from the East Prussian town of Pillau, remembered the devastation when he visited Hamburg many months later. "What I saw in Hamburg made you completely sick. I saw buildings completely destroyed, with the bathtub sitting in the rubble still intact. That is still in my mind. The city was completely destroyed. We had to walk between paths in the rubble. In some places it was impossible to walk."[16]

Of course there had been some Allied losses too, despite the use of Window. In all, Bomber Command lost eighty-seven planes in its four raids. For the Kirkham family of Vancouver the night of the firestorm was especially tragic. Two of its sons — Ernie and Tom — died aboard crippled bombers that crashed into the North Sea while trying to limp back to England. Lennie Rogers of Port Colborne, Ontario, died that night the same way. Ironically, his brother had disappeared without a trace into the North Sea four months earlier.

That the Allies had suffered losses couldn't begin to comfort the Germans, who were reeling from shock at what had happened. Pilot Adolf Galland said later, "The wave of terror radiated from the suffering city and spread throughout Germany. Appalling details of the great fire were recounted. The glow of the fires could be seen for one hundred twenty miles. A stream of haggard, terrified refugees flowed into the neighbouring provinces. In every large town people said, 'what happened in Hamburg yesterday can happen to us tomorrow.' Berlin was evacuated amid signs of panic. In spite of strict reticence in official communiques, the terror of Hamburg spread rapidly to the remotest villages of the Reich."[17]

Galland's statement was no exaggeration. Berliner Marie Vassiltchikov told her diary on July 28 that "Hamburg is being bombed daily. There are very many victims and it is already so badly hit that practically the whole town is being evacuated. There are stories of little children wandering the streets calling for their parents. The mothers are presumed dead, the fathers are at the front, so nobody can identify them.... The fate of Hamburg arouses great anxiety here for last night Allied planes dropped leaflets that called upon all women and children in Berlin to leave at once, as they did before the raids on Hamburg began. This sounds ominous. Berlin may well be next."[18]

German fighter pilot Heinz Kroll, who flew over Hamburg the day after the firestorm, was utterly appalled by what he saw. "The British by night and the Americans by day in a series of massed air attacks have practically destroyed this great city," he wrote in his diary. "Entire sections of the city have been devastated by nightly British phosphorus incendiary bombs.... During my flight I observe the great fires that are still raging everywhere in what has become a vast area of rubble. A monster cloud of smoke rises up to three thousand feet above the fires, fanning out to a width of some ten to twenty miles, as it slowly drifts eastward to the Baltic Sea, seventy miles away. There is not a cloud in the sky. The giant column of rising smoke stands out starkly against the summer blue. The horror of the scene makes a deep impression on me. The war is assuming hideous aspects."[19]

CHAPTER 7

THE BATTLE OF BERLIN

As hundreds of Canadian airmen jammed noisily into a cavernous aircraft hangar one afternoon in the late summer of 1943, a hushed silence suddenly spread through the crowd. On a stage in front of them, Air Marshal Arthur Harris marched up to the microphone. Harris almost never visited the bomber squadrons, so the men knew instantly that something big was up. He didn't keep them waiting. "More than half of you won't be here in the next few weeks," he began.[1]

Pilot Doug Harvey, who had joined the RCAF at age twenty, remembers the remark instantly got everyone's attention.

"We are about to begin a series of raids that will demand the best from all of you," Harris continued. "We know there will be tremendous losses, but it has to be done. You've done a splendid job, but the real test is still before you. We must beat Germany to her knees."[2] By the time he was finished, the man who had opened his address by telling his audience he was about to send half of them to their deaths was being cheered wildly. The reaction may seem strange, looking back half a century later, but the fact is the airmen were willing to risk their lives, provided they could be convinced that what they were doing was going to help win the war.

The bomber boys knew Harris was a fighter, and they'd follow him anywhere. What they didn't know was that he was about to launch a series of raids that would go down in history as the Battle of Berlin. Until now, although the war was more than three years old, the German capital had not been hit very hard by Bomber Command. There had been sporadic attacks since 1940, but because the city was so far from England the raiders had to lighten their bomb loads so they'd be able to carry enough fuel to get there. Besides that, Berlin was the most heavily defended target in the Third Reich. That had also deterred the Allies from going after it in force. Indeed, American reporter William Shirer, who had lived in Berlin prior to the American entry into the war, had once told his diary "the British bombings have not been very deadly. The British are using too few planes — fifteen or twenty a night — and they have to come too far to carry really effective, heavy loads of bombs."3

Now Harris planned to change all that. In a memo to Prime Minister Churchill he predicted Bomber Command could wreck Berlin from end to end by April 1, 1944. "It will cost us four hundred to five hundred planes," he wrote. "It will cost Germany the war."4 Churchill was sceptical, but he authorized the offensive anyway. It was a long shot at best, but if Harris could force the Nazi regime to throw in the towel by the spring of 1944 there'd be no need for the D-Day invasion, which was planned for that June. No need, either, for a long and bloody land campaign to liberate Europe.

Many historians have blasted Harris for being recklessly optimistic heading into the Battle of Berlin. Whether destroying the enemy capital would force Germany to surrender or not, however, the fact remains that it was a target of great importance. For one thing, it was the seat of government. Hitler lived there, as did most of the Nazi leadership. It was also home to the Gestapo headquarters, the Foreign Office, the Propaganda Ministry, and the Reich Chancellory. More than that, it was an important industrial centre. There were steelworks, iron works, and textile plants, along with war factories that produced 25 per cent of the German army's battle tanks and half its field artillery. On top of that, there were three important aircraft factories, plants producing U-boat engines, and facilities that were responsible for fully a third of Germany's output of electrical equipment. If all that wasn't enough, Berlin was a communications and rail centre of note.

It was also a fat, juicy target. One might even say it was sprawling, covering as it did 400 square miles (800 if you counted its suburbs). With a population of four million people it was the largest city in the Third Reich. It was, indeed, the third-largest metropolis in the world.

The first of nineteen assaults on Berlin took place on the night of August 23, 1943, when 727 aircraft, led by Canadian master bomber Johnny Fauquier, attacked the city. The master bomber was the pilot who had to find the target and mark it. It was his job to fly low, identify the aiming point, and then drop green flares on it. After that he released his bomb load, which was made up entirely of incendiaries, to make it still easier for those who came behind him. It was, by far, the most dangerous job in Bomber Command, not only because you had to fly lower than the other airmen, but also because the master bomber didn't get to fly in and out of the target area as quickly as possible. He carried extra fuel so he could circle the city after dropping his bombs, directing others to the aiming point by radio.

With the highly skilled Fauquier marking the target, the bombers struck hard, killing almost 900 people, including sixty German soldiers. But the defences had been even more deadly than anticipated. Berlin was ringed by 7000 anti-aircraft guns, 3000 searchlights, and enough airfields to accommodate more than 200 fighters. In all, fifty-six bombers were blown to pieces. With nearly 400 airmen lost, it was Bomber Command's bloodiest night of the war to date.

Only five Luftwaffe planes were destroyed, but German fighter pilots who survived the raid recall a battle of savage intensity. Gunther Wolf shot down two Lancasters in six minutes before being sent down in flames himself by an alert tail gunner. "Don't ask me who hit us because I do not know," he told an interviewer decades later. "There was just one loud bang and the right engine was on fire, the canopy shattered."[5] Moments later, he was floating down into the burning city beneath his parachute.

Messerschmitt 110 pilot Peter Spoden had a similar experience. After shooting down one bomber he was wounded in the thigh by a gunner. He managed to bail out, but there were complications. Spoden's body banged heavily into the ME 110's tail unit and he became entangled on the outside of his own doomed plane as it hurtled towards the earth at 400 miles per hour. Only with great effort was he able to work himself free and parachute to safety. The narrow escape scarred him emotionally, and he would relive it in his dreams for years to come.

Canadian pilot Billy Day had a close call of his own. Conned by searchlights, he was attacked by three Focke Wulf 190 single-seater fighters right over Berlin. Day dove steeply to escape, and his tail gunner had the presence of mind to keep one eye shut as they plunged through the glare of the searchlights. Once Day pulled up, the gunner still had enough night vision to send one of the enemy planes spinning down out of control. The other two Germans made a hasty retreat. But Day and his crew weren't out of hot water yet. When they levelled off they discovered that their fuel tanks had been riddled with bullets, and gasoline was gushing out at an alarming rate. They considered bailing out, but decided instead to try to make it home, crossing the North Sea with the fuel gauges reading almost empty. By the time they landed in England the bomber had hardly a drop of fuel left in its tanks.

Canadian bomb aimer John Bailey had an even more harrowing experience. The pilot of his plane was critically wounded and the damaged bomber spun down out of control. Keeping cool, Bailey pulled the injured aviator out of his seat, took over the controls, and calmly flew home, making a perfect landing. Bailey, who had washed out of flight school the year before, was immediately awarded the Conspicuous Gallantry Medal.

The death toll in Berlin that night had been unexpectedly high. Fortunately, the city's wide boulevards had combined with the stone and brick construction of many buildings to prevent a firestorm, but there had been widespread damage nevertheless. Marie Vassiltchikov, a twenty-six-year-old broadcasting service worker, was horrified by what she saw, telling her diary, "There was a red haze over Berlin, and entire streets had collapsed."[6]

Others were bitter. Arno Abendroth, a fourteen-year-old schoolboy, recalled later the satisfaction he felt when viewing the broken bodies of four Canadian fliers. Rushing to the scene of a crashed bomber, he was held back by police. "They told me they had identified the bodies as Canadians. They weren't badly mangled but I do remember their deathly pale faces, chalk white. These were the first dead men of the war I had seen, but I must say that I had a deep satisfaction at the sight of those dead terror fliers. They were our enemies."[7]

While Abendroth was gloating over the Canadian corpses, hundreds of thousands of Berliners were packing their belongings and preparing to flee. More than a million people had left the city after the big raids on Hamburg, but most had returned a few weeks later, arriving home just in time to be caught in the first major attack on the capital. Now they were leaving for good. Rich Ruhr Valley industrialists, many of whom had been living for months in posh Berlin hotels, headed for small villages in the countryside. Many others, however, especially in Berlin's poorer sections, had no place to go. They would just have to ride out the storm as best they could.

Bomber Command was back on August 31, when 622 planes bombed through heavy clouds. This time luck was on the side of the Germans. A staggering forty-seven raiders were shot down, carrying 329 men to their deaths or imprisonment. On the ground, losses were light because the clouds were so thick they made it impossible to find a target even as large as Berlin. In all, only seventy Germans died, most of them in rural areas outside the city. Undaunted, Harris threw his main force against the enemy capital three nights later. This time, results were better. Six hundred Germans died in exchange for twenty-two bombers. The ratio had improved but Harris had lost 125 aircraft in less than two weeks. He pulled in his horns, giving his tired crews time to regroup while he planned his next move.

Air gunners at rear of a Lancaster bomber. Jim McCaffery (front), Jim Cook (back). Courtesy of the author.

When the offensive resumed, on November 18, 1943, the weather proved to be Bomber Command's biggest headache. Once again clouds blanketed the target, forcing the airmen to bomb blindly. As a result, high explosives were scattered over a wide area and fewer than 200 people perished. On the positive side, the overcast conditions kept the Luftwaffe grounded, and only nine bombers fell, mostly to flak.

Canadian tail gunner Jim McCaffery, who made one trip to Berlin, recalled the anti-aircraft fire over the capital as being intensely thick. "It was well defended. You can tell by the amount of flak at night. Flak gives little bursts of flame. Also, searchlights were quite thick. It was just a little bit like going into a corridor of hell, flying for hours across a quiet, black countryside and then plunging into a mess like that. Fire, reflections of light below and many, many probes of searchlights all about us."

Searchlights could be as unsettling as being shot at. "If one nailed an aeroplane the others would come and form like a teepee — a cone. I have seen aeroplanes caught in these cones and they are either attacked by fighters or become the centre of fire for flak. It can be a very bad situation."[8]

Then there was the risk of collision, which was magnified several times whenever bad weather limited visibility. Canadian pilot Bill Baker discovered that the hard way when he flew right into the tail of a Lancaster thirty miles from Berlin. The two machines came together with a sickening, metal-crunching crash. The rear gunner of the lead plane was killed outright, but the rest of the crew was able to bail out before the bomber crashed. The nose of Baker's plane, meanwhile, was missing, along with his bomb aimer, who had gone hurtling out into the night without his parachute.

Anyone else would have high-tailed it for home. But Baker decided to carry on. He managed to find the target but the bomb release wouldn't work, and he was forced to turn for home. His troubles, however, were far from over. Temperatures at 20 000 feet were hovering around -50 degrees Fahrenheit, and howling winds were cutting through the cockpit like a knife slicing through butter. After four hours Baker was almost frozen solid. He managed to make a safe landing, but lost several fingers on both hands to frostbite and never flew again.

The raiders returned four nights later in what would turn out to be Berlin's worst ordeal of the war. This time almost 800 bombers took part, dropping 2500 tons of bombs. Once again the city was covered in clouds, and the airmen had to rely strictly on guesswork. This time, however, they got lucky, and the vast majority of bombs fell smack in the centre of the city, killing 2000 people and leaving 175 000 homeless. One four-thousand-pound "cookie" did much of the damage when it scored a direct hit on an air-raid shelter, slaughtering 500 civilians. Another one hundred were crushed to death during a mad scramble down a narrow flight of stairs that led to another shelter.

There was no firestorm as such, but soon whole blocks were in flames. One tragedy followed another. Survivor Horst Hatwich remembers seeing an old blind man sitting in the middle of the street in a chair as his home burned to the ground. "That picture, of that old, helpless, blind creature in the firestorm made me feel very sad."[9] Turning away, he witnessed something every more terrible. A husband was savagely beating his wife with clenched fists, smashing her features to pulp for no apparent reason. The man, Hatwich concluded, must have been driven insane by the bombing.

Ingeborg Spie saw what may have been an even more gruesome sight as an elderly couple leapt from a burning apartment building and landed almost at her feet. "It was a noise you cannot describe, when people splash down like that; they lay there like broken dolls."[10]

German Armaments Minister Albert Speer was one of millions who took shelter that night. After the raid he emerged just in time to see flames devour his ministry building. "In place of my private office I found nothing but a huge bomb crater," he wrote in his autobiography. Jumping into a car, he drove frantically through the streets in a bid to inspect important war factories. What he saw gave him a start. "We drove over streets strewn with rubble, lined by burning houses. Bombed-out families sat or stood in front of the ruins. A few pieces of rescued furniture and other possessions lay about on the sidewalks. There was a sinister atmosphere full of biting smoke, soot, and flames. Sometimes the people displayed that curious hysterical merriment that is often observed in the midst of disasters. Above the city hung a huge cloud of smoke that probably reached twenty thousand feet. Even by day it made the macabre scene as dark as night."[11]

Hitler, for his part, shrugged off the damage, despite the fact his own private rail car had been destroyed. Speer tried to impress upon him how much destruction had been wrought, but the Führer interrupted him with the wave of a hand, asking the armaments minister how many tanks he could deliver to the army next month. After another all-out attack on the capital four nights later, Speer would have to report that tank production had suffered a major setback because the biggest tank factory in Berlin lay in ruins. About 800 civilians also died, and there was widespread panic in the city because the world-famous Berlin Zoo had been hit, sending dozens of lions, jaguars, leopards, giant apes, and crocodiles into the streets. Police officers and soldiers were pressed into service to shoot the beasts, but for days people were afraid to wander into parks or go swimming. Propaganda Minister Josef Goebbels noted in his diary that the raid also destroyed dozens of important industrial buildings. Hitler, he added, seemed more concerned about the loss of the old Assembly Hall, which was a Berlin cultural landmark.

The German capital had been badly mauled, but Harris knew it hadn't been destroyed, and he wasn't about to let up. He sent 478 planes to Berlin on December 2 and almost 500 more on December 16. Still not satisfied, he even ordered an attack on Christmas Eve. To Helga Schmidt, who was a fourteen-year-old schoolgirl, the December 24th raid was the cruelest blow of all. "My brother was home from the Eastern Front and he had brought us presents and a big goose. After so many months of rationing we were all very excited. No one thought even the English would bomb us on Christmas Eve. It seemed so un-Christian. Our tree was decorated so beautifully, and I can still remember the smell of that bird. It filled our apartment. It's funny,

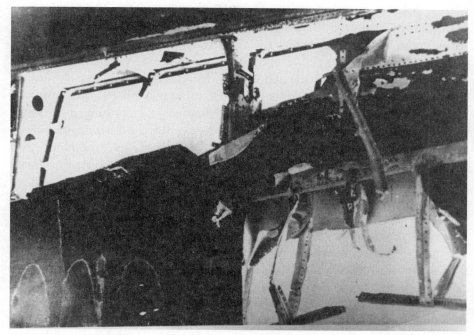

Battle damage to the wing of a Lancaster bomber, caused by three cannon shells from a German night fighter. Jim Letros was aboard this Lancaster, which made it back to England. Courtesy of Jim Letros.

but I can still remember the euphoria I felt. I was almost delirious with joy. I think under the stress of bombing people become unreasonably depressed about any little thing that goes wrong in their lives — and unreasonably happy about any sort of good things that happened. Anyway, the bombers came that night. We had to run for the shelter. Our building was hit by incendiary bombs and we watched it burn to the ground from across the street. My brother lost his arm later in the war, but I have to tell you I don't think I was ever more depressed than I was that Christmas."[12]

Eleven-year-old schoolgirl Ingrid Scheyk had a remarkably narrow escape around this time. "We were in a cellar when a bomber was shot down by flak and came down and crashed right on the building above us. The lady right next to us got squashed between the stones. All the exits were closed. It was dark and we could only see flames. We found a little hole and people were pushed into it from the back and pulled out of it from the front."[13]

With the New Year there was no respite. More than 400 bombers came on January 1, 1944, and almost that many were back the next night. With the weather now creating almost impossible flying conditions, however, many crews had trouble finding the city, and damage was relatively light. If the civilians got a break, casualties mounted steadily for both Bomber Command and the hard-pressed German night fighter force. Dozens of bombers were being shot down on every mission, and morale on many bomber stations was close to cracking. Some crews began dropping their bombs long before they reached Berlin so they could avoid the capital's awesome defences. Still others dropped parts of their loads into the North Sea on the way to the target so they could gain more altitude once they got over Berlin. Canadian pilot John Sheriff recalled morale plummeted so noticeably that some men openly cursed Harris in the mess. Gripped by fear, exhaustion, and anger, many were in no condition to carry on. Sheriff knew of three crews that were too mentally drained to continue. But they were left on operations, and two were quickly shot down.

Bomber Command had been accustomed to heavy losses in the past but this was different. The Battle of Berlin was draining the force white. It wasn't uncommon now to lose fifty planes a night over the target. Many more were crashing as exhausted crews tried to land in foggy weather after nine hours in the air. On one particularly galling raid the Germans shot down twenty-five Lancasters and thirty-nine others crashed over England. Some slammed into hillsides or struck trees or power lines as pilots tried to find their fog-bound bases. Others were lost when crews bailed out after giving up all hope of making a safe landing.

Then there were the icing problems. Freezing temperatures caked some planes in so much ice that the pilots couldn't climb beyond 14 000 feet. That made them sitting ducks for the flak and fighters. What wasn't known at the time was that the Luftwaffe was also taking it on the chin. In fact, the German Air Force had lost fifteen night fighters on January 1, mostly to bad weather. The next evening, ten black-crossed planes crashed in and around Berlin. Not long after that, twenty fighters were destroyed in a single night by severe icing problems. In all, close to 250 night fighters would be lost before the Battle of Berlin petered out. The majority crashed because of poor weather, but several dozen did fall to bomber gunners. On one particularly tragic night for the Luftwaffe, two leading aces were killed. Major Heinz Wittgenstein, who had eighty-three kills to his credit, perished at the hands of a tail gunner. And Hauptmann Manfred Meurer, a squadron commander with fifty-six victories behind his name, died when he flew too close to an exploding Lancaster.

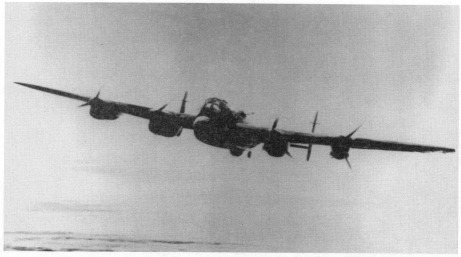

Lancaster bomber in flight with one engine knocked out. Courtesy of Jack Western.

Despite the frightful losses, airmen on both sides simply carried on, showing a remarkable degree of courage. Canadian pilot John McIntosh wouldn't quit even after a Messerschmitt 110 peppered his Lancaster with lead over Berlin, setting one engine on fire and damaging all four propellers. The bomber fell 12 000 feet before he was able to bring it under control. Amazingly, the German fighter was still in hot pursuit. This time, however, it ran headlong into a fusillade of slugs from McIntosh's two gunners and fell away in flames. With his tormentor dead, the Canadian nursed the critically damaged bomber all the way to England. Incredibly, none of the crew had been hit, although there were cannon shells in both gun turrets. McIntosh, who would be shot down and captured a few weeks later, won the Distinguished Flying Cross for his bravery.

Canadian pilot John Gray demonstrated the same sort of dogged determination on his first trip to Berlin. He lost an engine over France but decided to carry on anyway, even though it was doubtful he'd have enough fuel to get all the way to the target and back. He bombed the German capital, but, just as he'd feared, his fuel ran out over the English Channel and he was forced to glide in for a landing on the water. Gray, who was flying his first combat mission, ditched the bomber so masterfully that all seven airmen were able to get out and into inflatable rubber rafts. Waves were soon swelling twenty feet high, but the men hung on for dear life until they were rescued by a Royal Navy destroyer.

Canadian airmen pose at the rear of a Halifax bomber. Kneeling on the left is Daniel McCaffery, the author's uncle. Courtesy of the author.

Finally, on March 24, 1944, it was all over. Just over 800 bombers pounded Berlin, taking part in the nineteenth raid in seven months. A shocking seventy-two were shot down. That was enough even for Harris, who decided to call off the offensive before being ordered to do so by the High Command.

Who won the Battle of Berlin? According to the official history of the Royal Air Force, the campaign was a German victory. Bomber Command lost four hundred ninety-five planes — just five fewer than Harris had predicted. Furthermore, the Nazis did not surrender that April 1. In fact, the end of the war was still nowhere in sight. Still, while Bomber Command hadn't achieved its objective, it would be a mistake to think the Germans hadn't been hurt, and hurt badly. Just over 10 000 Berliners had died and the raids had wrecked dozens of square miles of the city. Damage to the main railroad station, which was important for moving both troops and supplies to the Russian Front, had caused serious disruptions. On at least one occasion thousands of tons of desperately needed supplies were held up for a week. And of course the loss of 250 German fighter planes was nothing to be sneezed at either. The truth is that Harris had placed unrealistically high expectations on the battle. That doesn't mean his men lost it. More appropriately, the Battle of Berlin might have been described as a draw.

If there's some doubt about who won the Battle of Berlin, there's no question whatever about who emerged victorious from Bomber Command's disastrous attempt to destroy the city of Nuremberg on March 30, 1944. There was a full moon that night, but Harris decided to send 795 bombers out anyway, hoping there would be enough cloud cover to allow the airmen to evade enemy fighters. He refused to cancel the mission even after a Mosquito reconnaissance pilot returned from an early evening flight over Germany reporting there were no clouds present.

What happened next was nothing less than a massacre. The bombers, caught in the moonlight and flying high enough to emit long white vapour trails, stood out like sore thumbs. Canadian tail gunner Daniel McCaffery, a veteran of the Battle of Berlin with two probable kills to his credit, recalled later it was almost like flying in broad daylight. For the first time in his tour of operations he could clearly see dozens of Halifax and Lancaster bombers all around him. The entire bomber stream was visible as it made its way across the continent. Even more disturbing was the fact that there wasn't a cloud in sight.

When the German fighters descended on them they did so with devastating force. Ace pilot Martin Becker had a field day, shooting down seven lumbering bombers single-handedly. In all, ninety-six Allied planes were shot down and seventy-one others were damaged, a dozen so seriously that they never flew again.

Amazingly, about the only place in Europe that had any cloud cover that night was the patch of sky over Nuremberg. The bombers that somehow made it through to the target couldn't find the city and most of their bombs fell in open country. In all, Bomber Command had lost 545 men in exchange for 129 Germans. Most of the enemy dead were civilians — only eleven Luftwaffe men were killed.

The documentary *The Valour and the Horror* is highly critical of Harris for sending his men out that night. Although some historians have come to his defence, arguing if he had waited for perfect weather conditions he'd almost never have mounted any raids, there can be no doubt that he — and he alone — was responsible for this terrible debacle. Why did he do it? No one will ever know, because Harris, who died in 1984, doesn't even mention the raid in his autobiography. About the best that can be said is that the air marshal was too aggressive that night. He'd mounted scores of successful raids in the past and would plan many more in the future, but on March 30, 1944, he had messed up, and messed up badly.

In any case, the Nuremberg raid demonstrated that, despite four years of raids, Germany was far from finished. Bomber Command was going to have to do a whole lot better if it hoped to bring the Third Reich to its knees.

CHAPTER 8

LIFE UNDER THE BOMBS

"We talked about nothing but air raids. The whole thing reminded me of a meeting of persecuted Christians in the Roman Catacombs."[1] Berliner Hans-Georg Studnitz scrawled that sad entry in his diary one night in 1943 after returning home from an unexpectedly depressing dinner party. His observation gives a good indication of what millions of ordinary Germans were feeling as the bomber offensive radically altered their day-to-day lives. So far, air raids had failed to break the spirit of the people, but they were making life miserable for an entire nation.

Like others throughout Europe, German civilians had feared aerial bombardment from the day war was declared. Air raid sirens had sounded in Berlin as early as September 2, 1939, when a rumour quickly spread that seventy Polish Air Force planes were approaching the capital. The Poles never did show, but Bomber Command, as we have seen, was over the city before the war was a year old. Those early raids caused few casualties and little in the way of material damage, but they had a profound impact on the population nevertheless. An 8:00 p.m. blackout was imposed immediately, and flashlights were bought up as fast as they could be put on store shelves. William Russell of the United States embassy noticed the blackout seemed to depress the general populace. "They all talk in whispers and low voices as they walk along the dark streets, almost as if they fear the enemy could overhear them and drop some bombs down on them," he wrote in his diary.[2]

Before long, the blackouts spread to every city and town in the Reich, which made getting around after dark a difficult proposition to say the least. In many communities the authorities handled the problem by painting curbs and street crossings luminous white and by covering cellar gratings with sandbags. To make sure they wouldn't bump into one another in the dark, people wore phosphorus buttons. For fanatical Nazis that wasn't good enough; they strutted about sporting swastika-shaped badges that glowed in the dark.

A German police officer guards a train load of vegetables. By 1945 food was in such short supply in some cities that it had to be guarded by police. Courtesy of Ulli Waschkowski.

Once the bombers began hitting oil refineries the situation got worse. The government moved to ration gasoline. Soon newspapers were chock-full of advertisements about cars for sale. With only twelve gas stations open in all of Berlin, however, there were few takers. Eventually, only top Nazi party officials, doctors, and leading industrialists drove anywhere. There were few taxi-cabs either, because people were not allowed to use them unless they were engaged in official government business, burdened by at least four pieces of luggage, or handicapped. Buses still ran regularly, giving off an eerie blue glow from their shaded lights. Tram cars ran too, but with their windows covered by black curtains, they were even more spooky looking than the buses. The few cars on the road had blackened headlights, except for tiny slits. Almost all street lamps were extinguished for the duration of the war. All of this, one visitor commented, made Germany's once-cheerful cities look like communities "lost at the bottom of the sea."[3]

Rationing of food, which started before the end of September, 1939, in response to an Allied naval blockade, was intensified as bombers tore up rail lines and smashed train stations, making it increasingly difficult to bring farm produce to the big cities. By the middle of the war potatoes, meat, dairy products, bread, rice, oatmeal, cream of wheat, tea, coffee, nuts, sugar, jams, eggs, fruits, and marmalade were all in short supply. Workers in heavy industry got extra food, but most civilians had to watch their diets very carefully. Before the fighting ended there was a critical shortage of food in some cities. "We had no food," Elke Gehrke recalled. "I remember finding a huge box of cookies by a garbage truck and they were the most wonderful cookies I ever ate. They must have been moldy, otherwise the garbagemen would have eaten them, but to me they were wonderful. I remember also my uncle got put in jail for stealing some potatoes. We had ration stamps… we were always hungry." After she was placed in an orphanage the situation got worse. "You just had everybody living in one room. We got turnips— that was the only food we saw, morning, lunch, and evening. Until this day I can't stand them. People in this country [Canada] can't comprehend what it was like to have nothing to eat."[4]

Ingrid Scheyk remembers people begging for meals. "There was no food. We had to go from house to house asking for food. We ate grass. You steal. You run in the night and steal milk from farmers. You steal potatoes in the night. People ate cats and dogs. It's the only way we survived. We had nothing. No grease, no coffee to drink. People took acorns and roasted them on a pan. You roasted them, grinded [sic] them up, and made coffee. You couldn't believe what we lived on. Dog meat is so sweet. You had to get used to it."[5]

The greatest ordeal, however, wasn't the lack of food and gasoline, or the depression caused by living with a permanent blackout. For most people the worst indignity was being forced to huddle helplessly in a humid shelter, often curled up in the fetal position, as bombs shrieked down out of the darkness. "While bombers droned overhead, I felt insignificant, like a rat trapped in a cellar," Kitzingen resident Winfried Weiss wrote later. Weiss, who was only seven years old when he experienced his first air attack, feared most being trapped inside his cellar as the flames came for him. "Fear rose from my groin and bowels, shot upward searing my arms and legs. For a moment I felt immense, as if I were about to escape my body," he said, reconstructing the events of one particularly fearsome raid.[6]

Ulli Waschkowski was only five when the war ended, but he still vividly recalls the terror he experienced in the air-raid shelters of Insterburg, a town in East Prussia. "It is my belief that you cannot really express in words the horror and fright that I endured as a child during those raids. It is an experience that goes beyond my — and I would think most people's — ability to describe. The horror started with the mandatory air raid drills during which we children had to wear gas masks. I remember being near panic as I was afraid of choking under the mask. Even years later I almost panicked when I was diving and not able to breathe. Also, the sound of air

Ulli Waschkowski (third from left), a German schoolboy and his family. Courtesy of Ulli Waschkowski.

Ulli Waschkowski (front) and his sisters. Courtesy of Ulli Waschkowski.

raid sirens, which were activated at 12 noon every Saturday until the sixties, gave me goose bumps.

"The actual raids happened during the nights only. It usually started with the sirens going off, after which we children were chased out of our beds and taken down to the basement. In a specially equipped room with steel doors we had to sit on benches and... wait. Then the horror came to its climax. We were sitting there listening to the noises of the airplane engines, the exploding bombs, the anti-aircraft fire, the shattering glass, and the roaring fires. This feeling of total helplessness, of not being able to do anything at all, was absolutely frightening. Even at my young age I realized what all this meant — the next moment could bring your death. I have heard soldiers on leave from the front say that they would have preferred to be out in the front lines because there you could at least do something like move, or shoot back, instead of just sitting there waiting."

Like most bombing victims, Waschkowski can recall one incident that was more terrifying than any other. "One outstanding moment during the bombing was when one night directly opposite our house a big compressed air bomb exploded. The shock wave was so strong that the firmly locked steel door of our shelter room flew open. For days after the raids we went out to look at the damaged houses in our neighbourhood. I vividly remember that once we looked in awe at the big crater that an unexploded bomb had left in front of the local hospital. I also remember that we used to inspect buckets filled with sand and [placed] in the attic, which were to be used against phosphorus incendiary bombs."[7]

Those who survived the air raids did so for a variety of reasons. Some had strong wills to live, managing to escape from smoke-filled buildings, or even structures that had been turned into raging infernos. Others seemed to possess a powerful sixth sense that alerted them to impending danger. Still others were just plain lucky. Schoolgirl Ria Kurr relied on all three factors to get her out of tight jams. Her first narrow escape came on a train ride home from a visit to her grandfather's house in Bamburg. "Grandfather acted funny at the train station when he sent us off," she said in a 1994 interview. "We weren't worried. It got so you couldn't worry about it. Then the train halted outside Schweinfurt. All of a sudden we heard planes. Why they bombed us I haven't got a clue. They dropped three bombs on us. One landed in front of the train and tore up the tracks. Another landed on one side of the train in a field and the other landed in a river on the other side. We were kneeling in between the benches and praying the rosary. My mother had one arm around me and one around my sister. It was a horror but it wasn't a frightening horror. It [saying prayers] gave us sort of a protection. It takes your mind off of it. One hour later the train was back in Bamburg. Grandfather said, 'I knew you would be coming back.' He was not demonstrative but there were tears in his eyes."

In that episode Kurr seems to have been saved more by good luck than anything else. But her next close call was averted because she could sense danger. "I had a dream in 1944 that Kitzingen was going to be bombed. I was one of those weird kids that had all those premonitions. We moved Christmas week. Christmas is very important in Germany. You don't do anything silly like moving." But the family's decision to listen to her premonition proved to be a lifesaver. Two months later Kitzingen was bombed and a neighbour child that Kurr had followed everywhere was killed. To this day she is convinced she would have perished along with her friend, Marianne, had the family not moved away. "During daylight bombing raids all through the war if you could run home in time they let us out of school, and we would run like the dickens. Otherwise, if you lived far away, you went to the

German schoolgirl Ria Kurr. Courtesy of Ria Kurr.

cellars. It's a wine-growing region, and the cellars are deep. Marianne was afraid to run home. She suffocated in a cellar… the doors were almost welded shut. She was one of our closest friends."

Kurr's closest brush with death came just before the close of hostilities. "Towards the end of the war in 1945 we moved to Neustadt. We had a little garden plot there. We went to the nursery and had trays of plants in our hands. We were walking home up a street with sidewalks on one side and a ditch on the other. We heard the airplanes. The warning alarms had sounded. Then we heard them coming down and they started shooting at us. Anybody who comes down that close could see we weren't soldiers, for Pete's sake."[8]

German army secretary Ann Hosseld was also caught in the open by strafing Allied aircraft. "I was wounded by machine-gun fire," she told the author. "I was shot through my left arm and had ten pieces of steel in my body, one in a lung and a few in other places. They were strafing the highways and I was wounded. I was in hospital for six weeks."[9]

Many found a hospital bed offered little in the way of safety. Nurse Edith Brackelmann was tending the sick at St Joseph's Hospital in Paderborn one winter night in 1945 when Bomber Command attacked. "They bombed the hospital to the level floor. We went down the stairs so fast we couldn't get dressed. Some had no shoes. We were just interested in getting the patients outside. The whole hospital was in flames…. As we were carrying them down the stairs windows were blasted out. Some people were hit by hundreds of pieces of glass." Once outside, the staff and patients lay flat in the snow. "We were outside on the grounds, we couldn't even make it to the bunker. It was really, really bad. The noise was absolutely terrible. How can I describe it? Of course some people died. Old ladies died of shock and heart attacks."

Eventually, they made their way to a bunker, but their ordeal was far from over. With bombs exploding outside, the nurses worked throughout the night trying to save the wounded. "People were cut really badly. We had to amputate legs and hands... we went through hell."[10]

Reaction to the air raids varied from person to person. Some, numbed from repeated attacks, became almost blasé about them. "You got used to it," survivor Ingrid Scheyk explained. "You can't run. You have to ride it out. There's nothing you can do. Either they get you or they don't."[11]

Some became so accustomed to bombings that they carried on almost as if nothing unusual was happening. Student Hiltgunt Zassenhaus, for instance, emerged from a Hamburg shelter after the great firestorm raid of 1943 and headed off to a nearby university to write an exam that had been scheduled for that day. She was covered in red dust, her eyes still stung from the smoke, and her throat ached every time she swallowed. Climbing over streets clogged with rubble, she reported to class. Astonishingly, the professor was waiting for her!

Others did not adapt so well. Werner Kluger, who was fourteen years old when the war ended, did not easily adjust to being bombed. "As we sat in the cellars made of stone with arched ceilings, lights were flickering, plaster was falling. You could hear the bombs whistling. We were scared but soldiers said as long as you can hear them whistling and exploding you're OK. That was sort of comforting." His worst experience came when planes were going after a gas factory only a few hundred yards from his shelter. "If they had hit it I wouldn't be talking to you today. Believe you me it was frightening. We knew it was for real. I remember they dropped a time bomb that fell in the factory yard right beside a tree. About two hours after the raid it exploded and a big piece of tree root fell in our yard. And because the tree was beside a brick wall, it was raining bricks all over the territory." Fortunately, no one was outside at the time and the Kluger family escaped unscathed.[12]

Trudy Ambridge also found the raids difficult to cope with. "I shall never forget the fear every time that siren started and you had to get up, put several layers of clothing on, grab your little case, which always stood packed handy with another change of clothes, and ran for the shelter across the road." Over time even she learned to adjust. "I think by 1945 we got so brazen about the whole situation that you didn't care anymore, and just stayed in bed and hoped for the best. I think most people in Germany had had enough of all this by then, and would have welcomed anyone who ended this misery and for it to never happen again."[13]

A black market sprang up in some places, where the authorities were inclined to turn a blind eye to it. Frankfurt resident Inge Neame recalled, "Coffee was scarce but you could often get it on the black market by bribing your butcher."[14] But Ann Hosseld found a different situation in Mannheim. "The food got less and less and we all got very thin. But there was no black market because there was the death penalty on it. Not many took the chance. It was the same with looting during the blackout. And it was carried out on the spot, which was a good thing… they [criminals] couldn't be allowed to take advantage of it."[15]

Of course, the greatest danger to the average German didn't come from a firing squad or hunger, but from the continuous bombing. People discovered they were at risk whether they lived in a big city or a tiny country village. Rural resident Trudy Ambridge confirmed that in a letter to the author. "I was only nine years old when the war began, but I vividly remember a lot of bombing raids," she wrote. "We lived just eighteen kilometres outside Hannover, which was a very industrial city, and also on the flight path to Berlin. In the latter part of the war the bombers used to fly across our little village almost non-stop. The American bombers came by day, and the British ones during the night. Of course, I was still in school at that time, and as soon as the siren was heard we were sent down the local mine, one hundred thirty-nine steps down slippery stairs. There was a room down there where we could sit and wait until the lights were switched on and off, which was the signal for the 'all clear.' As there was only one entrance we always hoped that nothing would hit it. There was no way out. We also had manholes along the main road in case there was an attack on vehicles, which used to be the targets for the fighters. As we had to cycle to school, these were used very frequently."

Some of the greatest danger for county folk came when Allied bombers had to take evasive action. "I was very glad we lived in the country, which only became a target when the anti-aircraft guns became too 'hot' for the bombers and they got into trouble. Then they seemed to drop their bombs anywhere. One time nine bombs fell into some field. We were very lucky. If they had fallen a shade further, we would all have been wiped out. Apart

German children steal coal from a moving truck in 1945. There was a serious shortage of coal and food in some German cities late in the war. Courtesy of Ulli Waschkowski.

from the craters they left, the next day lots of mushrooms sprouted in the fields, and we managed to pick baskets full. So we made the best out of that situation."

Youngsters found other ways to cope as well. "Apart from being scared, we tried to make the best out of the situation. The American bombers often carried extra fuel tanks, which were shaped like small weather balloons and painted silver. Very often they discarded them. We collected them and the handy boys cut them in half and we had a boat. They made little seats and paddles, and off we went to the local river for the ride. The only handicap was that you had to sit very straight, otherwise the 'boat' would overturn and the seats would float away. In this way we spent hours having fun and tried to forget the nasty things which were happening."

Ambridge remembers the bombings disrupted life in many ways. "We had lots of people living with us who were bombed out of Hannover. Our classes in school swelled to seventy or more children. I still have great admiration for our teachers who tried their best to cope with this onslaught and managed to teach us despite having their and our sleep interrupted almost every night. And there was no getting out of doing your homework. Somehow we accomplished this in between sitting in the shelter and sleeping."[16]

German boys at Rostock. Hans Richter is in the second row in uniform. Courtesy of Hans Richter.

Survivors saw both residential and industrial areas ravaged by bombs. Hans Richter remembers raiders once damaged an aircraft plant where his father worked while, at the same time, doing harm to residential districts in Rostock. "We were huddled in the basement and heard the bombs exploding," he said. "On that occasion one of those blockbusters, as they were called, hit and destroyed an apartment house like ours, about one hundred yards away. It was during one of these raids that a Lancaster crashed with howling engines about a half mile away in the woods. The next day I went to the crash site, the wreckage was still smouldering and I saw the burned bodies of the flight crew. Apparently they had no chance to bail out."

A year later the fourteen-year-old Richter, who was by now training to become an aircraft mechanic, witnessed the destruction of Rostock's main airplane factory. "It was an overcast day, I was standing with some colleagues on the dunes by the sea. We could hear the bombers overhead. The first prematurely released bombs exploded in the sea, the next bombs fell into the river a few kilometres away and then we saw the inferno as the aircraft plant was destroyed. At that time the raids were mostly carried out by B-17 bombers and it was obvious that military targets could be accurately located through a complete cloud cover."

Near the end of the war Richter often witnessed Allied aircraft flying overhead in broad daylight, virtually unchallenged by German flak or fighters. Hiding in nearby woods when the sirens sounded, he saw huge fleets of bombers flying overhead. "On sunny days we saw the B 17 formations coming in from the Baltic Sea, flying south towards Berlin. They were flying low enough that we could see the U.S. Air Force stars on the wing underside and we counted about two hundred or more. About ninety minutes later the formations returned flying north towards Denmark. We found it amazing that there was no anti-aircraft activity when those overflights took place, but then we realized there was very little defensive equipment in our area. At that time probably all available equipment was employed at the eastern and western fronts."[17]

Werner Kluger doesn't remember the bombing doing much damage to military or industrial targets in his home town of Jaegerndorf. "I recall they hit the railroad station tracks once, and the tracks were bent like corkscrews. Our town had a big locomotive yard and they tried to hit it because everything moved by rail. And we had munitions factories but I don't think they ever hit them. They never managed to hit the gas factory or the munitions factories but they destroyed enough homes and things like that."[18]

Ulrich Dankworth, on the other hand, lived in a community where both industrial and residential areas were flattened. "I grew up in downtown Magdeburg, an industrial city located approximately one hundred fifty kilometres west of Berlin," he told the author. "The industrial areas in my home town were regularly bombed with very few civilian casualties." Later in the war, bombs began landing all over the city. Dankworth has never forgotten the terror of those attacks. "I was only four years old when my mother lifted me out of my bed and carried me down to the air raid shelter every time the sirens warned the citizens of an impending night raid. She and the other tenants of the house were always calm and never made the children aware they were scared. I can still smell the musty air in this small, always overcrowded shelter and can still hear the thundering noise of the exploding bombs in the nearby suburbs."

The raids became so fierce that people soon began fleeing the city. "I just turned five when my mother with her four young children moved to a hamlet twenty-five kilometres away. I believe most families with children were evacuated to escape the intense bombing." Not long after the Dankworth family escaped, Magdeburg's residential downtown area was utterly destroyed. "My mother, my brother and sisters, and thousands of others witnessed from a safe distance of twenty-five kilometres the placement of the flares (we called them 'Christmas trees') marking the targeted area, and then the intense bombing with incendiary bombs, of the residential heart of the city. I remember my mother saying over and over again, 'Why did they destroy the houses?' Everybody in the village was stunned. A big plume of black smoke was visible for days but I did not, of course, comprehend what happened until we saw with our own eyes, in June, 1945, nothing but ruins in the city centre. Other parts of the city, even suburbs next to the armaments factories, were spared on that particular raid."

Even today many Germans can't understand why the Allies sometimes went after residential districts. "I know the historic, residential downtown areas of almost thirty other German cities were also specifically targeted for destruction, not just Dresden, Hamburg, and Cologne," Dankworth said. "Believe me, it really hurts deep down" to hear the claims of some that civilians were not deliberately bombed.[19]

Ulli Waschkowski recalls that raids on his home town of Insterburg always seemed to be directed at the city core. The city itself was devoid of any industry. "It is also worth mentioning that my parents owned a piece of property right next to the air force base outside of Insterburg... as far as I remember that base was never attacked by the bombers. My parents also owned an apartment building with six apartments for families of army members. Interestingly, the building received a direct hit during the first attack on Insterburg."

Waschkowski said many civilians took bloody vengeance on any Allied airman who had the misfortune to parachute safely into the city. "There was a great amount of anger at the crews of the bombers. As far as I know a number of shot-down airmen were 'lynched' by furious civilians."

"Personally, today I feel no animosity against anyone who took part in these bombings. There is though one question for which I have not found an answer, and probably there is none: Why did the Allies who were fighting for a just cause without any doubt, have to resort to the same inhumane and barbaric means as the Germans? Or is there an answer: evil creates evil."[20]

Austrian Elisabeth Frey thought the raids were justified, despite the fact she was nearly killed by bombers on more than one occasion. Frey, whose grandmother was Jewish, had been rounded up and forced to work in a munitions factory. "They took us there in a train and it was bombed," she recalled. "I remember mostly Polish and Ukrainian women were on board. They were

German children flee the cities by train to escape the bombers. Courtesy of Ulli Waschkowski.

prisoners too, but I'm sure the guys in the planes wouldn't know there were prisoners on board. Over one hundred fifty people died. The train was filled with blood, just running like a river. I'm seventy-four years old and I cannot forget it. People should know even those in prisons had to suffer. But it's wrong for people to blame the airmen. They were just trying to end the war quickly. In the camps we were praying for the boys to liberate us. They had to do what they had to do. My attitude is they [the Germans] started it, they should have known the world wouldn't let them get away with it."

As the war dragged on the raids began affecting Germany in ways that no one could have foreseen. Most of the able-bodied men were in the armed forces, and now women were increasingly being employed to work in factories, clean up bomb damage, and even to operate anti-aircraft guns and searchlights. As a result, many young people had virtually no adult supervision. Teenagers had more freedom than ever before, and that led to inevitable problems. Records in the city of Munich, for example, show many teenage girls were having sex as early as age fourteen. In one case, three boys and three girls, all thirteen years old, were caught in a group sex act. Two boys, one thirteen and one sixteen, were accused of having group sex with three nine-year-old girls. One sixteen-year-old boy was arrested as a male prostitute. With so many men away at the front, he had been doing a brisk business prior to his arrest. There were also reports of teenage girls engaging in "unnatural sexual intercourse" with French slave labourers. One girl having sex with German soldiers told her mother she was only doing what Hitler wanted — trying to produce more children for the state.

In a bid to get their children away from both bombs and temptations of the flesh, many German parents shipped them off to Hitler Youth summer camps in the countryside. In all, 1 200 000 people — most of them children — fled the cities. The exodus saved many lives, but it was carried out with considerable difficulty. Trains and ships that could have been moving troops and supplies around the countryside were used to get civilians away from built-up areas. In all, nearly 1200 special trains made trips to rural areas. Seventy-eight ships were also involved in the evacuation.

The vast majority of Germans — including most children — didn't go anywhere. They had to live with the constant fear of bombings. For many, it wasn't just the raids that were hard to take. "There were no dances, all the men were gone," Ann Hosseld said. "It was very dreary. You couldn't buy any clothes and that bothered me a great deal. I couldn't visualize life after the war. You couldn't imagine it ending."[21] To take their minds off the situation many turned to music. People went out in blinding snowstorms to hear concerts in churches or community halls. Classical music was popular with the older generation, but, much to the chagrin of the Nazis, American and British swing music was liked best by many young people. Movies were another diversion, but most were tiresome government propaganda films.

For those working in war factories there was almost no life at all. Men worked seventy-two hours a week, often relying on pep pills to stay awake on the job. Women and youths employed in such places were expected to put in sixty hours of labour. Often, many people went straight from work to the nearest bomb shelter. There were even reports of people being married in bunkers.

Others, however, shunned the shelters and wouldn't leave their homes for anything. Many refused to give up familiar surroundings even after their homes had been damaged by Allied planes. Berliner Ruth Andreas-Friedrich said people she knew preferred to stay in bomb-damaged homes simply because they were home. "If they destroy our living room we move into the kitchen. If they knock the kitchen apart, we move over into the hallway. If only we can stay at home. Even the smallest corner of home is better than any palace in some strange place."[22]

The Nazis tried to boost public morale by publishing stories of civilian heroism. One newspaper told of a teenager who rescued his father from a burning building and then urged its adult readers not to shame themselves by letting children teach them about valour. Others tried to whip up hatred for the enemy, calling the Allied fliers "air pirates" and dismissing the United Kingdom as an "island of murderers."[23] But many ordinary people weren't buying the propaganda. There were jokes such as "What's the difference between India and Germany? In India one man [Ghandi] starves for millions. In Germany, millions starve for one man [Hitler]." Or: "Dear Tommy, please fly further on your way; spare us little miners for today. Fly instead against those people in Berlin; they're the ones who voted Hitler in."[24]

Some became so disgusted they lost all faith in the regime. "We were afraid mother was going to wind up in a concentration camp because she couldn't keep her mouth shut," Ria Kurr recalled. "She was known as an agitator. I wasn't allowed to go to the Hitler Youth. Mother got a medical certificate for me. I wanted to go because my friends were there. But we would go to church every day. They used to say, 'Hum, you're too sick to go to the Hitler Youth but not too sick to go to church.'"[25]

Those who survived the bombings have vivid and horrifying memories that have not faded with the passage of the decades. George Busch, who was just thirteen years old in 1945, still recalls his first air raid. He was caught on the toilet and was late making his dash for a shelter. As he came out into the street, he was nearly trampled to death by a runaway horse team that came bolting straight for him. Once he got to the shelter, he found, "It was no pleasure. Everybody was praying. I was mostly with women and old people. The men were all gone."[26]

"To this day I cannot stand dark rooms," Elke Gehrke says. "And every time I see pictures of the war in Yugoslavia or Africa I see myself as a child and my head aches with pain. I recall my childhood and to us it was all death and it was horrifying. Your life is never the same."[27]

The Germans who found the bombing campaign easiest to cope with were undoubtedly those on home defence duties. They faced extraordinary danger because the men and women who operated the anti-aircraft guns, searchlights, radar stations, and fighter planes couldn't hide in shelters. They were right out in the open when the bombs were falling, and scores of them were killed or maimed. But at least they didn't feel helpless. Instead of huddling like rats in a cellar, they were fighting back.

German pilot Franz Stigler. Courtesy of Franz Stigler.

Indeed, almost every night about one million German home defence personnel swung into action as word was received that the bombers were on their way. Luftwaffe artillery personnel scrambled to operate the 20 693 anti-aircraft guns, popularly known as flak (which was an acronym for Fliegerabwehrkanone). At the same time, sausage-shaped balloons, known as rubber flak, were sent aloft to dangle curtains of steel cables around factories and railroad stations. Such protection, it was thought, would prevent low-flying aircraft from getting too close to those targets. While all of this was going on, saucer-shaped radar units spun north and west to search the heavens for intruders, their every move matched by the king-sized reflector drums of the searchlights.

At first, the anti-aircraft personnel were all adult men, but as the war dragged on they were joined more and more by teenage boys, women, and even Russian prisoners of war. Whether they were men, women, boys, or POWs, they were very courageous — and very good. Heinz von der Hayde, a fire-control lieutenant at an anti-aircraft command centre in Berlin, recalled his crew was able to shoot so rapidly that during one raid they went through 900 rounds of ammunition. Their barrels became so hot that the guns could only be handled with asbestos gloves. The next day "nearly every barrel had to be changed. Some were bent with the heat; others had the rifling worn out."[28]

A good flak crew could fire and reload an 88-millimetre cannon with almost blinding speed. Gunther Lincke recalled that with the aid of headphones, electrically set gun elevation devices, and a Russian loader, his crew could fire a round every eight seconds. The gunners were by no means just dishing it out, however. They were taking punishment too, as teenager Heinrich Moller found out while operating a rangefinder in a Berlin flak tower. On one particularly awful night, he remembers holding his fire as the bombers thundered directly overhead. As they had done so often in the past, the Germans refrained from shooting in the hope that they could trick the airmen into thinking they weren't over the target. For several anxious moments he held his breath, praying the ruse would work. Seconds later, he heard the unmistakable shrieking sound of bombs coming down right on top of him. "They seemed to fall all over the surrounding area at once. There were thousands of incendiaries; a whole lot of them fell on top of both our tower and the gun tower, about three hundred on each. Across at the gun tower it looked just like a fireworks display. There were at least ten of them near me. We had two gunners killed. One had his head bashed in by an incendiary bomb falling right on top of his steel helmet; that shattered his brains."[29] Coming hard on the heels of the firebombs were high explosive bombs. Soon the whole area was engulfed in flames, and a firestorm developed. Muller, who stuck to his post throughout the ordeal, had to tie himself to the tower rails to prevent being sucked into a wall of flames.

As good as the flak crews may have been, they were by no means the main threat to Bomber Command. Without a doubt that honour belonged to the German fighter pilots. Flying twin-engine Junkers 88s, Messerschmitt 110s, or Heinkel 219s, they outmatched the Lancasters and Halifaxes in every way imaginable. An HE 219, for example, was armed with six cannons, including four awesome 30-millimetre guns firing shells that appeared to Allied airmen to be almost the size of pumpkins. A one- or two-second burst from that formidable arsenal would pulverize any bomber it hit. The ME 110 didn't have as much firepower, but it came equipped with cannons that fired upward! This allowed the pilot to fly straight and level immediately below the bomber, where he was out of the vision of the rear gunner. Using this technique, German pilots shot down hundreds of Allied airmen who never knew what hit them.

Besides the superior armament, the fighters were much faster and more agile. Needless to say, with as many as 1000 bombers attacking a city at once, a good German fighter pilot could have a field day. The most success-

German pilot Franz Stigler, who shot down twenty-eight Allied bombers. Courtesy of Franz Stigler.

ful Luftwaffe night fighter ace, Heinz Wolfgang Schnaufer, shot down an incredible 121 bombers. Nicknamed the "Night Ghost," he destroyed five Lancasters in one mission on the night of May 25, 1944. Nine months later, on February 21, 1945, he bagged nine Lancasters in one twenty-four-hour period. Incredibly, he survived the war without suffering so much as a scratch. Another ace, Helmet Lent, sent 102 bombers down in flames. In all, two dozen night fighter pilots scored fifty or more kills each. By way of contrast, the top Bomber Command gunner, Canadian Peter Engbrecht, shot down five German fighters. Most gunners seldom even fired their guns, and those that did rarely hit anything.

Like fighter pilots of all nations, the Luftwaffe pilots tended to be a cocky, sometimes even swaggering breed, but like the bomber crews, they were mostly just boys. Studying photographs of them you see happy, self-assured individuals who painted their planes with colourful personal markings. The single-seater fighter pilots seemed to favour yellow noses and, on the fuselages, illustrations of playing cards such as hearts, spades, or diamonds. Some went in for symbols of Mickey Mouse or other Disney characters. In fact, Mickey Mouse was exceedingly popular in Germany throughout Hitler's rule. At Christmas, 1939, propaganda minister Josef Goebbels had even given the Führer eighteen Mickey Mouse movies and had recorded in his diary that Hitler, a big fan, was "very happy" to receive them. "I hope that this treasure will bring him joy and relaxation," he wrote.[30] The two-seater fighter pilots, on the other hand, favoured pictures of bright red and yellow roosters painted just below the canopy.

Most of the German pilots, it's safe to say from reading their letters and diaries, had little interest in politics. Their elders had taught them since childhood to believe in Hitler and the Nazis, but for most their real passions were flying and girls.

Certainly ace Franz Stigler was no goose-stepping fanatic. "I was flying since I was twelve years old," he told the author. "My father was a pilot and my teacher in Grade 5 was a pilot. I loved flying." Asked if politics was ever discussed in the mess, he replied, "We didn't know what politics was. I had a girl's name on my plane — and the coat of arms of Berlin." Asked the name of the young lady whose moniker was inscribed on his ME 109, he quipped, "it changed with the girl."

As the war dragged on, the airmen became disgusted with the Nazis. There were whispers about what was going on in the concentration camps, but "not very much was known about it. Anyway, if anyone tried to do something about it, he wouldn't have lasted too long."

Stigler, who shot down twenty-eight Allied planes, believes the Luftwaffe pilots relaxed between sorties much the same way as the bomber crews did. "We did all kinds of stuff to relax. You were in the middle of a fatal fight — when you got back to the base you had to relax somehow. We turned to drinking, girls, all of us on both sides."

Stigler said every German pilot he knew had friends and relatives who were being bombed. But few felt any lasting animosity towards the bomber crews. "We just tried to keep them away from our cities. We were soldiers and they were soldiers. We did our job and they did theirs. There was no bitterness."

Sceptics might be inclined to suspect that Stigler has simply mellowed with age. The truth is he had no ill feelings towards his opponents, even during the height of the air war. He proved that conclusively on December 23, 1944, during what may have been the most amazing single moment during the entire five-and-a-half-year bomber offensive. Taking part in a daylight mission against American aircraft, Stigler shot down two B 17s before returning to base to refuel. As he was waiting to take off again, a badly damaged bomber limped across the sky, only 300 feet above his head. Taking off in hot pursuit, the ace quickly overtook his slower adversary. But as he closed in for the kill, Stigler suddenly hesitated. He couldn't bring himself to open fire. Three of the big plane's four engines had been knocked out, and the tail gunner, whom Stigler could see clearly, was obviously wounded. "I just couldn't shoot because I could see the man was bleeding very badly." To slaughter a helpless opponent just wasn't in his make-up. Pulling up directly alongside the damaged bomber, Stigler found himself face to face with the startled American pilot — Lieutenant Charles Brown. Neither man seemed to know quite what to do. No one had trained them to fly wingtip to wingtip with the enemy. Gesturing with a gloved hand, the German pointed towards Sweden. He wanted the B 17 to land in that neutral country, where its crew would be interned for the duration of the hostilities. Uncertain about what to do next, Brown banked away and flew back to England. Stigler realized the Allied plane was getting away but he deliberately let it escape. Back on the ground, he wisely said nothing to anyone about the episode.

Nearly half a century later a curious Brown, anxious to discover the identity of the Messerschmitt pilot who had spared him, wrote to a German magazine, providing details about the bizarre encounter. Stigler saw the letter and immediately called the American. The two former enemies arranged to meet in a Seattle hotel (Brown lives in Miami and Stigler is now a resident of Surrey, British Columbia). Although it had been decades since they'd last seen one another, Brown instantly recognized Stigler, and the two quickly became fast friends. The American, in fact, even managed to talk the Federation of European Combatants into bestowing the prestigious Star of Peace on the old German ace. It was a fitting tribute to a man whose story reminds us that there was plenty of humanity — and bravery — to be found on both sides.

Regardless of how much common decency there may have been in ordinary Germans, the fact remained that the Third Reich was still a monstrous regime. And Arthur Harris and the American air commanders were determined to keep throwing their bombers at it until it was utterly destroyed.

CHAPTER 9

THE BOMBER BOYS

As tough as the bomber offensive was on German civilians and military personnel, there was one group that suffered even more — the Allied bomber crews.

The airmen had joined up looking for adventure, or out of a sense of patriotism, but few had any real idea what they were getting into. Before long, it became obvious to most that their chances of survival were slim. Each man had to complete thirty operations before he could go home, and the life expectancy at one stage in the war was only seventeen.

There were so many ways you could get killed that most found it best not to think about it. If enemy fighters or flak didn't get you, there was a good chance you'd be killed in a mid-air collision with another bomber. Or you'd be hit by a string of bombs coming down from an aircraft flying overhead. Or your plane would slam into an English hillside as an exhausted pilot tried to locate a fog-bound airfield.

"A lot of our casualties were collisions, or bombs falling on people," bomb aimer Jim Letros said. "There were a lot of accidents. We came back one night and were doing our circuit to land, waiting our turn, when I saw a light in front of us and yelled for the pilot to dive. He did, the aircraft swooshed over our heads and hit the guy behind us head-on. There was burning and flaming debris everywhere."[1]

Many men died in the most bizarre ways. A tail gunner from New Zealand was so overcome with fear that he threw up into his oxygen mask, then suffocated when the vomit froze at high altitude, cutting off his air supply. Tail gunner Jack Western recalls a man being decapitated by a whirling propeller blade right on the airfield. "He went walking, or running, down the runway at night. It was silly. Nobody knows yet why he was there." He also recalls a distraught airman committing suicide after receiving a "Dear John" letter from his girlfriend. On still another occasion, a man was killed when the incendiary bombs he was loading into the belly of a Lancaster sud-

Jack Western, tail gunner. Courtesy of Jack Western.

denly broke free and came down on top of him. "All they found was a black patch and a hat."

Western had several almost hauntingly surreal experiences. The first came before he'd even completed training. "We were shot down while we were training," he said. "We did three months training as a crew and at the end of that you had to fly one trip over enemy territory that you were not officially given credit for. It didn't have to be very far over, but it had to be over enemy territory. That night we were flying a Whitley bomber on a diversionary raid, which meant the main force was going to three or four different targets. Our objective was to take pictures of enemy gun positions just on the opposite side of the Canadian lines in France. The Whitley doesn't fly very fast at the best of times and when the German 88s fired up we got hit in both engines."

During that moment of extraordinary danger, the airmen relied on humour to quell the rising panic. "You make insane remarks like 'tail gunner to skipper, I think we're on fire,'" Western recalled. "He says, 'you're kidding?' He's sitting right beside the engine and of course he can see it's on fire. That kind of banter was going on to break the tension. I don't know what would have happened if we didn't do that sort of thing because you're frightened to death. Anybody who tells you they're not frightened is lying."

The pilot turned for home, but the plane was rapidly losing altitude. When they got down to 12 000 feet he issued the order to bail out. Western didn't like the idea one bit. "It was kind of stupid, bailing out in the black of night into the English Channel. I talked the crew out of it. I could swim and might have had some chance, but not very much. And I was the only one who could swim." So they continued to head for England, losing altitude all the way. Eventually, the battered Whitley crossed the channel, but now the pilot was losing his valiant struggle to keep it airborne. Finally, the machine gave up the ghost and dove straight for the ground.

At such moments many people report seeing their lives pass before their eyes, but not Jack Western. "I said something that begins with 'Oh God and Our Father.'" Seconds later he heard the pilot cry out, "Brace yourselves!"

The crash was spectacular. "There was a noise, a flash, a blinding flash. We severed some power lines and then there was a slight bump such as you get coming down an elevator with a poor attendant. The plane totally disintegrated. The tail fell off, the wings fell off, and the engines fell out. The tail was up in an apple tree. The front of the plane finished up fifty feet from an old lady's front door. She lit a candle and came out to see what it was all about. There was fuel everywhere and they very quickly told her to put it out. I was thrown out. They found me some distance away in a ditch filled with water. My Mae West (lifejacket) kept me afloat."

The next thing Western remembers is lying soaking wet, covered in blood, inside a house. "Then I was in an ambulance with a WAAF (a female volunteer attached to the Royal Air Force) holding my head. I recall that she had little clothing except a great coat. I was nestled to a nice breast and then threw up all over it. Next thing I remember was I was looking at a bright light and someone in white said, 'nothing we can do for him.' A female said, 'if he's going at least we can clean him up.' Next time I woke up I was in a bed. And it was daylight. Someone came to me and asked if I wanted anything. I could not speak. I tried to lift my head and I found it could not move. Several days later, power came back to my body and my speech slowly returned. My wife, then my fiancée, told me she was there at the hospital and fed me very scarce grapes. I don't even remember the grapes, that's the worst of it."

After his recovery, Western was posted to 153 Squadron to begin one of the most event-filled tours of duty in the history of Bomber Command. There were satisfactory moments, such as the time he participated in the raid that put the German battleship *Admiral Scheer* out of commission. "Our photo [a picture taken from Western's plane] showed a direct hit between the funnels. We know we dropped a cookie right smack on top of that battleship. It never sailed again."

A Canadian-built Lancaster bomber and crew. Air crew (standing), from left to right: Norm Fenerty, bomb aimer; Les Hauxeel, wireless operator; Joe Eissen, navigator; Vern Martin, pilot; Russ Gray, mid-upper gunner; Jack Western, tail gunner; Dennis Baker, flight engineer. The three men kneeling in front are unidentified ground crew. Courtesy of Jack Western.

Death was a constant companion. Once, as he flew over a Luftwaffe airfield on a daylight raid, Western saw two close friends killed right in front of him. They were flying in a nearby Lancaster that took a direct hit from an anti-aircraft shell. "The guy who slept next to me fell right out of the plane. He wasn't wearing a parachute because there was no room for it in his turret. The plane fell smack in the middle of a farmhouse. You could see white rings going out and, when the smoke cleared, there was no farmhouse. We were friends, as much friends as you could get to be. To see them both killed, literally right in front of your eyes...."

On another occasion he had the misfortune of over-hearing a heart-wrenching exchange between a critically wounded tail gunner and his pilot. "Someone aboard another plane had pushed the wrong button and their conversation went air-to-air. We could all hear their conversation.

We heard an explosion, then 'Oh God! Oh Mother! I'm hit!' He started yelling for his mother. It was the tail gunner. The pilot ordered the crew to abandon the aircraft. The next thing we heard was the mid-upper gunner saying 'I can't get the rear gunner out.' The skipper said, 'You bail out, I'll try to land.' The tail gunner was saying, 'I can't get out! My legs!' The pilot says, 'Don't worry, I'm staying with you. You'll be OK.' Then we heard a big bang and everything went quiet. That was enough to unnerve people, especially because it had been a rough raid. We got back home and flaked out. The lights were out and we were all asleep and the next thing we hear is the horrible scream of a guy yelling, 'Oh God! Oh Mother! I'm hit!' The kid sitting across the room from me is sitting up in bed, his eyes closed, and screaming all the words we'd heard of that tail gunner and his pilot. He went through the whole thing. We didn't touch him. When a guy is in that state you don't touch him. The rest of us didn't get to sleep that night."

An even more terrible scene awaited Western after he returned from one raid and spotted a badly damaged Lancaster parked a short distance away. "I saw the rear turret and the mid-upper turret were both a real mess. The rear turret was shot to pieces. As I walked up to the plane, and I swear this happened, the tail gunner waved at me. At that moment one of the crew took me away and put me in a truck. 'You shouldn't be here,' he said. Then I heard a scream. The top half of the tail gunner came off and the bottom half remained [inside the turret]. He was hacked in half. As soon as he defrosted he fell in half. I was so sure I had heard him scream."[2]

Needless to say, some found the pressure more than they could bear. They simply refused to fly any longer. Those who gave up paid a terrible price, however. They were officially designated as LMF, or lacking in moral fibre. In other words, they were branded as cowards. Most were stripped of their rank and shipped off to clean latrines, work in coalmines, or serve in the army. They were shunned by old friends, and their family members felt confused and embarrassed.

Most airmen were appalled by the practice of publicly humiliating men who were clearly suffering from battle fatigue. "I thought it was too cruel," commented bomb aimer Jim Letros. "We were all human beings. It had nothing to do with moral fibre. You just cracked. Our mid-upper gunner cracked one night just as we were going into the target. He started screaming, 'Get the hell out! We're going to be killed!' I saw fellows break down who couldn't get back in the aircraft."[3]

A Canadian Lancaster bomber crew. Standing, from left to right: Johnny Walker, Johnny Norrington, Bill Dean, Gord Bullock, Lyle James, Lionel Wright, Bob Irvine, and David Bernett. Kneeling in front are unidentified members of the ground crew. Courtesy of Lyle James.

Jack Western felt LMF "was a load of crap. I met in the cookhouse guys who had spaces on their arms and chests where there had been stripes and wings. I talked to one guy who had twenty-odd flights to his credit. He had reached a point where he could no longer fly. To go before three penguins [airforce officers who did not fly] and have them say you were lacking moral fibre… these were people who had never gone on these trips. They were psychiatrists but not aircrew. The first time somebody shot a real shell at me I realized I was nuts [to have volunteered]. They decided one guy who had done forty ops was a coward. It was crazy. That guy was suffering from mental and physical fatigue. There's a lot of difference between battle fatigue and being a coward. That's just being a human being."[4]

Pilot Lyle James, who flew damaged planes home on ten separate occasions, has a different opinion. "I can't excuse LMF. People think that's harsh but if we could get out just by saying you didn't want to fly anymore you'd have twenty men lined up and I'd be at the head of the line. I know I'm in the minority in that view."

James believed most airmen handled the strain well. "Everybody was conscious that each trip could be your last. Everybody knew that. But there were only two instances on our squadron of people who cracked up, out of thirty crews. I think they were under remarkable control." Often men returned from particularly hair-raising missions vowing never to fly again, only to go right back into the fray after they'd calmed down. "Our mid-upper gunner told me 'I'll never fly again' several times. He'd say, 'They can shoot me, I don't care.' But he always did [show up for every mission]."[5]

Some men, however, clearly carried on long after they should have quit. Airman Charles LaForce recalls a friend who was so mentally exhausted that he had a premonition of his own death. "I had gone back to the locker room to get a good-luck talisman and he was sitting on the bench, one flying boot on and the other hanging from his hand. I said, 'C'mon Carrothers. They'll go without you.' He said, 'To hell with it. Let them go.' I think he knew he was going to die. We got one of those lorrie girls [a female truck driver] to drive us, him to his aircraft and me to mine. We had just taken off with Wing Commander Marshall behind us. There was such a flash of light even at two thousand feet and about five miles from the airfield, that I was ready to bail out if the pilot had said 'go.' Carrothers and his crew had blown up coming down the runway. All that was left was a thirty-foot crater in the runway. I could hear his voice and was embarrassed to cry like a child. I was a pallbearer and there wasn't a lot left to carry. Probably the weight of a few bags of sand. I can still hear him teasing our signals officer, Taffy Lewis. 'I was out with your girlfriend last night, Taffy.'"[6]

Jack Western, too, remembers men who were in no shape to stay on operations. By continuing to fly after their nerves were shot they were putting the whole crew at risk. "I saw a guy in the mess slowly tearing newspaper strips. He'd drive you nuts. He'd get the newspaper so it would go from one end of the room to another in one piece. There were amazing reactions from people. Some literally couldn't put a cigarette in their mouth, they were shaking so much. Yet they'd go in the plane and didn't show any reactions. Some went out at night and got absolutely polluted."

Some thought it took more courage to go LMF than it did to continue on operations. "The biggest scare I ever got was when they charged me with desertion in the face of the enemy," Jack Western says. He was late returning to base from leave, getting back just in time to discover the squadron was leaving on a mission without him. "I drove up to the station and was told at the gate, 'You're late. There's a battle order on, you're going to be charged.' I was shown as AWOL [absent without leave]. I drove over to my billet, grabbed the locker key and threw my clothes on just as the crew was pulling out. I actually flew the mission. The next thing I knew two MPs [military police officers] were waking me up, saying, 'You're under arrest.' I'm taken to the CO's office and he says I'm charged with desertion in the face of the enemy. Fortunately, I had enough sense to take my logbook with me. I said, 'I flew that mission and my skipper can verify it.'"

The experience helped convince Western that it took a great deal of courage to face the stigma that went with simply quitting and being branded LMF. "I was scared to bloody death [on operations]. I was. I was frightened. The point was — was I more frightened of what would happen if I went LMF or of flying? I've never been able to reconcile that. For me personally, was it a braver thing to go LMF or was I a coward for not going LMF?"7

Those who pressed on may have conquered the fear of being publicly humiliated, but there was no getting away from the terror a man felt when he was being shot at. Bomb aimer Miles Tripp has written perhaps the best description of what it was like to be under fire of any of the 125 000 men who flew with Bomber Command. Recalling in his memoirs the day his Lancaster was shot up over Cologne, he wrote, "I was still clutching the bomb release when a delayed wave of shock made my body almost unbearably hot with a prickling heat, and my face felt as though it was being jabbed by a hundred pins. Gradually, the tingling heat disappeared but then my body started to tremble and I couldn't control the shaking of my legs. Any residual dreams of glory faded and forever vanished in the daylight over Cologne. From now on survival dominated my thoughts."8

Lancaster pilot Ron Pickler was comforted by a belief that he'd somehow get through. "I wouldn't say you were scared because you always thought it [death] would happen to someone else." Flying over a hotly defended area could be extremely stressful nevertheless. "I remember distinctly going through the target feeling ice cold drops of perspiration falling off my chest onto my arms. I had a new pair of gloves on in which the palms were soaking wet. So you knew you were under strain."9

Bomb aimer Jim Letros believes most of the airmen were able to carry on because of their fatalism. "At one time half the crews that started didn't finish. You just acquired a fatalistic attitude." Their youth also helped. "I was eighteen when I went in and twenty-one when I went out. You were young, otherwise you couldn't do it."

Some also had an exceptionally strong will to live. Letros was on one raid where his pilot practically refused to be shot down. "We got conned [by searchlights]. The pilot had to go into pretty violent evasive action. I remember him saying, 'God damn it, they're not going to get us!' When we got hit he threw the plane into a straight dive. From twenty-six thousand feet he dove to fourteen thousand. On the way down he was yelling at me to get rid of the bombs and I did. We dove so steeply that we were out of control and the flight engineer had to help him pull out." When they eventually levelled out, they found they were free from the searchlights and flak.[10]

Just as was the case with many German civilians who survived air raids, the Bomber Command boys who lived to see the end of the war had more than their share of luck. Jim Letros saw six bombers get shot down in front of him on the way to Nuremberg, and a German night fighter put three cannon shells through the port wing of his Lancaster, but he escaped unscathed. Tail gunner Daniel McCaffery had an even more narrow brush with disaster when a jagged piece of shrapnel tore the bottom of his turret and passed between his legs. "I nearly got my backside shot off — or worse," he recalled.[11] Mid-upper gunner Bill DuBois was on an operation in which shrapnel smashed into his turret, hitting both his guns but missing him. "We came back once with a main spar cracked and with holes all through the plane, but we never lost anybody. We were very fortunate because we saw planes beside us get blown to pieces." During some daylight raids late in the war, he saw flak so thick he was convinced "we'd never get through. But we did."

Early in their tours the airmen were extremely vulnerable, but as they gained experience, they became harder to kill. Members of a crew that survived half a dozen sorties were soon working well as a team. "Everybody had a job to do," DuBois said. "You had to keep your eyes open for collisions. Can you imagine eight hundred bombers flying over a city with no lights on? You were just straining all the time, blinking for silhouettes of other planes." Once, on a daylight mission, he called out a warning to his pilot when another Lancaster appeared directly above them, about to unload "six tons of bombs."[12]

Pilot Lyle James was flying over Gelsenkirchen one night when he saw a full load of bombs hit a Lancaster one hundred feet off his starboard wing, crushing it "like a leaf." During a raid on Cologne a stick of high explosives passed so close to his own plane that he could clearly read the markings on the individual bombs. And he just missed a collision with another bomber over Duisburg when his 19-year-old mid-upper gunner, Bill Dean of Windsor, Ontario, called out a last second warning. "It was so close that as Bill screamed, 'go down skipper' I immediately threw it into a wild dive, and as I looked over my shoulder, I could see the props of another Lanc missing our twin tails by inches." Before his tour was over, he would also narrowly miss a head-on crash with a German Dornier 217 night fighter. "He was flying against the stream, and at the same altitude as we were. We missed each other by about fifty feet. We had holes in both the rear and upper turrets. Bill Dean had holes that narrowly missed his head. A piece of red-hot shrapnel fell into his flying boot, burning him. And hydraulic lines to the rear turret were severed, rendering it inoperable."

On at least two other occasions teamwork saved his bacon. During a trip to Aschaffenberg, James tossed the big Lanc all over the sky in a desperate bid to shake off a pair of German fighters. With his gunners calling out warnings, he was able to keep out of harm's way. "Tracers were flying both over and under our wings, but he didn't put a scratch on us." Finally, mid-upper gunner Bill Dean got in some bursts of his own and both fighters fell away, one trailing flames from its port engine.

On another trip the crew was saved thanks to the combined efforts of James and flight engineer Johnny Norrington. "Just as we were approaching the target, a Lancaster about a hundred feet in front of us blew up in a blinding fireball. I had no recourse but to fly directly through this inferno, and when we came out on the other side of it, there was burning oil and bits of debris on the windscreen and the leading edges of the wings. At this time, the mid-upper gunner called to say that there was smoke coming from our port wing. It was not smoke, but gasoline, leaking at the rate of eighty gallons per minute from two of our petrol tanks that had been shot open, possibly by the same shell that brought down the other Lanc. The big danger here was the flames burning on the front of our aircraft, but these shortly flickered out and we proceeded to bomb the target. Our flight engineer rendered sterling service. He immediately switched our fuel lines onto the damaged tanks, so we could use up as much fuel from them as we could, before they ran dry. As the danger of an explosion was imminent, I ordered the crew into their parachutes, just in case. After we had cleared the target area, I was still quaking and, just as I was starting to calm down, right off our port wing tip there burst a black puff of flak. Instinct took over, and I rolled about thirty degrees to starboard at the same time diving away. As I looked over my shoulder, I could see six more flak bursts stitching right along the path that we had been flying. I have always wondered if that unseen gun crew ever knew how close they came to shooting down a Lanc before breakfast that morning. We returned to base with seventy-four holes in our aircraft and fifteen minutes fuel left in the tanks. As we landed, control tower, seeing the state of our poor old plane, ordered us to proceed to the graveyard [the scrap heap for planes damaged beyond repair]."[13]

Watching out for collisions and falling bombs was all part of a night's work for the gunners, but their main role was to keep a sharp eye out for enemy fighters. In fact, seeing them first was the key to survival. The tail gunner had to be especially alert because the Germans usually attacked from the rear. Jim McCaffery recalls continuously moving his guns across, up, and down, making quick reversals whenever he thought he saw something in the dark. "To turn right or left you used a control column since all the movement was governed by hydraulics," he said. The triggers for his four machine-guns were also on that column, "which was like a short handle-bar on a bicycle." The area directly in front of his face didn't have any glass, giving him better visibility. "When you looked into the gun sight you saw an illuminated ring with an illuminated dot in the middle of the circle. There was no glass between that gun sight and the great outdoors." McCaffery saw fighters about four times during his tour. He tried to avoid shoot-outs because his machine-guns were no match for their cannons. Nor were they always reliable. Once three of his four guns jammed when he opened fire over the English Channel. "I was an armed lookout who tried to spot them before they saw us. Whenever I saw one I'd call out, 'fighters in the vicinity' and the skipper would dive a few hundred feet, losing them in the dark. They seldom followed because there was no shortage of targets for them in the bomber stream."[14]

Sometimes, the only warning a gunner would get of an impending attack would come when a star he'd been looking at suddenly disappeared. When a fighter did attack, it did so with unexpected suddenness. Daniel McCaffery made that clear when he was asked to reconstruct the actions in which he was credited with two enemy aircraft probably destroyed. "Don't ask me to describe it, it all happened too fast," he said.[15]

If the enemy didn't pose enough danger, there was always the weather. The airmen quickly discovered that flying at 20 000 feet in mid-winter could be a bone-chilling experience. This was especially true for the gunners, who sat in partially opened turrets. Precautions had to be taken to avoid perspiring before take-off because any sweat could freeze, causing frostbite. At 20 000 feet, icicles six inches long occasionally had to be pulled from oxygen masks, and airmen had to keep blinking to keep their eyelashes from freezing. On one of Jim McCaffery's operations, the temperature dipped to -56 degrees Fahrenheit. To stay alive, gunners relied on thick socks, a warm pullover sweater, an electrically heated inner suit, an outer suit, three pairs of gloves, and flying boots. Just for good measure, Jack

Canadian tail gunner Daniel McCaffery.
Courtesy of the author.

Western wore a nine-foot-long scarf around his neck and smeared vaseline all over his face. In addition to all the clothing, the airmen brought along a surprising array of other items. Western wore sunglasses to help him maintain his night vision. "I also had a knife in my boot to cut the parachute cords in case it got caught in a tree. In my pockets I carried two chocolate bars, two flasks of coffee, two or three sugar candies, and chewing gum. Chewing constantly cleared your ears. You constantly had to hold your nose and swallow as you climbed, to equalize the pressure. We also took pills to stay awake. And you had a pill to stop you from going to the bathroom. Going to the bathroom in a Lanc was a contortionist's job."[16] To relieve themselves the airmen had to find a portable toilet in the bowels of a darkened fuselage. Getting in and out of their cramped turrets was no easy task. Some didn't bother with the toilet. Jack Currie saw that on his first raid. "Somewhere near Aachen, as I was assimilating a first sight of hostile flak and searchlights, McLaughlin loosened his safety straps and parachute harness. The roar of the slip-stream deepened as he opened his side window about six inches. Ponderously, deliberately, he turned to the window and set his left knee on the parachute seat. I had no idea what he was doing, and glanced back at the flight engineer for reassurance. Impassive eyes between helmet and oxygen mask told me nothing. I returned, fascinated, to McLaughlin, whose attitude suddenly took on a familiar shape. Holding himself sufficiently far from the window to avoid frostbite or dismemberment, he made use of the slipstream's suction to achieve his purpose."[17] Some men were afraid to go to the toilet for fear that the enemy would show up and catch them literally with their pants down. Once, after a nine-hour round trip to eastern Germany, Jim McCaffery returned to base in desperate need to urinate. He had stayed at his guns until the plane had safely landed, only to discover the aluminum doors behind him were jammed shut. "My urge was so great that I kept pushing anyway and crumpled those little doors. I pulled myself out of the turret and relieved myself under the aircraft. The next day, I was summoned by the armaments officer and asked what had happened to the turret doors. I gave him some cock-and-bull story about a threatening emergency over enemy territory and he accepted it."[18]

Preparations for the operations were elaborate. "Normally, on a daylight raid you would have the military police come to the billet and take a roll call, making sure you were awake," Jim McCaffery said. "You acknowledged, and you knew then that you had to be at the briefing room at a certain hour. The navigators and wireless operators were briefed ahead of us because more information had to be absorbed by them. We went to the briefing room and the intelligence officer would tell us what to expect in the way of defences. The weather officer would tell us what to expect in the way of weather. In both cases there was a fair amount of guess work. They couldn't possibly know. Then the bombing leader would describe the target."

"Briefing being over, we went to the crew locker rooms where we put on our flying clothes. We then went out and got into trucks and drove across the airfield to be deposited beside our aeroplane. Everybody got aboard, tested his equipment... every engine was run up and tested out by the skipper and the flight engineer. Then the engines were shut down and we all left the aeroplane to stand around underneath for perhaps half an hour or so. But then a flare would be fired from the tower or we would otherwise be signalled to re-enter the aeroplane and one by one we revved ourselves out on the perimeter track, circled the concrete all the way around the aerodrome, and took our place in line."

The operation was often scrubbed at the last moment. "For every mission that was actually carried out, we were briefed, taken out to the aeroplane, run up and tested our equipment and then were told, 'this one is scratched.'

I don't know whether they did it because there was a legitimate reason or they did it just to keep us on our toes." Most likely, England's notoriously bad weather was the key factor. "There were days when the weather was so socked even the birds were walking," McCaffery said. Once, the fog was so thick that his pilot clipped the top of a tree with his wheels, and they set down with a large branch stuck in the landing gear.[19]

If the mission wasn't cancelled at the last minute, the take-off of a squadron of Lancasters could be an awesome sight. Pilot Lyle James recalled that after the control tower fired a signal flare "the whole station would immediately come to life, with first one, then another Rolls Royce Merlin engine whining, then coughing, and then settling into a quiet roar, which increased second by second, until all 128 engines, each of 1250 horsepower, were all singing their songs. Then the flight leaders would slowly wheel their big bombers out onto the perimeter tracks, followed by their flights, and eventually two long lines of Lancasters would be circling the drome, looking for all the world like circus elephants as they made their way to the take-off point, where one by one, they rolled down the runway, slowly gaining speed, then taking off so gracefully into the dark sky."

When it was his turn to roll, James would always say a "quick but fervent prayer for a safe return." Then the brakes would be locked, and he'd "apply all the power you could give her." Then he'd "release the brakes, and the struggle would begin to hold her straight until you could get the tail up, then get all of this thirty-two tons of 100-octane gas, high explosives, and seven tense young men up to one hundred thirty-five miles per hour in little over a mile, then into the pitch blackness at the end of the runway, and up into the air! It always seemed to me that once we had taken off, got the wheels and flaps up, and then throttled back to climbing revolutions, that about a quarter of the trip was over."

The first part of the journey was usually uneventful. The crew had time "to settle down, the navigator to find his true winds, the bomb aimer would be doing test runs on various targets as they passed beneath him, while the engineer computed our fuel use. All of this time the gunners would be keeping a close watch for our own aircraft, to avoid a collision."

On the way home, the crew usually started to relax about half way across the North Sea. At that point of the mission, James always found himself thinking "with luck I might finish this trip and live to see another day."[20]

Between flights, there wasn't a great deal to do. "The RAF didn't go overboard when it came to providing recreation," Jim McCaffery said.

"Travelling troupes of entertainers sometimes put on shows in the recreation hall and the men went into nearby towns once or twice a week to visit pubs and dance halls." Often, however, the only entertainment was found in the mess. "The English are all excellent conversationalists, and an Englishman with a pint of beer and an hour to kill... conversation was one of the great recreations. And oh, of course, there were a lot of nice-looking girls in England, too."[21]

Besides drinking, talking, and chasing girls, the airmen relied on practical jokes to get their fun. Jack Western recalls, "Once we rigged a guy's bed so it would collapse. He got in it and the bed went crunch. With another guy we took his bed apart and put it in the rafters. We spread his gear all out. He comes rolling in at 2 a.m. and can't find his bed. We said, 'it's the next one down!' It's half a mile away. But off he goes. He comes barrelling in and a female voice says, 'What the hell's going on?' He's in the WAAF quarters. Next morning we go to breakfast and he's not there. They'd fastened him to a bed, painted him red, white and blue, and put him up on top of the air raid shelter. He was always on time after that. Before then, he'd always be coming in late, saying, 'Wakey, wakey, you bastards!'"[22]

As for food, Jim McCaffery said, "We ate well. The British public received one fresh egg a month, the armed forces one a week, and flying crews got one fresh egg every time we flew, whether on operations or training. There was plenty to eat. There was not a great deal to complain about, except the Brussels sprouts. They must have grown in profusion in England because they never seemed to have a shortage. We got so many that it was a good twenty years after I got home before I could eat one again. But overall, I'd say the food was adequate, considering that millions of tons of shipping and thousands of men were on the bottom of the Atlantic attempting to bring it to us."

English eating habits took Canadians some getting used to. "We had breakfast and lunch, but supper was tea. If you went into the mess any time between 8 p.m. and 9:30 p.m. you would find a big tankard of tea, cheese, and butter and margarine. They followed the English habit of having supper late."[23]

Regarding the touchy subject of killing civilians, reactions of the airmen varied widely. Certainly none of them had joined the air force expecting that they'd be involved in the killing of non-combatants. Asked why he signed up, Jim McCaffery said, "At the time, it was the thing to do. Ever since 1936 we had been fed a steady diet of bad news about Nazi Germany

Lancaster bomber pilot Ron Pickler.
Courtesy of Ron Pickler.

and Hitler. And it was no question about motivation. We knew he was a devil, followed by devils." Furthermore, farming bored him. "I didn't think Hitler would have any greater terror for me than being brought up in the 1930s on hard work. And there was a certain glory attached to it. I suppose all 18-year-olds go in with foolish notions."

The Valour and the Horror had argued that the airmen didn't know their bombs were being directed at civilians. They were, the documentary suggests, duped by the High Command into carrying out raids against residential districts. But the men who flew the raids say they knew civilians were dying. "We were nearly always told the targets were marshalling yards but I think most of us knew that these were just the general target area," Jim McCaffery said. "They [the High Command] didn't care if in catching these marshalling yards they killed a few thousand people and knocked over a few thousand homes and set a few thousand fires. It turned out after the war that Bomber Harris believed that he could do great damage to German production by simply burning down their houses in the winter months."[24]

For most men the task at hand was made easier by what became known as the "morality of altitude." You dropped bombs into the dark and, although you saw fires far below, it was all very impersonal. "It was so remote," pilot Ron Pickler said. "We really didn't think what happened when the bombs landed. I didn't anyway."[25]

For some, like Englishman Jack Western, that the Luftwaffe had bombed his home town made it a little easier for him to raid German cities. "I had no qualms whatsoever," he said. "We were told the targets. If anybody in their right mind thinks you can take five hundred airplanes and bomb an oil refinery and not expect civilians aren't going to get hurt... you've got to have rocks in your head. We knew we were killing civilians, but didn't they kill our civilians first? Think of the millions of people they whacked out in Russia and the thousands in Warsaw. I had no compunction. I was going to London once and I saw a Yank in the train who had come right out of Germany. He showed me pictures of a concentration camp that he'd taken with his own camera. It was nauseating."

Western even went so far as to drop pop bottles on the Germans from his rear turret. "I'd drop six of them out and they'd whistle all the way down. Can you imagine what that would sound like on the ground? Up would go the air raid sirens. Everybody would go into the shelters. Afterward, people would be looking for unexploded bombs. It created panic."[26]

Canadian pilot Lyle James was another untroubled by his role. "I've never lost a moment's sleep about it. I'm proud of what I did. When I saw those little kiddies in the tube, night after night in London... and people with baby carriages who were strafed by the Luftwaffe in Bournemouth. We were fighting a battle for survival. They were after world domination and they came damn close to achieving it. They had plans for a 2000-mile rocket to bomb New York." James added that many cities were so highly industrialized that they were legitimate military targets. "You take Essen, with the Krupp Works right in the centre of the city. They made torpedoes, JU 88s, tanks. Eighty-eight thousand people worked there and they were as important as soldiers at the front."[27]

Mid-upper gunner Bill DuBois has a similar opinion. The Germans, he points out, were bombing Allied cities before Bomber Command hit the Third Reich. "They started the war. As far as I'm concerned, they're responsible for fifty million deaths. We didn't want the war. Every time I flew over Germany I wasn't shaking my fist in anger at them. I had a job to do." Civilians were killed, he concedes, but that couldn't be helped. "You can't send a thousand bombers over a city and expect to hit only industrial or military targets. Anybody who thinks civilians don't get

Canadian mid-upper gunner Bill DuBois.
Courtesy of Bill DuBois.

killed in war aren't living on this planet. Anybody who says war is a sanitary exercise is crazy. War is the closest place to hell you'll ever get without being there."[28]

Others, however, were troubled — during the war and after — by what they'd seen and done. Airman Charles LaForce, who had seen English children huddling in London's subway system during the 1941 blitz, couldn't help thinking about the German youngsters under his bombs. "After I had participated in my own bombing raids," he wrote in 1994, "I wondered how many Hans and Fritz and Gretchens I had helped to kill or maim. I comforted myself with the knowledge that Hitler et al. made no effort to move women and children to the country, as Britain did. Hitler refused to break up the home industries and they weren't making chocolate bars there. At that time, Bomber Command was the only part of the military able to fight back. By this time the Germans had exterminated millions of Jews and killed millions of Russians during the invasion of the U.S.S.R. Besides, they were trying to kill me all the time so the philosophy became 'do it to them before they do it to you.' While I was writing this a series of thunderstorms passed by and so I had noise accompaniment to help me remember those stupid, terrible times."[29]

A group of Canadian airmen. Bomb aimer Jim Letros is at the far right. Courtesy of Jim Letros.

Bomb aimer Jim Letros is also troubled when he thinks about what his bombs may have done. "It bothers me. Quite often I think about it. I rationalize it. That's the way it was — man's inhumanity to man. You had to be there to understand the feelings at the time. War is war. There was terror bombing." Still, he believes the bomber offensive was worthwhile. "It broke the back of the Germans. It's hard for people to understand today. They were trying to kill you and you were trying to kill them. You had to get into a certain way of thinking, otherwise you couldn't carry on."[30]

It's safe to say most of the airmen believed they were doing a job that had to be done. And the vast majority were willing to stick with it, no matter how dangerous it became.

They were incredibly brave young men who were willing to put their lives at risk whenever their society asked them to. If there is any blame to be laid for the decision to bomb cities, surely none of it belongs on the doorsteps of the airmen who flew the raids.

CHAPTER 10

THE RAID ON DRESDEN

The time had come to finish the job. Senior Allied commanders were in agreement about that much as the summer of 1944 approached. In the West, Germany had endured two solid years of heavy aerial bombardment. Cologne, Hamburg, the entire Ruhr Valley, and a great deal of Berlin had been destroyed or seriously damaged. In all, Arthur Harris claimed, Bomber Command had wrecked no less than forty-five cities. Even when his tendency to exaggerate was factored into the equation, it was obvious the Third Reich had been badly hurt. Harris wanted to keep pounding away at fifteen major cities that were still largely intact, still insisting that carpet bombing could cause the collapse of civilian morale and force surrender without the need for an invasion of western Europe. But the High Command wasn't willing to wait any longer before opening a second front on the ground. It had decided to launch an amphibious assault along the coast of France on June 6, 1944. In preparation, it ordered Bomber Command to carry out a continuous series of raids on German army positions near the shore and on airfields, railroads, ammunition dumps, and bridges in both France and Belgium. Harris objected strenuously, pointing out four-engine bombers would be hard pressed to hit such small targets with any degree of accuracy. Civilian casualties in Nazi-occupied Allied nations would be heavy, he warned. This time, however, Harris was overruled, and Bomber Command began preparing for a new offensive that would be almost as controversial as the one it had waged over German residential areas.

Actually, this wasn't the first time Harris had been ordered to put Allied civilians at great risk. In late 1942 and early 1943 Bomber Command was ordered to carry out area attacks against the French seaport towns of Lorient and St Nazaire in an attempt to destroy German U-boat bases. The submarines, protected by thick concrete pens, were undamaged, but both cities were flattened and hundreds of French men, women, and children were killed.

That destruction was only a taste of what was coming. It all started on April 9, 1944, when a raid aimed at a German army supply station in the French town of Lille went terribly wrong, leaving nearly 500 civilians dead. Another 464 French perished less than two weeks later at Noisy-Le-Sec when bombs intended for railroad yards crashed into nearby residential areas. Belgium, too, felt the impact of Allied bombs, with almost 300 civilians being killed or wounded during an attack on train sheds at Malines.

When the invasion came the attacks reached a bloody crescendo. Because the targets were so close to England it was possible for Allied fighters to escort the bombers all the way to the target and back, which meant the raiders could operate in daylight for the first time in years. Night after night and day after day, the airmen rained tens of thousands of tons of high explosives down on France and Belgium. Indeed, Bomber Command flew as many sorties in the first week after D-Day as it had mounted during the first nine months of the war.

Civilian casualties were inevitable. A Lancaster or Halifax couldn't hit a small target with the same pinpoint precision as a single-seater fighter-bomber or two-seater dive-bomber. In many cases the airmen were sent after highly dubious targets such as roads, which were difficult to hit and easy to repair. "They aimed not to kill Germans but to cut roads, which the French knew was impossible," French historian Jean Quellian said fifty years later: "Everyone wondered: why?"[1]

Many bombs directed at roads fell into quaint country towns, killing scores of people. "We were forgotten, left to our own devices," recalled Frederique Legrand, who was just a child when missiles aimed for a bridge near Caen killed her parents and hundreds of others inside the city. Orphanages were soon so packed that the French government didn't recognize many as wards of the nation until 1964. By then, recognition amounted to a certificate. "Relatives helped raise me and my sister and brother. But we were different from other kids," she said. "No one seemed to know what Normandy suffered."[2]

German soldier Franz Cockel got a first-hand look at the bitterness some of the French felt as Allied bombers destroyed their homes. As he fled from the battlefield nursing a wounded hand he was suddenly surrounded by French civilians. "I expected them to tear me apart. One man pulled out a dagger, but he pointed it to the sky. 'This is for the Americans,' he told me."[3]

In all, 14 000 French and Belgian civilians were killed by Allied bombers during this period.

Norm Anderson, a Canadian army soldier who was accidentally bombed by Allied planes in 1944. Courtesy of Norm Anderson.

Nor were civilians the only victims of "friendly" bombs. Canadian soldiers were pummelled by Lancasters as they closed in on enemy troops near Falaise. With the two opposing armies almost nose-to-nose it was exceedingly risky to use heavy bombers, but the Lancs were sent in anyway. In all, seventy planes attacked the 12th Canadian Field Regiment and the 30th Field Company. When the bombers appeared overhead the soldiers fired off yellow signal flares to ward them off. Tragically, the Pathfinders were carrying yellow flares to mark the target and dozens of planes dropped their loads in the midst of the Canadians.

One of the soldiers caught in the raid was Corporal Norman Anderson of Forest, Ontario. "We were sweeping for mines when we heard banging behind us," he recalled. "We turned and saw these damned bombers dropping bombs." The men dashed into a tunnel at the bottom of a quarry. Moments later bombs were slamming right into the quarry. "The concussion would lift you off the floor, pretty near," Anderson said. "They bombed the wrong place. They wiped the artillery out."

When the smoke cleared, sixty-eight soldiers were dead or wounded, and dozens of tanks, trucks, jeeps, and field guns lay in ruins. Many more would have been killed if not for the fact that men took shelter in the quarry tunnel or in slit trenches that had been dug just hours beforehand to guard against German artillery. Despite what happened, the soldiers remained surprisingly

141

stoic, realizing accidents were an inevitable part of war. "It wasn't the first time something like that happened," Anderson said. "We got bombed, or strafed, by American fighters the week before. It wasn't all that unusual."[4]

The airmen, however, were not to be blamed for any of these debacles. Many put their own lives at great risk, flying extremely low in order to bomb as accurately as possible. The diary of Russell McKay, a pilot from Ontario's north country who took part in several raids over France, proves that conclusively. There are repeated entries such as "concussions of exploding high explosive bombs rocked us violently," or "some aircraft came home holed by bomb fragments."[5]

Nor would it be fair to insinuate the bombers did nothing but kill Allied civilians and Canadian soldiers. So many bombs were falling that the airmen couldn't help but do some serious damage to the German army as well. Two notable successes should be recalled. In one case, bombers so badly cratered a road junction that two German tank divisions couldn't get through to launch a planned June 30 counter-attack on Allied troops near Villers. Lancasters employing 1200-pound Tallboy bombs collapsed a railroad tunnel, preventing a frustrated German tank division from reaching its objective. There were dozens of less dramatic victories as well. For instance, Nazi motor torpedo boats were prevented from attacking the invasion fleet after their bases were all but obliterated by air attacks. V-1 rocket sites near the Pas de Calais were put out of action by bombers, thus sparing London from further damage from the infamous buzz bombs.

Regardless of how effective they were at this stage of the war, there's no doubt whatever that the airmen who carried out these raids were among the bravest of the brave. In fact, two Canadians won the Victoria Cross, the country's highest gallantry award, during this period. The first was won just one week after D-Day for an almost unbelievable display of self-sacrifice by twenty-seven-year-old Winnipeg native Andy Mynarski. Mynarski, a soft-spoken fellow with boyish good looks, had had a hard life. He'd been forced to drop out of school at age sixteen after his father died so he could help his mother support a family of four children. But if there was a hard edge to him as a result of his early travails, he never showed it to any of his crewmates. Posted to 419 Squadron, RCAF, he'd flown a dozen missions as a mid-upper gunner by June 13, 1944. His best friend, tail gunner Pat Brophy, recalled later the crew was apprehensive as it prepared for its thirteenth operation on June 13th. As they sat on the grass at sunset, awaiting orders to board the plane, Mynarski found a four-leaf clover, and the mood changed. "Twirling the good luck token like a tiny prop, he turned to me," Brophy wrote later. "Here Pat," he said. "You take it."

Two hours later they were flying over Cambria in bright moonlight, looking for railroad yards. Then it happened. A JU 88 night fighter appeared out of nowhere, its guns blazing. Two engines on the Lancaster burst into flames, and fire erupted inside the fuselage between Mynarski and Brophy. The pilot ordered the crew to bail out, and Mynarski immediately left his turret. He was about to jump out a side door when, for some unknown reason, he glanced back towards the rear of the bomber. At that moment he took in a frightening scene. The door to the rear turret was jammed shut, and Pat Brophy was trapped helplessly inside. What's more, if he was going to attempt a rescue the Manitoban was going to have to plunge straight through a wall of fire. He knew, too, that the pilotless Lancaster might explode at any moment. Lesser men would have gone out the escape hatch, but not Mynarski. Brophy tells best what happened next. "Instantly, he turned away from the hatch — his doorway to safety — and started towards me. With the aircraft lurching drunkenly, Andy couldn't keep his feet. He got down on hands and knees and crawled — straight through blazing hydraulic oil. By the time he reached the tail his flying suit was on fire." Brophy shouted to Mynarski to save himself, but the gallant gunner grabbed an axe and began swinging furiously at the jammed doors. They still refused to open. "Wild with desperation, he tore at the doors with his bare hands," Brophy recalled. "By now he was a mass of flames below the waist."[6]

Mynarski looked as if he was ashamed to leave without his friend, but Brophy waved him away, realizing there was nothing more that could be done. Stumbling back through the burning fuselage, Mynarski made his way to the escape hatch. By now his upper body was on fire and his parachute was in flames. Nevertheless, Andy Mynarski wasn't quite ready to jump. He paused for a moment, turned to face Brophy and saluted his pal before leaping out into the night.

The Lancaster, which was on automatic pilot, eventually glided down and crashed. Amazingly, Brophy was thrown clear and lived to tell the tale of Mynarski's incredible courage. Mynarski himself couldn't tell anyone what had happened because his burning parachute had only partially opened and he hit the ground with great force. French civilians came to his rescue, but he died later that night from his burns and internal injuries.

If Mynarski's story isn't enough to convince even the most cynical individuals of the great courage possessed by the bomber crews then the tale of

Attack on the port of Kiel, Germany, on September 15, 1944. Photo was taken from the plane of Canadian pilot Lyle James. Much of the city was burned out. Courtesy of Lyle James.

how Calgarian Ian Bazelgette won his VC might do the trick. The twenty-five-year-old Lancaster pilot was attacking V-1 rocket sites in northern France on the evening of August 4, 1944, when his plane ran into a storm of anti-aircraft shells. Two engines were knocked out, and fires broke out all over the bomber. The bomb aimer lost an arm and one of the gunners was overcome by toxic smoke. Bazelgette, who was master bomber for the raid, continued his attack, marking the target with flares and then dropping his own bombs. Moments later the crippled machine went into a hideous spin. Somehow, he managed to pull the plane out of its death dive, but the flames were spreading rapidly and it was obvious they couldn't possibly make it back to England. The Canadian ordered his four unhurt crewmen to bail out and then sat in the burning Lancaster for several agonizing seconds trying to decide what to do next. Should he jump himself and leave the bomb aimer and mid-upper gunner to die? Or should he attempt a near-impossible landing in a darkened farm field below? The temptation to save himself must have been overwhelming but Bazelgette rejected the easy option, located a pasture in the inky darkness and headed in for a crash landing. He was gambling he'd have enough time to set the bomber down before it exploded. After that, he'd just have to hope he'd escape the crash-landing unhurt and still have enough time to drag two wounded men out of the flaming wreck. Sadly, he never got the chance. Moments before the wheels touched down, the fuel tanks erupted, turning the bomber into a fireball. Ian Bazelgette and the other two men were both killed instantly.

By mid-September Paris had been liberated and the German army was being pushed back across France. It was clear Bomber Command was no longer needed to ensure a successful invasion, so Harris was allowed to send his planes back to Germany. This time, however, the High Command ordered him to concentrate on knocking out the enemy's oil industry. It was hoped that by blasting the refineries and storage depots to rubble Bomber Command would ground the Luftwaffe and put German tanks and trucks out of action. Harris was livid. He wanted to continue the carpet bombing of cities. It was too late to prevent an invasion, but he still hoped he could bomb the Germans out of the war before it became necessary to cross the Rhine River. Once the Allied armies were inside Germany, he knew enemy troops could be expected to fight with fanatical determination. If the Germans could be forced to surrender before that happened, tens of thousands of Allied lives might be spared.

To get around the oil directive Harris interpreted it very liberally, ordering area attacks on cities that housed the oil industry. Just for good measure, he simply defied orders from time to time, occasionally sending his men out to blast targets that had nothing to do with oil. Nevertheless, several oil refineries were knocked out at this time, putting both the German army and the Luftwaffe in a precarious position.

As the Lancasters and Halifaxes headed back to Germany, Bomber Command had never been more powerful. Losses over France and Belgium had been relatively light compared with the Battle of Berlin, and with new bombers rolling off production lines in both Canada and England, Bomber Command had grown by 50 per cent since the beginning of 1944. What's more, new technology was now available, making it easier to find and bomb smaller objectives. One German city after another now succumbed to the bomber fleets. Many were smaller towns that had never been attacked before. They had narrow streets and old wooden structures that would burn like cordwood.

Darmstadt, a small city of virtually no industrial importance, was the first to go. It was all but removed from the map on September 11, 1944, with the death toll surpassing 12 000. The raid could be partially justified from a military point of view, however, because Darmstadt was crowded with German soldiers on their way to the Western Front. In all, more than 1000 infantrymen were killed that night.

Frankfurt and Stuttgart, two cities in southern Germany, were lashed with bombs the next night. In the former, fires raged out of control for three days,

Raid on anti-aircraft gun emplacements at Domberg, Germany, on October 29, 1944. Note bomb craters below. Arrow on right shows a string of bombs descending from the plane of Canadian pilot Lyle James. Courtesy of Lyle James.

leaving 500 dead. In the latter, almost 1200 died. Bremerhaven was destroyed before September was out, and Brunswick was all but annihilated in mid-October. In fact, 150 hectares of the city were burned out and 561 citizens were killed. The beautiful university town of Bonn, home of famed composer Ludwig van Beethoven, was ravaged three nights later. Dozens of historic old buildings were lost, but Beethoven's home was saved by firefighters who scrambled onto the roof to knock away incendiary bombs. Today, it still stands, serving as a museum that houses artifacts connected to the great master. Freiburg was next to go, with 3000 dying there in one night.

Raids also continued in Nazi-occupied countries with decidedly mixed results. An attack on the big German submarine base at Bergen, Norway, killed 113 Norwegian civilians, including sixty children, but it also damaged three U-boats and sank two German surface vessels. Another raid in Norway produced one of Bomber Command's greatest triumphs of the whole war. Thirty Lancasters armed with Tallboys capsized the mighty bat-

Messerschmitt 163, a German fighter plane.
Courtesy of the author.

tleship *Tirpitz* in Norwegian waters on November 12, 1944, drowning 1000 sailors.

Pilot Bob Knight flew through "huge lumps of flak that came off the *Tirpitz*" in order to get in close to the target. After dropping his bomb he should have streaked straight for home, because enemy fighter planes might have shown up at any moment. But he couldn't tear himself away from the incredible scene unfolding below him. "We could see the *Tirpitz* was actually mortally wounded. We stayed for quite a time, which was rather foolish, because of the possibility of fighters above and flak below. But I felt I had to see her go. She was a beautiful ship and well, it was really sad."[7]

Bomber Command, which had dropped just 10 000 tons of bombs on the Third Reich in 1940, had dropped more than 50 000 tons a *month* throughout 1944. That figure, however impressive, would pale beside the monthly average that would be achieved in 1945.

The new year opened with yet another directive from the Air Ministry. This time, in addition to oil targets, the powers that be wanted Bomber Command to go after jet-plane factories and plants that were building the so-called *schnorkel* submarines. The Luftwaffe was now receiving an alarming number of hot new Messerschmitt 262 jets that were 125 miles per hour faster than the speediest Allied fighters, and the German navy was getting new U-boats that could travel faster and stay under water longer than the old models.

Harris complied with the order, but just as he had done in late 1944, he continued to order the occasional area attack. When Chief of the Air Staff Charles Portal suggested he stop carpet bombing cities altogether, Harris threatened to resign. Portal, worried about Harris's enormous popularity with the British public, backed down. The area raids, which were of rather dubious value at this later stage of the war, would continue.

At first, most of the raids were confined to the Ruhr Valley, which had been partially rebuilt the previous autumn. Results were often gratifying. At Duisburg on the night of January 22, 1945, a large force of Lancasters knocked out both a benzol plant and a major steelworks. Six days later Cologne, which had been spared for months, was raided in broad daylight. The Luftwaffe failed to respond, but German flak gunners were ready and waiting.

As he approached the target, pilot Eric Wannop reported later, the sky over the city was completely cloudless and a wintry sun was shining brightly overhead. They were as exposed as fish in a barrel and moments later they found themselves wading through a sea of exploding black puff-balls. Other pilots climbed or dove to avoid the flak but Wannop held his course, figuring there was no way to escape the barrage. All around him planes were being hit. Three Lancasters exploded in flames and crashed. Still the formation pressed on. Wannop was reaching for the bomb door control valve when a shell went off directly in front of him. "I saw the brilliant flash... heard the crump... crump... and instinctively ducked. We sped through the thick, black pall of smoke as shrapnel spattered the aircraft from nose to tail. At the same time the plane kicked and bucked like a rodeo bronco."[8]

Wannop's Canadian rear gunner, Jim McCaffery, saw half the port rudder get blown off only yards from his turret and heard the terrifying sound of shrapnel riddling the bomber in forty places. "It was like somebody had heaved a great handful of gravel on a wall," he said. "I saw smoke coming from the engines as it passed me and heard the flight engineer call for people to get ready to bail out. We were right over the target. It wasn't a very happy prospect." In fact, that may well have been the understatement of the war because angry German civilians were now routinely lynching downed Allied airmen. Crews were being warned to give themselves up to soldiers or police officers if they came down inside a city. In some cases, German soldiers and policemen had been known to keep mobs of civilians away from downed airmen at gunpoint.

In any case, as the crew prepared to bail out Wannop held the plane level long enough for bomb aimer Ron Evans to unleash their deadly cargo.

Bomb aimer Ron Evans. Courtesy of the author.

At the same time, flight engineer Jerry Stocking activated automatic fire extinguishers, dousing flames in the burning engines. It looked doubtful that they'd be able to get back to England, but the airmen decided to get as far away from Cologne as possible before taking to the silk. Soon they were out of flak range, but their problems were far from over. "Two engines were knocked out," McCaffery recalled. "Both were on the starboard side of the aeroplane, which made it that much worse. A Lancaster will fly and maintain altitude with two of the four engines working. It can even land with only one engine; but it's made that much harder if two good engines are on the same wing. One side of the aeroplane is dead."

They crossed into France and made straight for an abandoned Luftwaffe airfield at Juvincourt. McCaffery held his breath as they came in. "It was landing the beast that was one of the most dangerous parts, because one side of the aeroplane was pulling; the other dragging. It was easy to turn sideways and develop a smash-up landing. But my skipper was a superb pilot and he was able to set it down OK. He received the Distinguished Flying Cross for his actions during that emergency."[9]

As he got out of the plane McCaffery could see German fighter planes scattered all over the field. The enemy had obviously left in a hurry, leaving behind aircraft that had been damaged or for which there was no fuel. He was warned not to go near the black-crossed machines because of the danger of booby-traps but the teenager couldn't resist climbing into the cockpit of a nearby Focke-Wulf 190 fighter. His immediate impression was

*A Lancaster bomber. Air crew (standing), from left to right: Jerry Stocking, Jim Cook, Bob James, Eric Wannop, Ron Evans, Jim McCaffery, Bill Body.*Courtesy of the author.

that there was no way his low-calibre machine-guns could penetrate the thick glass in front of a German fighter pilot's face. Moments later his thoughts were shattered by an unexpected crash that nearly made him jump out of his skin. Glancing quickly around, the gunner spotted an RAF mechanic who had just slammed a wrench down on the Focke-Wulf's wingtip. Not needing another reminder about the possibility of booby-traps, he took his leave.

Back in England, meanwhile, Wannop's crew was reported missing in action. The station padre even asked the congregation at Sunday evening service to pray for them. Seconds later, he was passed a note informing him that they were safe in France. Turning to the worshippers, he said, "Never in all my years in the service of God have my prayers been answered so quickly."[10]

Bomber Command now turned its attention to cities deep in eastern Germany that had never been raided before. This would be the final attempt to bomb the Germans into surrendering. With the Wehrmacht now fighting desperate defensive actions inside both its eastern and western borders, it was felt a series of crushing blows against cities such as Wiesbaden, Dresden, Chemnitz, and Potsdam would create such chaos that the Nazi regime would finally collapse. Weisbaden was the first target of what was code named "Operation Thunderclap." Over 500 bombers attacked the place on February 2, failing to hit five plants producing arms but managing to savage a vast residential area. About 1000 people died, and hundreds more were injured.

Now came Dresden, by all odds the most controversial raid of the whole war. Dresden, a beautiful 700-year-old city of splendid rococo architecture, historic buildings, churches, and monuments, was known throughout Europe as the "Florence on the Elbe." World famous for its pottery, it had been left at peace throughout the war, leaving many of its 600 000 permanent inhabitants under the mistaken impression that the British government had secretly agreed not to bomb it, provided the Luftwaffe left Oxford alone. Still others believed Prime Minister Churchill had personally ordered Dresden spared because he had a relative living there. The rumours were all false, of course, but ordinary Germans had no way of knowing that and, as a consequence, Dresden was viewed as a sanctuary. Indeed, its population had ballooned to 1 300 000 by February 1945 as swarms of refugees poured in from the east, fleeing the advancing Red Army. A staggering 200 000 of them lived in a tent-and-shack city in Dresden's Grossen Park, which rivalled Vancouver's Stanley Park in acreage.

Although conditions were crowded and Russian troops were only seventy miles away, the ancient city was in a festive mood on the evening of February 13. It was Carnival Night — when youngsters dressed in adult costumes to celebrate an annual holiday. Back in England, 800 Lancasters were being fueled and loaded with hundreds of thousands of tons of bombs, most of them incendiaries. As the afternoon waned, more than 5000 airmen filed into briefing rooms to get the low-down on where they would be going that night. For most, the target came as a shock. Pilot Eric Wannop couldn't believe it. "To me, Dresden wasn't associated with war. Like every schoolboy, I had been taught that it was famous for its pottery."[11] Tail gunner Jim McCaffery remembers the fear that was created when the men realized just how far behind enemy lines they'd have to fly. "I remember that we were in the briefing room and that a large map on the wall with a piece of cord, strung from one end to the other, showed the sort of dogleg course of the trip across the continent. It was clearly a very deep penetration... and that long line across the map caused a lot of apprehension among the

Pilot Eric Wannop with his wife and daughter. Courtesy of the author.

aircrew. Nobody said anything, except my skipper seemed quite ill at ease, even though he was mostly cool. He said, 'Mac, tonight we've *got* to watch for fighters.' I thought that was a rather unnecessary remark. That was my job, watching for fighters. I had a personal interest in seeing that they didn't get to shoot me down."

McCaffery recalls being told Dresden was being destroyed for political purposes. "As far as Dresden goes, that was the first time that the commander of the station came and gave us a political reason for the raid. It only happened just prior to take-off at the briefing for the Dresden raid. The station commander rarely attended briefings. This was left to the squadron commanders and other senior officers. He came, I think probably on orders from higher command, to explain to us that the Nazis had convinced the German people that at the end of World War I their armed forces had remained still on foreign soil and basically undefeated, and that they — the German forces of World War I — had been betrayed by politicians at home. He then pointed to the cord running across the map and the city of Dresden and then he said, 'there are going to be a lot of people in Dresden tonight who are going to find out that war can be a very nasty thing. Never again will any future German government be able to say that the country was fairly well intact but still defeated.' In other words, we were given a political reason for this deep penetration, the one and only time in my experience that that was done."[12]

At a nearby airfield, bomb aimer Miles Tripp was being told Dresden was jammed with one million refugees. The information disturbed him enormously. "During the briefing I remembered newsreels taken early in the war and in my mind's eye saw a long stream of French refugees, their possessions piled on handcarts and prams, scattered in panic as bombs fell. The memory was instant and vivid and left me feeling disturbed, and the recollection of that moment has never left me."[13] But disturbed or not, Tripp and more than 5000 other airmen soon found themselves thundering down runways on their way to a date with history.

Harris sent 244 Lancasters against Dresden in the first wave, with another 529 coming behind in a second strike force. If all went well, the initial assault would set large fires, and the second wave would appear just in time to catch firefighters in the open.

As the first planes approached Dresden at 10:30 p.m. the airmen braced themselves for a hot reception. Strangely, nothing happened. There were no fighters and almost no flak. The menacing anti-aircraft guns perched on adjacent hillsides were mere papier-mâché props. The Germans had been so sure that Dresden would never be bombed that they'd long since sent the real guns to the front for use against Allied tanks. At nearby Luftwaffe airfields, meanwhile, fighter pilots were late in scrambling because of a communications mix-up. In all, only twenty-six fighters got airborne, with most of them taking off too late to intercept the bombers.

Quickly realizing there was no opposition, the master bomber ordered pilots to descend. The Lancasters came in unmolested, dropping 800 tons of bombs through a thin layer of clouds.

German schoolboy George Busch, who was on the outskirts of the city along with scores of other refugees from the province of Silesia, suddenly saw red fireballs shooting up from Dresden's old town district. "I could see everything. The night was as bright as the day and the whole earth was shaking like an earthquake. We were just on the edge of it."[14] Within minutes the city's narrow streets had been transformed into a furnace.

Schoolboy Gerhard Kuhnemund was caught right in the eye of the storm. "The whole of Dresden was an inferno," he said later. "In the street below people were wandering about helplessly. I saw my aunt there. She had wrapped herself in a damp blanket and, seeing me she cried out... The sound of the rising firestorm strangled her last words. A house wall collapsed with a roar, burying several people in the debris. A thick cloud of dust arose and mingling with the smoke made it impossible for me to see... time and again we stumbled over corpses."[15]

Within minutes the crackling fires came together, creating a firestorm that shot temperatures up to an estimated 1100 degrees Fahrenheit. Just as had been the case at Hamburg two years earlier, whirlwinds of unbelievable force swept people off their feet. Student Bodo Baumann watched in horror as a firefighter was lifted from a bridge and tossed into a wall of flames. It looked for all the world as if he'd been grabbed by the invisible hand of a giant. Thousands more perished in similar fashion, and tens of thousands were suffocating in airless shelters.

The second wave of bombers was now approaching. It had taken off around 9:30 p.m., climbing steadily to 19 000 feet before making its way across France and part of Nazi-occupied Czechoslovakia. Swinging into eastern Germany, it made straight for Dresden. There may not have been much flak over Dresden itself, but such a large force couldn't possibly fly that deep into enemy territory without suffering some losses, and anti-aircraft gunners at various locations along the route picked off three Lancasters.

As the survivors approached Dresden they had no difficulty locating their target. Canadian bomb aimer James Letros recalled, "It was terrible. You could see fires two hundred miles away. The whole sky was lit up."[16] Englishman Miles Tripp found the light from the fires so intense that when he got within a half dozen miles of Dresden he could clearly see the black outlines of other bombers. "The streets of the city were a fantastic latticework of fire. It was as though one was looking down at the fiery outlines of a crossword puzzle; blazing streets etched from east to west, from north to south, in a gigantic saturation of fire." Sickened by the sight, he instructed his pilot to head south of the dying city. As soon as they were past the fringe of the inferno he thumbed the bomb release, hoping his incendiaries would land harmlessly in the countryside. "I couldn't forget what we had been told at briefing, or the newsreels of German bombing atrocities."[17]

Whether Tripp's compassionate act saved any lives that night will never be known. What is known is that the second wave of bombers arrived over Dresden at 1:30 a.m. on February 14 — Saint Valentine's Day — and proceeded to drop another 1800 tons of bombs. The devastation caused by such a pounding cannot be captured by statistics or adjectives. Only the stories of survivors will suffice. Margaret Freyer, a twenty-four-year-old nurse, was huddled fearfully in a cellar, expecting it to collapse on top of her at any moment. When she finally emerged she saw total ruin in every direction. "I saw only burning houses and screaming people... all I could hear was the roaring of the flames. I could hardy see, due to the flying sparks, the flames and the smoke." She went stumbling off in search of her missing fiancé and encountered still more horror. "What I saw is so horrific that I shall hardly be able to describe it. Dead, dead, dead everywhere. Some completely black like charcoal. Others completely untouched, lying as if they were asleep. Women in aprons, women with children sitting in prams as if they had nodded off. Many women, many young girls, many small children, soldiers who were identifiable as such only by the metal buckles on their belts, almost all of them naked. Some clinging to each other in groups as if they were clawing at each other." She could not grasp the meaning of it all because so many of the dead were mutilated babies. And the corpses lay close together, almost as if they had been deliberately set down, street by street.[18]

Helga Sievers, a Red Cross nurse, fled from a burning building only to be greeted by the firestorm. Half blinded from the smoke she got down on her belly and crawled away, eventually taking shelter in a school cellar. As the last planes retreated she came outside and shook her fist at the sky, crying out, "You bloody Americans, bloody British." Realizing the futility of her actions she headed home, walking at first, but then breaking to a full gallop as she approached the front door of what had been her home. The house was nothing more than a pile of smouldering rubble but, thankfully, her parents were alive, waiting for her on what was left of the front steps. Later, she went to the marketplace where bodies were being burned to guard against disease. "I thought they were logs," she said in a 1994 interview. "Then I was filled with horror."[19]

George Busch also ventured into the city shortly after the bombers left. "We were snooping around like teenagers do. We saw bundles of burned people in the street. They were all charred bodies. The streets were still smouldering and smoking. I was coughing. It wasn't a nice sight. I don't even want to think about it."[20]

There were bizarre scenes near the Dresden Zoo, where bombs blew the doors off cages, freeing dozens of exotic animals. A dead leopard was found hanging in a tree, perched above the bodies of a pair of naked women. Zookeeper Otto Sailer-Jackson came across an ape that extended its arms to him. Both were bloody stumps without hands. Mortified, he drew a revolver and put the poor beast out of its misery.

As the bombers headed for home, meanwhile, the airmen experienced what Eric Wannop remembers as "a spine-chilling feeling. The whole city was ablaze from end to end. It was like looking at a sea of liquid flames, inspiring by its intensity. It was so bright at bombing height that we could easily have read a newspaper."[21]

Jim McCaffery got his best look at the inferno as the bombers headed back to England. "It was like one big patch of the world on fire. A solid mass of fire. The city burned for seven days. The bombs that we dropped consisted of incendiary bombs and four-thousand-pound high explosive bombs to mix it up. That fire was visible for two hundred miles. The glow in the sky was visible even further than that."[22]

The return journey was by no means totally safe. Four more Lancasters were shot down, and another two crashed on landing in England. In all, the destruction of Dresden had cost Bomber Command nine planes and sixty-three men. More than that, however, it also cost the force its hard-won reputation. Word quickly spread about what had happened, and there was widespread revulsion. Many ordinary Britons had visited Dresden before the war, and they knew it had been a beautiful, historic city of little industrial importance. For once the Allied newspapers didn't try to minimize civilian casualties, reporting that as many as 70 000 might have died. In fact, the death toll was closer to 135 000. One American reporter went so far as to write openly that Bomber Command was using "terror" tactics against German civilians in a bid to hasten the end of the fighting.

Even Winston Churchill, who had approved the raid, was shocked by what had happened. He issued a memo to his chiefs of staff that said in part, "The destruction of Dresden remains a serious query against the conduct of Allied bombing." In future, he added, bombers should concentrate on industrial and military targets "rather than on mere acts of terror and wanton destruction, however impressive."[23]

In Germany, where one would have thought people would have grown accustomed to such horror, there was renewed despair. Berliner Ruth Andreas-Friedrich wrote in her diary, "Last Thursday they devastated Dresden most terribly... there was hardly a whole house left in the city, and all the splendour of a centuries-old civilization had gone up in smoke. Thousands of people met their deaths; they ran like burning torches through the streets, stuck fast in the red-hot asphalt, flung themselves into the waters of the Elbe. They screamed for coolness; they screamed for mercy. Death is mercy. Death is good when you are burning like a torch. Dresden was a glorious city, and it's a little hard getting used to the idea that Dresden, too, no longer exists. I felt like crying."[24] Nazi propaganda

Bombs hit Emmerich, Germany, on October 7, 1944. Photo was taken from the plane of Canadian pilot Lyle James. Courtesy of Lyle James.

minister Josef Goebbels did break down and weep when he heard the news.

Despite Churchill's memo, some area bombing raids continued to be carried out. The night after the attack on Dresden a major force of bombers went after Chemnitz, a city noted for the making of underwear and cars. Heavy clouds made accurate bombing a problem, and the city escaped largely unscathed. Other communities were less fortunate. Pforzheim, a town famous for making jewelry and clocks, was gutted on February 23. Schoolboy Werner Bachmann was there and recalls that virtually every building in the city was destroyed. "Before the sirens went the bomber planes had marked a square over the city with what we called 'Christmas trees' [flares]. All the bombing planes did was fly into the square and let go. Twenty-five thousand, mostly women and children, were killed in the next hour. It was mainly the fires that did it. There was such a fire that there was a firestorm from the oxygen rushing in to feed the flames. I was in a bunker on the outskirts of the city. I remember praying a lot and keeping my head low. My age then was twelve years."

Bachmann survived more than one raid on the town, but not all his relatives were so lucky. "One time a bomb hit my uncle's home two blocks away. I went over and found only his lower body in the rubble. Since we only had wooden clogs, I took off his leather shoes and wore them for the next five years."[25]

Hildesheim, a medieval town of no industrial importance, was next on the hit list. It was flattened with the loss of 1600 people. Even Wiesbaden, which was known mostly for its spas, was smashed, mainly because Bomber Command wanted to deny the German army a safe haven where exhausted troops could snatch a few days' rest. Vienna, one of the world's most beautiful cities, was hammered too, with one string of bombs destroying the much-loved opera house, which had opened in 1869. Citizens of the Austrian capital seemed to take the loss of this cultural treasure, which contained 160 000 costumes and sets for 120 plays, harder than they did news of setbacks from the front. After the war, the city made its reconstruction a top priority, and when the new Opera House opened in 1955, it was seen as a sign that the war was finally over.

At the end of February Allied troops had occupied most of the Ruhr Valley, but Bomber Command found plenty of other targets. March became the busiest month of the war, with more than 67 000 tons of bombs being dropped. There was a heavy price to be paid. The Luftwaffe had been all but driven from the skies, but it was still capable of making the odd surprise appearance. German fighter pilots proved that on the night of March 4 when they followed the bomber stream all the way back to England, shooting down twenty Lancasters right over their own airfields. Gunners were supposed to stay alert from the time of take-off until landing, but, in truth, many found it impossible to maintain a sharp lookout for up to nine hours at a time. Most weren't paying strict attention after they got over the United Kingdom. Indeed, after one Lancaster was shot down over its own airfield it was discovered that the tail gunner had already unloaded his guns. "He was too anxious to get out," gunner Jack Western said.[26] In what may have been an even bolder move, the German fighter arm made a by then almost unheard of daylight appearance on March 31, shooting down eleven bombers over Hamburg.

By the beginning of April the war was clearly all but over, but still Bomber Command didn't let up. Hamburg was hit yet again on April 8 and Potsdam, a Berlin suburb that had not been bombed before, was devastated on the 14th. Canadian mid-upper gunner Bill DuBois took part in the Potsdam operation, discovering the Germans were still capable of making life miserable for the attackers. In fact, searchlights were so thick "it was almost like daylight... that was really hairy."[27] But only one bomber was lost in exchange for 5000 more Germans.

The Third Reich now lay in ruins from end to end, leaving few worthwhile targets, but Harris continued to send his men out in strength. In an almost obscene show of force, he dispatched just under 1000 bombers to wreck the naval island of Heligoland on April 18. Two days later, oil storage facilities at Regensberg were bombed. Bremen was smashed by almost 800 bombers on April 22, just days before it was captured by Allied troops.

What may have been the most satisfying raid of the war occurred on April 25 when Lancasters carrying the 12 000-pound Tallboys went after Berchtesgaden, Hitler's notorious Eagle's Nest retreat in the Austrian Alps. Tail gunner Jack Western got a unique view of the operation as his plane flew between snow-capped peaks. "It was a fantastic sight. There were mountain ranges we couldn't fly over because we were so loaded down with bombs, so we flew right through them. I only saw things after we'd flown through and I thought, 'I hope this valley doesn't have a dead end.'" At one point three German fighters approached, but they were driven off by Swiss anti-aircraft fire. At least one of the Focke-Wulfs was hit and seen going down trailing black smoke. A few minutes later the Lancasters struck. As Western looked on, a huge explosion rocked the Eagle's Nest, which disappeared in a cloud of smoke.[28]

Hitler, who was holed up in his Berlin bunker, didn't have long to mourn the loss of his favourite retreat. Five days later, with Russian troops literally just down the street, he blew his own brains out. The war in Europe was now all but over, and Bomber Command turned its attention to more pleasant duties — dropping food on starving Dutch civilians in parts of Holland still occupied by the Germans. Most of the eastern Netherlands had been liberated by the Canadian army, but German troops still stubbornly clung to large portions of the west. They weren't prepared to surrender until they were ordered to do so by Hitler's successor, Admiral Karl Doenitz. So while the opposing armies waited for the new leader of what was left of the Third Reich to act, people in Holland were dying.

Fortunately, the German army commander in Holland was not a fanatical Nazi, and he agreed to a temporary ceasefire that would allow Allied planes to fly over hostile territory to drop food. "The Germans allowed what was called a 'corridor of innocence,'" explained Jim McCaffery, who took part in several of these mercy flights. "Through their lines we low-flying bombers would dump food. We flew over enemy territory but there was an agreement that we would not be fired on." In one eight-day period 2835 Lancasters and 124 Mosquitos dropped 6672 tons of food in what was dubbed "Operation Manna."

For the battle-hardened fliers these missions were exhilarating. They took off so loaded down with food that some loaves of bread actually fell out of turrets or partially closed bomb bays. "Those aeroplanes had six thousand pounds of food in the bomb bay," McCaffery said. "We came in at the lowest possible air speed at a height of about five hundred feet and opened the bomb bay doors gradually, and sacks and cans were dropped. I suppose twenty per cent was destroyed when it hit the ground, but still, if only five thousand pounds remained edible it helped these starving people. We dropped food in a field outside The Hague and then, gradually gaining altitude, flew over the city. A long stream of Lancaster bombers on a mercy mission instead of a killing mission. It was certainly a very exalted day. Our wireless operator fired off every flare he had in his flare crate. Every one of the Lancasters was firing these flares. We saw people in the streets waving bedsheets, waving arms."[29]

Jack Western flew so low that "dodging the chimney pots was one of the hazards. We could actually see tulips bending in the wind. We were coming out not much more than fifty feet up. At one point we passed a very large windmill and I looked *up* to see people in the windmill above us waving. It was amazing. We supposedly saved five million people. That's when we were saving people rather than killing them. We dropped coffee, tea, sugar, milk, chocolate, flour, dried eggs — all in sacks. The people spelled out the words 'thank you' with sheets. It was really emotional. Ever see a bunch of guys cry?"[30]

Almost as gratifying was Operation Exodus, in which the bombers were used to ferry 75 000 former Allied prisoners of war back to England. After the First World War many ex-POWs had spent months waiting to be repatriated and the High Command wanted to avoid a repeat of that situation. Once again there were heart-wrenching scenes. Jim McCaffery recalled landing in France at Juvincourt airfield, the same place where he'd made an emergency landing just a few months earlier, to pick up a load of Indian soldiers. "After we got back to England one of my jobs was to stand in the doorway just inside the crew entrance and see that everybody got down the ladder alright. The first of these Indians came up to me and looked at me and he stuck out his hand — a long, bony, skinny hand, I thought, and shook my hand. Each one of those twenty-six men shook my hand as they left. I believe that was one of the most heart-warming things that every happened to me in the service. These men had been in prison camps for years, and we were the angels bringing them home."[31]

When the Germans finally surrendered, on May 8, 1945, there were wild celebrations on the bomber stations. McCaffery remembers it this way: "It was a joyful day for everybody and when we got home to our squadron [after dropping food on Holland] I took my clothes off in the crew room and walking up

Tail gunner Jim McCaffery poses near a German V-2 rocket in 1945, just after the end of the war. Courtesy of Jim McCaffery.

to the Sergeant's Mess, there was a speech by the prime minister on the radio and over the public address system they played 'God Save the King.' I came to a stop and stood at attention. A man driving an RAF truck came to a stop beside me in honour of the anthem. When it was over we saluted each other and grinned and we both carried on our way. That night there was considerable stout ale drunk. I had never seen these staid RAF chaps get so wild. They even built a big bonfire in the front of the Sergeant's Mess and I believe there were two or three bicycles thrown on it. But it was a great time."[32]

Bomber Command now planned to send men and planes to the Pacific theatre to help the United States Army Air Force finish off Japan. The Americans, however, didn't need any help. They'd already firebombed just about every major city in that country, including Toyko, claiming hundreds of thousands of lives. When the Japanese still refused to give up, President Harry Truman ordered the newly developed atomic bomb to be dropped. So it was on August 6, 1945, that a single airplane with a single bomb destroyed the city of Hiroshima, killing 58 000 people outright, with another 81 000 dying slow deaths later from shock, radiation burns, and other wounds. Three days later, another atomic bomb fell on Nagasaki, killing 75 000 more people. That was enough even for the fanatical warlords who ran Japan. They accepted Allied surrender terms and the Second World War was finally over.

CHAPTER 11

THE CONTINUING CONTROVERSY

Was Bomber Command's relentless five-and-a-half-year war against Germany immoral and wasteful? Or did it play a key role in toppling one of the most evil regimes in history?

Those questions have been raised from time to time ever since the Second World War ended fifty years ago this year. Word about what the bombers had done to Germany spread quickly as millions of ordinary Canadian, American, and British servicemen occupied the Third Reich in the spring of 1945 and began writing letters home, describing the terrible carnage they could see all around them. Soon newspaper reporters were on the scene as well, spreading the story around the globe. The journalists didn't pull any punches. Writing for London's *Daily Mail*, for example, reporter Walter Farr left no doubt that residential districts of Cologne had been targeted. "The place is a shambles, every bit of it. So far, after an hour's tour of the city streets, I have not come across a single house, shop, restaurant or hotel that is not destroyed or partially damaged. Except for the cathedral, all of us who knew Cologne before would never recognize the city. The damage to Cologne is such that it may take thirty years to make it look like a city again."[1] To many in the victorious nations the reports came as something of a shock because the Allied High Command had been issuing press releases throughout the long conflict insinuating that the bombers had been hitting mostly military and industrial targets. People knew some German civilians had been killed, but they assumed the deaths had been accidental, and they had no idea just how widespread the slaughter had been.

Before long both the British and Americans had teams of experts on the scene recording the damage. What they found was appalling devastation. Seventy cities had been pulverized by Bomber Command and the American

Women clear bomb damage in 1945 Berlin. Few men were available, as they were at the front. Courtesy of Ulli Waschkowski.

Eighth Air Force. Many had been totally destroyed. Hundreds of thousands of civilians were dead, millions more were homeless, and countless historic buildings, monuments, and priceless cultural treasures had been lost. Even some of the most ardent proponents of area bombing couldn't help but feel sympathetic to the victims. Sir Charles Portal, one of the masterminds of the bomber offensive, expressed regret for what he had helped unleash after touring the ruins of the Berlin suburb of Potsdam just a few weeks after the war ended. "Harris removed the town of Potsdam in half an hour one night in April," he wrote, "I have never seen anything so complete and scarcely a bomb outside the town proper. The whole thing is the finest possible object lesson against starting wars but I came away feeling very sorry for those people and when I eventually said so I found all the others felt just the same."[2]

General Lucius Clay, deputy American military governor in Berlin, expressed similar feelings when he arrived in the wrecked German capital two months after the last bomb had fallen. "Wherever we looked we saw desolation. The streets were piled high with debris which left in many places only a narrow one-way passage between high mounds of rubble, and frequent detours had to be made where bridges and viaducts had been destroyed. The Germans seemed weak, cowed, and furtive, and not yet recovered from the shock. It was like a city of the dead."[3] The stench of rotting flesh was everywhere and people engaged in massive clean-up operations found corpses in the rubble every day for months.

It would be an exaggeration to say there was a public outcry when people in the Allied nations began to realize just how badly Germany had been mauled. Hatred for the former Nazi regime ran deep, and many believed the Germans had received their just desserts. This sentiment was only intensified when the concentration camps were liberated, and the world found out about the Holocaust. Still, there was a subtle, unofficial backlash against the bomber boys. When the British government announced a list of postwar laurels for its top military commanders, Arthur Harris's name was conspicuous by its absence. A suggestion by Harris that his surviving aircrews should receive special campaign medals was flatly rejected. He was bitter about the snub for the rest of his life and for good reason. In all, more than 55 000 airmen had been killed and nearly 20 000 others had been wounded or captured. In other words, 60 per cent of his men had become casualties, making Bomber Command by the far the hardest hit branch of all the Allied forces. He guessed, quite correctly, that he and his men were being ignored because the very government that had sent them out on their extraordinarily dangerous missions was now ashamed of what had been done.

Over the years the controversy over the morality of bombing has flared from time to time, as more and more people began viewing the killing of civilians as an immoral act. In 1946, when Harris admitted in his memoirs that his men usually aimed their bombs for the centre of the town they were attacking, there were angry denunciations of him in left-wing British newspapers. Respected historian Sir Basil Liddell-Hart went so far as to call the bomber campaign "the most uncivilized method of warfare the world has known since the Mongol devastations."[4] The debate died down for a time after that, but surfaced again in 1963 when controversial British author David Irving published a shocking book called *The Destruction of Dresden*. It revealed in graphic detail what had happened to the Saxon capital in February, 1945. The book gained considerable attention, at least partly because it pointed out, for the first time, that more civilians had died at Dresden than had perished in the atomic bombings of either Hiroshima or Nagasaki.

Strangely, although it had been debated for decades in other countries, the controversy over the bomber offensive never received much play in the Canadian media. Despite the fact that Canadians had played a pivotal role in the campaign, most people viewed it as a British–American affair. All that changed, however, in 1992 with the release of *The Valour and the Horror*. The video brought the debate to the attention of a whole new generation of Canadians, most of whom had never even heard of it. At virtually the same time, two events in Europe helped rekindle the subject on that continent. The first came on May 30, 1992, when the British government at long last got around to honouring Arthur Harris by unveiling a statue of him right in the heart of London. The commemoration, coming on the fiftieth anniversary of the famous 1000-plane raid on Cologne, caused a storm of protest in both England and Germany. A few demonstrators even went so far as to toss red paint on seventy- and eighty-year-old Bomber Command veterans who had turned out for the event. Emotions ran even higher a few months later when Queen Elizabeth visited Dresden. Angry crowds booed and pelted her with eggs.

Over the years critics of the bomber offensive have collectively made the following charges:

- Bomber Command deliberately ignored military and industrial targets in favour of the ruthless slaughter of innocent German civilians.
- The bomber offensive failed to break the morale of the German people, which had been one of its chief objectives.
- Bomber Command failed to destroy or even seriously damage industries vital to the Nazi war machine.
- The bombing of Germany actually prolonged the war by diverting planes away from the battle fronts, where they could have served a much more useful purpose.

So what is the truth? Did Bomber Command deliberately target civilians? The answer to that question has to be an emphatic *yes*. No one who has conducted even the most superficial examination of the evidence could possibly conclude otherwise. The minutes of British War Cabinet meetings and memos sent to Bomber Command headquarters from those meetings make it perfectly clear that residential areas were often priority targets. Further evidence is found in the United States Strategic Bombing Survey (USSBS), an exhaustive probe carried out shortly after the war by more than one thousand American civilian and military personnel. Among other things, the survey found the Allies had dropped 1 300 000 tons of bombs on Germany. Some 676 846 tons — or 34 per cent of that total — had been released over cities. Twenty-six per cent had been aimed at transportation targets, 19 per cent fell on industrial premises, and 20 per cent on "tactical targets." Furthermore, only one in five of the bombs dropped on cities had been released from American aircraft. The rest had come from Bomber Command. Besides that, there are the words of Arthur Harris himself. Harris made no attempt whatever to duck the issue in either his private or public writings. In his autobiography he says matter-of-factly that during the Battle of the Ruhr "the aiming points were usually right in the centre of the town… the objective of the campaign was to reduce production in the industries of the Ruhr at least as much by the indirect effect of damage to services, housing and amenities, as by any direct damage to the factories or railways themselves."[5] He was even more blunt in an October, 1943, memo to the undersecretary of state for air, complaining bitterly about the government's attempts to cover up what his men were doing. Referring to a raid on Kassel in which the newspapers had been told the bombers had blasted a locomotive works and an aircraft factory, he said the destruction of those facilities was not nearly as important as the fact that "Kassel contained over two hundred thousand Germans, many of whom are now dead and most of the remainder homeless and destitute." The goal of the bomber offensive, he continued, was "the obliteration of German cities and their inhabitants." He went on to express the fear that morale among aircrews would plummet if the government insisted on sugar-coating what they were doing. "When they read what the public are told about it they are bound to think, and do think, that the authorities are ashamed of area bombing."

As far as Harris was concerned the government should have admitted publicly that the aim of his offensive was "the destruction of German cities, the killing of German workers and the disruption of civilized community life throughout Germany. It should be emphasized that the destruction of houses, public utilities, transport and lives; the creation of a refugee problem on an unprecedented scale; and the breakdown of morale both at home and at the battle fronts by fear of extended and intensified bombing, are the aims of our bombing policy. They are not by-products of attempts to hit factories."[6]

In discussions with U.S. Army Air Force General Ira Eaker, Harris insisted the raids on residential districts favoured by Bomber Command were more effective than the American policy of trying to hit only industrial and military targets. "You destroy a factory, and they rebuild it. In six weeks they are in operation again. I kill all their workmen, and it takes twenty-one years to provide new ones."[7]

How many people died under the bombs? The figure 593 000 is mentioned in most histories, but that only includes those killed within the borders of Germany prior to Nazi expansion. When you factor in Austria, the

Sudetenland, and the Rhineland, the number jumps to 635 000, including about 570 000 civilians. The balance of the victims were slave labourers, Allied prisoners of war, or German military personnel. And while this book only deals with the bombing of the Third Reich, it should not be forgotten that Bomber Command and the USAAF killed 64 350 civilians in Italy and 900 000 more in Japan. In all, about 1.6 million Axis civilians perished in air raids.

Property damage in Germany was almost incalculable. Some 3 700 000 homes had been destroyed, and millions more were seriously damaged. In all, about seven million people were left homeless.

We have established that civilians were intentionally targeted and indeed killed in vast numbers. But it must be remembered that the Allies only turned to area bombing after other methods had proved to be all but useless. For two-and-a-half years Bomber Command had tried without success to hit military and industrial targets. The technology simply didn't exist to permit accurate night bombing of small targets, and it was impossible for unescorted bombers to survive in the daylight skies over Germany. The only options were to abandon the offensive or resort to area bombing. Rightly or wrongly, the Allies chose to carpet bomb every German city within flying distance of England. Essentially, there were two objectives — to disrupt German war industries by destroying the cities they were located in and to weaken the morale of the population so that ordinary Germans would rise up against the Nazis and sue for peace.

The question about what impact the bombers had on morale is a tricky one. From a statistical point of view the best evidence comes from the USSBS. American personnel interviewed five hundred Germans shortly after the war in a bid to find out what impact air raids had had on civilian morale, and their findings make for fascinating reading. Among other things, the exercise showed 83 per cent of Germans went into the Second World War with either "high" or "medium" morale. Six years later, only 21 per cent reported their morale was still in one of those two categories. Fully 78 per cent said their spirits were "low." But only 36 per cent thought bombing was the most significant factor in the drastic mood swing. The rest blamed the general military situation, personal losses, or internal dissension.

Undoubtedly the bombing helped lower morale, but it clearly wasn't the only reason why the average German was feeling so depressed by the spring of 1945. In any case, morale never fell so low that it caused anything even remotely resembling a general uprising against Hitler.

Besides the statistical evidence, we have the testimony of survivors. Two dozen Germans interviewed by the author are virtually all of the opinion that bombing did not break morale. Typical of their comments were the following:

> The way the government was set up even if it had broken your morale there wasn't anything you could do. If you said anything you could be sent to a concentration camp very quickly. It was absolutely useless to try to break morale. Most of us would have liked the war to end. We didn't want it to start. I saw people who made only slightly critical comments on the street get taken away by the Gestapo. Two women on the street were complaining about the soup kitchen when the man beside them turned up his collar and said, "I'm Gestapo, you two are coming with me."
>
> — Former Frankfurt resident Inge Neame.

> As far as I know it didn't demoralize the people. It may have been difficult to tell from my point of view because I was just a teenager, but I thought it brought people together.
>
> — Former Rostock resident Hans Richter.

> Bombing did not break morale. The Nazis told us the Allies planned to show Germany no mercy if they won the war. It was a lie but with them bombing our cities we could easily believe it. If anything the bombing made us all the more determined to win because we feared Germany would be destroyed if we lost.
>
> — Former Hamburg resident Heidi Schaefer.

> There were many of us who were anti-Nazi but with both Nazis and anti-Nazis being bombed, it brought us all together.
>
> — Former Berlin resident Helga Schmidt.

> The morale of the people never really was demoralized. The bombing scared them for awhile, then they just

packed up [their fears] and kept going. People were
tough. They became almost used to it.
— Former Sudetenland resident Werner Kluger.

The best evidence on the subject, of course, is the fact that the Germans didn't surrender until Allied soldiers had made it all the way to Berlin. In other words, they didn't give up until their country was physically occupied and virtually all their fighting men had been either killed or captured.

Without question, then, the critics are correct when they say Bomber Command failed to break the morale of a tough and courageous German people.

Next comes what may be the most important question of all: Did the bombing seriously disrupt the Nazi war machine? If the bombers didn't force Germany to surrender did they at least *help* to bring the Third Reich to its knees? Critics claim the manufacture of guns, tanks, trucks, and planes sky-rocketed in Germany throughout the war. Indeed, the statistics would seem to bear that out. German arms production tripled between 1942 and 1944. The Nazi aircraft factories, which built only 15 000 warplanes in 1942, managed to produce almost 25 000 in 1943, and more than 40 000 the next year. Tank production, which stood at 760 a month at the beginning of 1943, reached an incredible average of 1600 per month by mid-1944. And all of this happened at a time when the bomber offensive was reaching its peak.

On the surface, it looks as if the bombers failed to do any real harm to the German war machine, but the evidence is misleading.

It's true that the Germans were able to keep their factories working by rebuilding them with amazing speed and by working feverishly to relocate them away from the cities. Some 140 even re-opened underground. Those who claim Bomber Command didn't hurt German industry aren't telling the whole story, however. What they don't say is that without the need to constantly rebuild and relocate factories, the highly resourceful Germans would have produced tens of thousands more weapons than they actually did.

The truth is that Germany made a dramatic shift in its economy at the beginning of 1942, deciding for the first time to go on a total war footing. At the time Nazi Propaganda Minister Josef Goebbels delivered a fiery speech in which he announced the Third Reich was going to gear up for what he called "total war." Until then, much of Germany's industrial production had still been devoted to peacetime goods. It may seem incredible that the Germans weren't producing arms flat out from the beginning of the war, but it's true. They did not expect a long war and had not prepared for one. This was amply demonstrated when Hitler sent his armies into Russia in June 1941 without any winter coats! Clearly he had expected to wrap up the campaign before the first snow flew. Once it became clear the Soviets weren't going to capitulate quickly, the Germans moved to dramatically speed up arms production.

Fortunately, at almost the exact same time that Germany's war industries moved into high gear, Bomber Command turned up the heat by reverting to area bombing. Before long, although arms production was tripled, it wasn't coming close to what the Nazis had planned for. Statistics for the year 1944 make the case best. During that year Armaments Minister Albert Speer had proposed to provide the German army with 14 000 new trucks a month, but during the best month only 8500 were built. He had proposed to produce 3200 tanks a month, but only 1800 rolled off the production lines during the best month. The Luftwaffe was promised 4800 new fighter planes a month, but got less than 3000. And so it went down the line. The army needed 800 000 000 bullets a month, but got only half that number. It wanted 6 000 000 cannon shells, but received less than 4 000 000.

Perhaps the production schedules were unrealistic in the first place. But all the evidence suggests bombing did hurt arms production. German records show absenteeism in war industries increased by 15 per cent after the bombers began raiding on a regular basis. And that was twice the pre-war rate. The situation was so bad, the United States Strategic Bombing Survey concluded, that German arms production would have been 2.5 per cent higher in 1942 if not for bombing. By 1943 it placed the drop-off at 9 per cent, and by 1944 at 17 per cent. The British Bombing Survey came up with similar figures. Albert Speer, who was in a better position to judge than anyone, believed bombings cut production by 10 per cent in 1943 and by 20 per cent in 1944. If those figures are correct, they represent an enormous loss to the Nazi war machine. Indeed, for those two years alone it would have amounted to about 10 000 fewer planes and 5000 fewer tanks.

To fully comprehend what the loss of that much equipment meant to the Germans it's important to remember that the tank was the principal weapon of the ground war. In his autobiography, Speer said one hundred tanks operated by a total of 500 men could easily crush 10 000 foot soldiers. So, 5000 tanks would have been capable of defeating half a million riflemen. On the Russian Front, where the Germans were outnumbered eleven to one at the end, the Wehrmacht needed every armoured vehicle it could get its hands on.

Another vital point the critics have overlooked is that the aerial bombardments forced the Nazi regime to concentrate more on the production of defensive weapons and less on turning out offensive arms. This was especially true in aircraft production. The record may show German airplane-building tripled during the height of the bomber offensive, but it also shows a dramatic shift in the type of machines being built. Prior to 1942 fully 62 per cent of the aircraft coming out of the Third Reich's factories were bombers. By the autumn of 1944 that figure had dwindled to a scant 8 per cent. Fighter plane production became by far and away the top priority. In other words, Bomber Command, with the help of the American bomber fleet, had put the Luftwaffe strictly on the defensive. Indeed, Speer went to his grave saying German bomber production would have remained above 50 per cent of total aircraft assembly work if not for the fact that fighters were so desperately needed to defend the Fatherland.

Again it's important to point out what all this meant on the battlefields. Essentially, it left the German army with very little in the way of air cover. As early as the spring of 1943 three quarters of the Luftwaffe was tied down on home defence. By 1944 the Germans had 2500 fighters and only 209 bombers in the West.

The mad scramble to produce more and more fighters also meant less effort could be expended on tank building. Karl Saur of the Ministry of Armaments and War Production made that clear in a 1944 speech to his staff. "The war cannot be won by aircraft, but aircraft are our immediate task, so we can create the possibility of producing tanks," he said. "We shall only end the war in the East with tanks… However, a pre-condition for this is one hundred per cent completion of the air force program, so that we can keep the enemy bombers out of the country in order to be able to continue production."[8] In other words, the only reason why the Germans were able to build 40 000 planes that year is that they gave easy-to-build fighter planes priority over both tanks and bombers.

Besides slowing down production of offensive weapons, Bomber Command forced the Nazis to spend an enormous amount of time and energy on air defence. In all, 1 000 000 men and 150 000 women were engaged in operating searchlight, anti-aircraft guns, and fighter squadrons. Another 1 000 000 to 1 500 000 people were engaged in repairing bomb damage. As far as Speer was concerned, Bomber Command had opened a second front in the West long before the D-Day invasion. "In the Reich and in the western theatre the barrels of ten thousand guns were pointed toward the sky," he wrote in his memoirs. "The same guns could well have been employed in Russia against tanks and other ground targets. Had it not been for this new front, the air front over Germany, our defensive strength against tanks would have been about doubled."[9] Furthermore, he said, a third of the nation's optical industry was tied up producing gun sights for flak crews, and half of Germany's electronics industry was engaged in producing radar and communications equipment for air defence. "Simply because of this, in spite of the high level of the German electronics and optical industries, the supply of our frontline troops with modern equipment remained far behind that of the Western armies."[10] Specifically, it meant German soldiers didn't have enough walkie-talkies, and artillerymen were short of sound-ranging devices.

Speer felt that bombers also denied the army badly needed new recruits. "There is no doubt that in the absence of air raids, it would have been possible to withdraw several hundred thousand more soldiers from the armaments industry at the end of 1943. A large portion of German skilled labour was required at the factories for bomb damage clearance, where their specialized knowledge and keenness to restore the plants made their presence indispensable after air raids. If no air raids had taken place, we should have been able to increase the proportion of foreign and unskilled labour." By 1944, he added, "Army training units were increasingly employed on bomb damage clearance work, leading to a reduction in the standard of training and to lengthening of training schedules."[11]

Perhaps most significant of all, Speer speculated in a 1971 interview, the bomber offensive created "an armaments emergency in Germany which ruled out a major program to develop the atomic bomb."[12] More than one historian who has examined the record has come to the same conclusion.

The air raids also caused massive damage to the Reich's oil industry during the last year of the war. American bombers attacking by day often set refineries on fire, making them easy targets for Bomber Command's night raids. As a result of this one–two punch, oil production came to a virtual standstill at times during the last winter of the war. The American bombing survey found "production from the synthetic plants declined steadily and by July 1944 every major plant had been hit. These plants were producing an average of 316 000 tons per month when the attacks began. Their production fell to 107 000 tons in June and 17 000 tons in September. Output of aviation gasoline from synthetic plants dropped from 175 000 tons in April to 30 000 tons in July and 5000 tons in September."[13] Indeed, the situation was so serious that Hans Richter, who was training to be an aircraft mechanic at that time, told the author he saw jet fighters come right out of factories and into storage because there was no fuel to fly them. The situation became so catastrophic that the entire Luftwaffe often found itself grounded for lack of aviation fuel. There was so little fuel to spare that training for new pilots had to be severely curtailed. As a consequence, thousands of poorly trained fliers were rushed into combat, where they were promptly massacred by the more seasoned Allied pilots. Canadian ace Russ Bannock commanded a fighter squadron that took full advantage of the situation, shooting down eighty German planes for the loss of just seven pilots. "And at least two-thirds of our losses were to ground fire," he said. "We were lucky. We had a lot of experienced pilots. They were more competent than the German pilots."[14]

The Third Reich's army suffered a similar fate. On the Western Front the Wehrmacht had threatened to make a major breakthrough during the 1944 Battle of the Bulge, but was stopped in its tracks by a lack of fuel. Frustrated panzer divisions had to sit idle for days at a time waiting to be refueled.

Some have argued all this chaos happened near the end of the war when it no longer really mattered. That logic, however, is faulty. The Germans didn't give up because of a lack of human resources. They still had millions of soldiers who would have been perfectly capable of dragging the war out for many more months than it lasted, had they been properly equipped. As it was, they were facing a situation where they were forced to use horse-drawn wagons to haul their equipment around. Arms production had fallen so short of requirements that some of them didn't even have rifles, never mind tanks. In fact, the production of rifles during one eight-month period in 1944 stood at 1 900 000 compared with battlefield losses during the same period of 3 500 000. Short of tanks, cannons, trucks, guns, airplanes, and even bullets, more than 3 000 000 German soldiers meekly surrendered to the Western Allies in the first four months of 1945.

What of the claim that the war could have been won more quickly had the bombers been employed in other theatres instead of over Germany? Most of those who advance this theory usually point to the Battle of the Atlantic to make their case. They argue long-range bombers could have escorted convoys far out to sea, attacking U-boats as they surfaced for air. There's some validity to the argument, because most of the ships sunk by submarines were lost in mid-Atlantic, well out of the range of non-bombing aircraft. There's another side to the story as well, and that's that bombing raids on Germany destroyed 207 U-boats at dockside or in shipyards. On top of that, it's estimated that damage to German factories disrupted production schedules enough to cost the enemy fleet more than one hundred submarines. Because each U-boat sank an average of three Allied ships during the war, it's safe to say Bomber Command saved about 900 transport vessels from a watery grave. These figures don't take into account the fact that by laying mines in the Baltic Sea and other German-controlled waters the airmen seriously disrupted the training of many U-boat crews. Mines laid by Bomber Command also sank or damaged more than 1000 enemy surface vessels. If all that wasn't enough, bombers sank six Nazi battleships, compared with only four sent to the bottom by the Royal Navy throughout the whole war.

At least one critic has argued that the bomber offensive actually delayed the invasion of Europe by a year by diverting resources away from the production of landing barges. Brian McKenna, one of the producers of *The Valour and the Horror*, advanced this theory in the Toronto *Star*, declaring that if "half the resources spent on bombers were used on landing craft, of which there was a severe shortage in 1943, then the invasion of Europe might have been advanced by a year, Germany defeated and perhaps three million Jews spared the Holocaust."[15]

This line of thinking assumes that conditions would have been virtually the same had the Allies hit the beaches on June 6, 1943, as they were a year later. In fact, circumstances would have been radically different. No invasion could have been guaranteed of success unless the Allies had absolute air superiority, and in mid-1943 they most definitely did not have anything of the kind. The Luftwaffe only started to go downhill in December 1943, when the Allies introduced the formidable new Mustang fighter. More than 1000 experienced German fighter pilots were killed, mostly by Mustangs, during the first four months of 1944 alone. By the time D-Day rolled around, the Luftwaffe was nowhere to be seen over the beaches. The Wehrmacht, too, was considerably stronger in 1943. The situation was still fairly stable on the Russian Front at that time, so it would have been possible for the Germans to rush reinforcements to Normandy. Indeed, the Germans were masters at moving large numbers of troops quickly by rail from one theatre to another. Had the invasion taken place in mid-1943 it might well have ended in bloody defeat. If that had happened it would have been years before the Allies would have been ready to try again. The

Germans, in the meantime, would have been able to concentrate all of their efforts on the Russian Front. They might even have been able to defeat the Russians and then force the West to negotiate peace. Far from saving European Jews, a botched invasion would have given Hitler the time he needed to finish them off completely.

In truth, Bomber Command did a great deal to secure victory for the Allies. But proponents of area bombing set themselves up for much of the criticism that has come their way by promising more than they could deliver. For years people like Harris and Portal had argued not that they could help win the war, but that they could win it by themselves. They created unrealistically high expectations, and when they failed to deliver, they were bound to be criticized. Still more censure was assured by not telling the public the truth about area bombing from the beginning. Had the High Command explained that the bombers were going after whole cities as a way of crippling centres of industry, government, and communications, most people would likely have understood.

What of the morality of bombing civilians? Did the Allies resort to evil means to achieve noble ends? This is a complex question for which there is no simple answer. My own opinion is that the bombing of heavily industrialized cities such as Essen, Hamburg, and Berlin could be justified because they helped win a war the Allies could not afford to lose. It must never be forgotten that when area bombing began in 1942 the democracies were on the brink of defeat. Nor should anyone forget what would have been in store for the world had the Axis powers been victorious. Even during the midst of a world war the Third Reich found the people and resources to round up and murder fourteen million people in Hitler's death camps. Humanity still remembers the 6 000 000 Jews who perished in those hideous places but few recall that the Nazis also slaughtered 3 000 000 non-Jewish Poles, 3 500 000 Russians, 1 000 000 Serbs, and 250 000 Germans in those same camps. Had Hitler won the war and been free to concentrate all of his energies on creating a so-called master race there is no doubt at all that he would have ordered the murder of tens of millions more victims. And hundreds of millions of people — including everyone in Germany — would have been forced to live out their lives under the heels of a brutal and repressive dictatorship. I am willing to accept that by bombing civilians the Allies lost some of the moral high ground they held in 1939. That, however, was infinitely better than losing the war itself.

All of this is not to say that Bomber Command's critics haven't made some important points. Far from it. Several of the cities bombed in 1945 were of little or no industrial or military importance. Many of them were flattened only days before they were about to be captured by Allied troops. The razing of Dresden, in particular, is a black mark on Bomber Command's record. Besides the fact that it contained very little industry and was crowded with refugees, Dresden was only a few weeks away from being occupied by the Red Army. Its destruction was an unnecessary and excessive show of force.

Even the firebombing of that beautiful old city, though, may have served some purpose. On that terrible night in February 1945 Bomber Command demonstrated to the world that warfare was no longer a practical way to settle differences between nations. It had shown a great city could be wiped off the map in a matter of only a few hours. Five months later the Americans drove the point home by destroying two Japanese cities with exactly two bombs.

Bomber Command played an important role in the defeat of one of the most evil regimes in history, but it did more than that. It also took the glamour out of war, once and for all. The romantic tales of combat that had become part of Western lore over the centuries were replaced by stories of old men, women, and children being burned to death in their cellars. They were innocents who had done no harm to anyone and who were incapable of doing any harm, even if they had wanted to. It may have been necessary to kill them to get at Hitler's war machine, but it was ugly, brutal work.

The great aerial bombardments of the Second World War were not forgotten by the postwar generation. Memories of Berlin, Toyko, Dresden, Hamburg, and Hiroshima kept the world's great powers from going to war with one another throughout the long years of the Cold War. Germany, once a warrior state that had invaded its neighbours in 1866, 1870, 1914, and 1939, is now a responsible, peace-loving nation. Today, wars only crop up in remote places where both sides know there is no threat of annihilation from the skies. Open confrontation between the great powers is all but unthinkable. As American President John F. Kennedy said in a 1961 speech to the United Nations, "Either mankind must put an end to war, or war will put an end to mankind."[16] That, in a nutshell, is the lesson Bomber Command taught the world.

NOTES

Introduction

1. Leslie Hannon, *Canada at War* (Toronto: McClelland and Stewart, 1968), p. 96.
2. Hannon, p. 96.

Chapter One

1. Aaron Norman, *The Great Air War* (New York: MacMillan Company, 1968), p. 44.
2. H.G. Wells, *The War in the Air* 1908.
3. David Nevin, *Architects of Air Power* (Alexandria, VA: Time-Life Books, 1981), p. 26.
4. Norman, p. 51.
5. Arthur Harris, *Bomber Offensive* (Toronto: Stoddart, 1990), p. 18.
6. Norman, p. 356.
7. Edward Jablonski, *The Knighted Skies* (New York: G.P. Putnam's Sons, 1964), p. 56.
8. Ronald Dodds, *The Brave Young Wings* (Stittsville: Canada's Wings Inc., 1980), p. 114.
9. Arch Whitehouse, *The Years of the Sky King* (New York: Doubleday, 1959), p. 78.
10. Norman, p. 381.
11. Norman, p. 381.
12. Dodds, p. 185.
13. Norman, p. 404.
14. Author interview.
15. Raymond Fredette, *The Sky on Fire* (Washington: Smithsonian Institution Press, 1991), p. 26.
16. Fredette, p. 58.

17. Fredette, p. 111.
18. Fredette, p. 72.
19. Fredette, p. 225.

Chapter Two

1. Nevin, p. 30.
2. Samuel Mitcham, *Men of the Luftwaffe* (Novato, California: Presidio Press, 1988), p. 9.
3. Nevin, p. 60
4. Nevin.
5. Nevin.
6. Nevin.
7. Nevin.
8. Martin Gilbert, *Second World War* (Toronto: Stoddart, 1989), p. 3.
9. Gilbert, p. 4.
10. Cajus Bekker, *The Luftwaffe War Diaries* (New York: Ballantine Books, 1966), p. 63.
11. Albert Speer, *Inside the Third Reich* (New York: Avon Books, 1971), p. 303.
12. Gilbert, p. 4.
13. The Reader's Digest Illustrated History of World War II, p. 24.
14. Bekker, p. 90.
15. Bekker, p. 143.
16. Nevin, p. 81.
17. Philip Ziegler, *London At War. 1939–1945* (Toronto: Knopf Canada, 1995), p. 113.
18. Harris, p. 51.

Chapter Three

1. Dunmore Spencer and William Carter, *Reap the Whirlwind* (Toronto: McClelland and Stewart, 1991), p. 6.
2. Martin Middlebrook and Chris Everitt, *The Bomber Command War Diaries* (London: Penguin Books, 1985), p. 58.
3. Middlebrook, Everitt, p. 131.

4. Daniel Dancocks, *In Enemy Hands* (Edmonton: Hurtig Publishers Ltd., 1983), p. 11.

Chapter Four

1. Max Hastings, *Bomber Command* (New York: Dial Press, 1979), p. 112.
2. Denis Richards, *Portal of Hungerford* (London: Heinemann, 1977), p. 189.
3. *Globe and Mail.* June 30, 1992.
4. Richards, p. 301.
5. *The Valour and the Horror*, CBC-NFB documentary.
6. Dave McIntosh, *Terror in the Starboard Seat* (Don Mills: General Publishing Company Ltd., 1980), p. 91.
7. Author interview.
8. Middlebrook, Everitt, p. 245.
9. Harris, p. 105.
10. Goebbels diary.
11. *Signal* magazine, 1942.
12. *Signal*, 1940.
13. Charles Whiting, *The Home Front: Germany* (Chicago: Time-Life Books, 1982), p. 137.
14. Whiting, p. 137.
15. Canadian Press. May 31, 1942.

Chapter Five

1. Ted Barris, *Behind the Glory* (Toronto: Macmillan Canada, 1992), p. 16.
2. Douglas Alcorn, *From Hell to Breakfast* (Toronto: Intruder Press, 1980), p. 25.
3. Robert Collins, *The Long and the Short and the Tall* (Saskatoon: Western Producer Prairie Books, 1986), p. 21.
4. Collins, p. 61.
5. Author interview.
6. Author interview.
7. James Williams, *The Plan* (Stittsville: Canada's Wings Inc.)
8. Williams.
9. Author interview.

10. Williams, p. 63.

11. Jack Currie, *Lancaster Target* (Markham: Paperjacks, 1993), p. 22.

12. C.F. Rawnsley and Robert Wright, *Night Fighter* (New York: Ballantine Books, 1967), p. 215.

Chapter Six

1. Harris, p. 118.

2. Guy Gibson, *Enemy Coast Ahead* (London: Michael Joseph Ltd., 1946)

3. Gibson, p. 288.

4. Alan Cooper, *The Men Who Breached the Dams* (Shrewsbury, England: Airlife Publishing Ltd., 1993), p. 84.

5. Cooper, p. 82.

6. Cooper, p. 87.

7. Gibson, p. 292.

8. Cooper, p. 105.

9. Brereton Greenhouse, Stephen Harris, William Johnston, and William Rawlings, *The Crucible of War 1939–1945* (Toronto: University of Toronto Press, 1994), p. 693.

10. *The Canadians at War. 1939–1945* (The Readers Digest Association of Canada Ltd., 1969), p. 383.

11. *The Canadians at War*, p. 380.

12. Author interview.

13. Author interview.

14. Author interview.

15. Author interview.

16. Author interview.

17. Adolf Galland, *The First and the Last. The Rise and Fall of the German Fighter Forces* (New York: Ballantine Books, 1967), p. 159.

18. Marie Vassiltchikov, *The Berlin Diaries. 1940–45* (London: Chatto and Windus Ltd., 1985), p. 82.

19. Heinz Knoke, *I Flew for the Führer. The Story of a German Airman* (London: Evans Brothers Ltd., 1953), p. 106.

Chapter Seven

1. Doug Harvey, *Boys, Bombs and Brussels Sprouts* (Halifax: Goodread Biographies, 1983), p. 72.
2. Harvey, p. 72.
3. William Shirer, *Berlin Diary. The Journal of a Foreign Correspondent 1934–1941*, p. 493.
4. Greenhous, Harris, Johnston, Rawlings, p. 730.
5. Martin Middlebrook, *The Berlin Raids. RAF Bomber Command. Winter 1943–44* (London: Viking, 1988), p. 338.
6. Vassiltchikov, p. 87.
7. Middlebrook, p. 338.
8. Karen McCaffery interview.
9. Middlebrook, p. 167.
10. Middlebrook, p. 169.
11. Speer, p. 376.
12. Author interview.
13. Author interview.

Chapter Eight

1. Hans-Georg Von Studnitz, *While Berlin Burns. Diaries. 1943–45* (Weidenfield and Nicolson, 1963), p. 11.
2. Terry Charman, *The German Home Front. 1939–45* (New York: Philosophical Library, 1989), p. 43.
3. Charman, p. 43.
4. Author interview.
5. Author interview.
6. Winifried Weiss, *A Nazi Childhood* (Santa Barbara: Capra Press, 1988).
7. Author correspondence.
8. Author interview.
9. Author interview.
10. Author correspondence.
11. Author interview.
12. Author interview.

13. Author correspondence.

14. Author interview.

15. Author interview.

16. Author correspondence.

17. Author correspondence.

18. Author correspondence.

19. Author correspondence.

20. Author correspondence.

21. Author interview.

22. Charman, p. 139.

23. Author interview.

24. Earl Beck, *Under the Bombs: The German Home Front* (Lexington: The University Press of Kentucky, 1986), p. 76.

25. Author interview.

26. Author interview.

27. Author interview.

28. Middlebrook, p. 153.

29. Middlebrook, p.153.

30. *Globe and Mail*. Dec. 24, 1992.

Chapter Nine

1. Author interview.

2. Author interview.

3. Author interview.

4. Author interview.

5. Author interview.

6. Author correspondence.

7. Author interview.

8. Miles Tripp, *The Eighth Passenger. A Recollection of Discovery* (London: MacMillian Ltd., 1978), p. 39.

9. Author interview.

10. Author interview.

11. Author interview.

12. Author interview.
13. Author interview.
14. Author interview.
15. Author interview.
16. Author interview.
17. Currie, p. 35.
18. Author interview.
19. Karen McCaffery.
20. Author interview.
21. Karen McCaffery.
22. Author interview.
23. Karen McCaffery.
24. Karen McCaffery.
25. Author interview.
26. Author interview.
27. Author interview.
28. Author interview.
29. Author correspondence.
30. Author interview.

Chapter Ten

1. Associated Press, June, 1994.
2. Associated Press.
3. Associated Press.
4. Author interview.
5. Russell McKay, *One of the Many* (Burnstown: General Store Publishing House Inc., 1989), p. 114.
6. *The Canadians at War*, p. 451.
7. Max Arthur, *There Shall Be Wings. The RAF from 1918 to the Present* (London: Hodder and Stoughton, 1993), p. 239.
8. Robert E. Wannop, *Chocks Away* (Lowesmore, England: Square One Publications, 1989), p. 88.
9. Karen McCaffery.

10. Wannop, p. 109.

11. Wannop, p. 120.

12. Karen McCaffery.

13. Tripp, p. 82.

14. Author interview.

15. Alexander McKee, *Dresden, 1945. The Devil's Tinderbox* (London: Souvenir Press, 1982).

16. Author interview.

17. Tripp, p. 82.

18. McKee.

19. Canadian Press. July 29, 1994.

20. Author interview.

21. Wannop, p. 122.

22. Karen McCaffery.

23. John Toland, *The Last 100 Days* (New York: Random House, 1970), p. 174.

24. Charman, p. 190.

25. Author interview.

26. Author interview.

27. Author interview.

28. Author interview.

29. Karen McCaffery.

30. Author interview.

31. Author interview.

32. Karen McCaffery.

Chapter Eleven

1. London *Daily Mail*. March 6, 1945.

2. Richards, p. 295.

3. Douglas Botting, *The Aftermath: Europe* (Alexandria, Virginia: Time-Life Books, 1983).

4. Larry Bidinian, *The Combined Allied Bombing Offensive Against the German Civilian. 1942–45* (Lawrence, Kansas: Coronado Press, 1976), p. 160.

5. Harris, p. 147.

6. Greenhouse, Harris, Johnston, Rawlings, p. 725.

7. Wilbur Morrison, *Fortress Without a Roof: The Allied Bombing of the Third Reich* (New York: St. Martin's Press, 1982), p. 37.

8. Dudley Saward, *Bomber Harris*. (London: Buchan and Enright Publishers, 1984), p. 310.

9. Speer, p. 363.

10. Speer, p. 364.

11. Saward, p. 312.

12. Saward, p. 308.

13. The United States Strategic Bombing Survey.

14. Author interview.

15. Toronto *Star*, June 18, 1994.

16. Justin Wintle, *The Dictionary of War Quotations* (Toronto: Hodder and Stoughton, 1989), p. 356.

BIBLIOGRAPHY

Further Reading:

Alcorn, Douglas and Souster, Raymond. *From Hell to Breakfast*. Toronto: Intruder Press, 1980.

Arthur, Max. *There Shall Be Wings: The RAF from 1918 to the Present*. London: Hodder and Stoughton, 1993.

Barris, Ted. *Behind the Glory*. Toronto: Macmillan Canada, 1992.

Beck, Earl. *Under the Bombs: The German Home Front*. Lexington: The University Press of Kentucky, 1986.

Bekker, Cajus. *The Luftwaffe War Diaries*. New York: Ballantine Books, 1966.

Bidinian, Larry. *The Combined Allied Bombing Offensive Against the German Civilian*. Lawrence, Kansas: Coronado Press, 1976.

Bishop, Arthur. *Courage in the Air*. Whitby: McGraw-Hill Ryerson, 1992.

Botting, Douglas. *The Aftermath: Europe*. Alexandria, Virginia: Time-Life Books, 1983.

Bowyer, Chaz. *History of the RAF*. London: Bison Books, 1977.

Byers, Andrew, ed. *The Canadians at War 1939–1945*. The Readers Digest Association of Canada Ltd., 1969.

Charman, Terry. *The German Home Front, 1939–45*. New York: Philosophical Library, 1989.

Collins, Robert. *The Long and the Short and the Tall*. Saskatoon: Western Producer Prairie Books, 1986.

Constable, Trevor and Toliver, Raymond. *Horrido!* New York: Ballantine Books, 1970.

Cooke, Ronald, and Conyers Nesbit, Roy. *Target: Hitler's Oil. Allied Air Attacks on German Oil Supplies, 1939–45*. London: William Kimber and Co., 1985.

Cooper, Alan. *The Men who Breached the Dams*. Shrewsbury, England: Airlife Publishing Ltd., 1993.

———. *Bombers Over Berlin: The RAF Offensive, November 1943–March 1944*. London: William Kimber and Co., 1985.

Currie, Jack. *Lancaster Target*. Markham: Paperjacks, 1993.

Dodds, Ronald. *The Brave Young Wings*. Stittsville: Canada's Wings Inc., 1980.

Frankland, Noble. *The Bombing Offensive Against Germany*. London: Faber and Faber, 1965.

Fredette, Raymond. *The Sky on Fire: The First Battle of Britain, 1917–1918*. Washington: Smithsonian Institution Press, 1991.

Galland, Adolf. *The First and the Last: The Rise and Fall of the German Fighter Forces, 1938–45*. New York: Ballantine Books, 1967.

Gibson, Guy. *Enemy Coast Ahead*. London: Michael Joseph Ltd., 1946.

Gilbert, Martin. *Second World War*. Toronto: Stoddart, 1989.

Greenhous, Brereton, Harris, Stephen, Johnston, William and Rawlings, William. *The Crucible of War 1939–45. The Official History of the Royal Canadian Air Force. Volume 3*. Toronto: University of Toronto Press, 1994.

Hannon, Leslie. *Canada at War*. Toronto: McClelland and Stewart, 1968.

Harris, Sir Arthur. *Bomber Offensive*. Toronto: Stoddart, 1990.

Harvey, J. Douglas. *Boys, Bombs and Brussels Sprouts*. Halifax: Goodread Biographies, 1983.

Hastings, Max. *Bomber Command*. New York: Dial Press, 1979.

Jablonski, Edward. *The Knighted Skies*. New York: G.P. Putnam's Sons, 1964.

Knoke, Heinz. *I Flew for the Fiiuhrer. The Story of a German Airman*. London: Evans Brothers Ltd., 1953.

Longmate, Norman. *The Bombers. The RAF Offensive Against Germany, 1939–45*. London: Hutchinson and Co., 1983.

McIntosh, Dave. *Terror in the Starboard Seat*. Don Mills: General Publishing, 1980.

McKay, Russell. *One of the Many*. Burnstown: General Store Publishing House Inc., 1989.

McKee, Alexander. *Dresden 1945: The Devil's Tinderbox*. London: Souvenir Press, 1982.

Middlebrook, Martin. *The Berlin Raids. RAF Bomber Command. Winter 1943–44*. London: Viking, 1988.

———. *Nuremberg Raid*. London: Penguin Books, 1986.

———. *The Battle of Hamburg. The Firestorm Raid*. Markham: Penguin Books, 1984.

Middlebrook, Martin and Everitt, Chris. *The Bomber Command War Diaries. An Operational Reference Book: 1939–45*. London: Penguin Books, 1985.

Milberry, Larry and Holliday, Hugh. *The RCAF at War. 1939–1945*. Toronto: CANAV Books, 1990.

Milford, Humphrey. *The RCAF Overseas*. Toronto: Oxford University Press, 1944.

Mitcham, Jr., Samuel. *Men of the Luftwaffe*. Novato, California: Presidio Press, 1988.

Morrison, Wilbur. *Fortress Without a Roof: The Allied Bombing of the Third Reich*. New York: St. Martin's Press, 1982.

Norman, Aaron. *The Great Air War*. New York: The MacMillan Company, 1968.

Rawnsley, C.F. and Wright, Robert. *Night Fighter*. New York: Ballantine Books, 1967.

Richards, Denis. *Portal of Hungerford*. London: Heineman, 1977.

Rumpf, Hans. *The Bombing of Germany*. New York: Holt, Rinehart and Winston, 1963.

Saward, Dudley. *Bomber Harris*. London: Buchan and Enright Publishers, 1984.

Shirer, William. *Berlin Diary. The Journal of a Foreign Correspondent. 1934–1941*.

Shores, Christopher. *History of the Royal Canadian Air Force*. Toronto: Royce Publications, 1984.

Signal. Hitler's Wartime Picture Magazine. London: Bison Publishing Co. Ltd., 1976.

Spaight, J.M. *Air Power Can Disarm*. London: The Air League of the British Empire, 1948.

Spencer, Dunmore and Carter, William. *Reap the Whirlwind*. Toronto: McClelland and Stewart, 1991.

Speer, Albert. *Inside the Third Reich*. New York: Avon Books, 1971.

Toland, John. *The Last 100 Days*. New York: Random House, 1970.

Trevor-Roper, Hugh, ed. *Final Entries, 1945. The Diaries of Joseph Goebbels*. New York: Putnam, 1978.

Tripp, Miles. *The Eighth Passenger. A Recollection of Discovery*. London: MacMillan Ltd., 1978.

The United States Strategic Bombing Survey. New York: Garland Publishing Inc., 1976.

Vassiltchikov, Marie. *The Berlin Diaries. 1940–45*. London: Chatto and Windus Ltd., 1985.

Von Studnitz, Hans-Georg. *While Berlin Burns. Diaries. 1943–45*. Weidenfield and Nicolson, 1963.

Wannop, Robert E. *Chocks Away*. Lowesmore, England: Square One Publications, 1989.

Webster, Sir Charles and Frankland, Noble. *The Strategic Air Offensive Against Germany, 1939–1945*. London: Her Majesty's Stationary Office, 1961.

Williams, James N. *The Plan*. Stittsville: Canada's Wings Inc.

Wolf-Moncheberg, Mathil. *On the Other Side. To My Children from Germany 1940–45*. New York: Mayflower Books, 1979.

Weiss, Winfried. *A Nazi Childhood*. Santa Barbara: Capra Press, 1988.

Whitehouse, Arch. *The Years of the Sky Kings*. New York: Doubleday, 1959.

Whiting, Charles. *The Home Front: Germany*. Chicago: Time-Life Books, 1982.

Ziegler, Philip. *London At War. 1939–1945*. Toronto: Knopf Canada, 1995.

Zassenhaus, Hiltgunt. *Walls: Resisting the Third Reich. One Woman's Story*. Boston: Beacon Press, 1974.

Newspapers

London *Times*

London *Daily Mail*

Toronto *Star*

Toronto *Globe and Mail*

Cologne *Zeitung*

Audio/Visual

The Valour and the Horror, 1992.

INDEX